DATE DUE

MR 20 '06			
OC 21 08			
NOV 3 0 2010			

Writing the World

Terra Nova Books aim to show how environmental and cultural issues have artistic components, in addition to the scientific and political. Combining essays, reportage, fiction, art, and poetry, Terra Nova Books reveal the complex and paradoxical ways the natural and the human are continually redefining each other.

Other Terra Nova books:

Writing the Future: Progress and Evolution

Writing on Air

Writing on Water

The New Earth Reader

The World and the Wild

The Book of Music and Nature

Terra Nova
New Jersey Institute of Technology
Newark, NJ 07102
973 596 3289
terranova@highlands.com
www.terranovabooks.org

Writing the World

On Globalization

edited by David Rothenberg and Wandee J. Pryor

A Terra Nova Book

The MIT Press
Cambridge, Massachusetts
London, England

MIT Press books may be purchased at special quantity discounts for business or sales promotional use. For information, please e-mail special_sales@mitpress.mit.edu or write to Special Sales Department, The MIT Press, 5 Cambridge Center, Cambridge, MA 02142.

This book was set in Berkeley Old Style Book by Graphic Composition, Inc., using Quark XPress, and was printed and bound in the United States of America.

Library of Congress Cataloging-in-Publication Data

Writing the world : on globalization / edited by David Rothenberg and Wandee J. Pryor.
   p. cm.
  "A Terra nova book."
  ISBN 0-262-18245-9 (hard.: alk. paper)
   1. Literature—Collections. I. Rothenberg, David, 1962– II. Pryor, Wandee J.

PN6014.W75 2005
808.8—dc22

                      2004062530

Printed on recycled paper.

10 9 8 7 6 5 4 3 2 1

Contents

Illustrations

The World as We Found It

David Rothenberg and Wandee J. Pryor

Things are supposed to be different this time. Not like they were before. Back then, one traveled far for objects—a new flavor, fabrics, spices, and gold. It was a time when the world seemed too vast to comprehend. Foreigners were shocked by the shade of another's skin, the colors of a marketplace, the smell in the streets. Back then, one small country might extend its borders nearly forever, claiming outposts all over the world. One little country could then appear as big as the whole planet and look at itself with great admiration and pride. That's the reason for imperialism, the business of empire. That's the way the far-off reaches of the world looked to those who saw themselves as the center, those who wanted to be bigger than the land they originated from, those who saw themselves as rulers and the rest of the world as servants or slaves.

But today we have new eyes. The tendrils of commerce and communication have spread far enough across the Earth that little is truly unfamiliar. Photography and television let us see it all. We know what the world looks like, and we find its richness astounding. We cannot dream of owning the world and all of its plenty, the lushness of India's history, the determination of the women of New Guinea, the cunning (*furbi*) of Italy. We are taught to celebrate difference—but the same movies are released all over the world at the same time. Advertising foists identical dreams on those it can reach, supporting the notion that one can do just about anything in a pair of cool new shoes. To those who lack access to glossy pictures, billboards, and television, this world seems impossibly remote.

Globalization is not supposed to be the new imperialism. It's the spreading of economy and culture all across the planet, so that there is no single power. Bankers smile as they say it, imagining emerging markets, capitalism welcoming in new tribes, new places to make and to sell the same goods. They propagate the idea that when the world finds we are all capable of conducting business the same way, a great peace will emerge. Is that what it's actually like?

Look at it a different way, and you see new chances for the old kind of exploitation, where a single country extends its borders to the far reaches of the world. Why do global corporations love China so much? Best place in the world to run a factory, because workers are not allowed to complain. Easiest country because, as *Nation* globalization correspondent William Greider aptly puts it, the old barbarisms of the industrial revolution can be put back to work for greater profits and an obedient, repressed workforce.

But some believe globalization will not let industry get away with such injustice for long. Information travels more freely today than in the not-so-distant past. Even the most ignorant American cannot really think our country is all that matters in the world. Everything we buy, say, or do is instantaneously linked to the far-off reaches of this globe as e-mails are sent, images are projected onto home entertainment centers, and phone calls are placed.

This anthology aims to show that globalization can be celebrated as a cultural concept, a willingness for different ways of life to learn from one another. When all of us learn enough about our differences to respect the diversity that exists, we will be unable to pretend we are the same. We will never accept the old innocence and ignorance bred by oppression and exploitation. It's time for us to listen to the many literate voices the world speaks. Bring it all together. People do not say or stay the same, and we can only grow by embracing what we hear.

This is the age of globalization, the century of a world interconnected when nowhere is all that far away from anywhere else. This is the time when the virtual world seems to dominate the physical world, so that minutes after a devastating earthquake in Iran, a friend can send a gratis message through the invisible Web that says: "Over there a crying man is hugging and kissing his dead daughter and wife, but his daughter's face still looks calm and beautiful. The man is looking up at the sky and shouting like an injured lion, while he is kindly holding two dead bodies in his arms. Dear friend, the earth got angry with those people, but why?"

We do not know why. We suspect nature still has no interest in us, as much as we try to honor and destroy it. We at Terra Nova have always considered nature in some form— air, water, evolution—and now you might assume we are tackling economics. Yet this is not a book about the expanding global market. Instead, it is a celebration of the global exchange of art and ideas.

Only the narrowest interpretation of globalization looks at the world's markets, assessing their fluidity and interdependence, adhering their flexibility to the same technologies that allow us to have friends in forbidden lands, one to which our nation refuses to grant diplomacy. Our computers, assembled by underpaid workers in a windowless factory in Malaysia, bear the name of a fruit, wholesome and American. The situation exploits them and spoils us, allowing us to buy something for what seems to be a reasonable price. Corporations are overjoyed to be able to expand their markets and to profit from the smooth flow of capital into new, eager, burgeoning economies. What evolves may be uncertain, but the development of something immense is definitely there.

Globalization is full of images of expansion. The world's biggest city emerges in an unknown province just outside Hong Kong. Twenty-six towns are merging into a megalopolis that has no name, which the Chinese government has given no name, refusing to admit it exists. In a few decades, 30 million people will live there, and the towns will have merged into the biggest city in the world, no longer distinguishable as separate entities, a giant place that's not even on the map.

In the discussion of globalization, there are endless stories and statistics. One of the world's biggest fast food companies, the parent of several of America's most favored brands, is now headquartered in China, where it expects the most expansion in coming years. "We are not an American company," explains the American CEO, who flies in once a month for meetings. "We are a global company." Every company wants to be that, since it promises so much range and monetary gain.

Protesters at the World Trade Organization summit in Seattle in 1999 alerted the world's globalizers that all might not proceed smoothly with their plans. The rest of us are becoming better educated on the ways that transnational corporations use the power of trade to set a worldwide agenda. In general, the haves of the world approve, while the have-nots remain excluded. The majority of the world's population still doesn't own a phone.

Globalization is a sexy promise available everywhere—but not to everyone. Access to the riches of the world is limited to those willing to change their lives, moving away from the local, the controlled, the closeness of food, family, and friends, to the international moneyed world. It is both promising and paralyzing. Few of us realize how much can be lost when we allow our identities to be influenced by a global image, a dream of prosperity that might never before have been coveted.

Corporations are efficient in the global marketplace, but they are also driven to compete. In competition we are encouraged to get away with as much as we can, because if we don't do it, someone else will, and we cannot afford to lose out, to do a little more with less—a cheaper labor force, more lenient labor laws. Business values are hard to retain in a cut-throat, fast-paced world. Companies pay their workers as little as possible far afield, and with far less regard for safety and rights than at home. These businesses don't waste their time worrying about the American workers whose jobs have been priced out of existence. These companies exist outside traditional morality, doing what they do simply because they *can*. No one stops them. No one stops us.

But we don't want to retell this familiar, important, and frightening story. We all know opportunity is wrought with temptation and difficulty. The optimists say the kinks will be ironed out! The pessimists say there's not enough to go around! The world's ailments come from overproduction, from ignoring the fact that even our miraculous, bountiful Earth has limitations. There is no way everyone in China can live as average Americans do. Something's got to give. Who wants to make do with less when the image of more continues to call out to us, wherever we are in the grand scheme of possession and consumption?

If there is any hope for us, it lies in the fact that globalization is much more than all of this. It is the dream of the global village, a world where we embrace the idea that all of our lives are interconnected. Global culture enriches us by linking individuals to individuals, forcing us to set aside differences in ideology, to ignore our fears and our sense of competition. Despite the grand technological gaps between North and South, it is still remarkable how the price of information is plummeting and that access to it becomes more fluid every day, despite efforts to have it controlled. The truth may still be guarded by the prejudices of the media, but alternate views are out there for us to find.

Politics, debate, and *conflict* are the words most often affiliated with globalization, but in this anthology, it is the poetry of cultural contact that speaks this truth. When Polish reporter Ryszard Kapuściński is introduced to a village chief with the highest compliment, "He is an African!" we are reminded that people all over the world know to look beyond appearances. When Audrey McCollum travels to New

Guinea, gradually improving her life and sensibilities along with those of several women in a remote village, we see how cultural barriers can vanish. When Hannes Westberg, shot and nearly killed by the Swedish police in a demonstration against the European Union top summit meeting, is still able to hope his ordeal may somehow point to a better world, we recognize the strength of our voices, that of both the individual and a unified group. When exiled Iraqi writer Najem Wali can suggest that "my Basra is really Marquez's Macondo standing in real life," we realize that some of the greatest truths lie in fiction. When young Ukrainian immigrant Inna Mattei looks at her new country and says, "New civilizations emerge in the estuaries of highways, they swing like gigantic flowers," we understand that there are times when poetry is all we have to frame our foreign experience, to translate the alien into the familiar.

Consider the two poems that begin and end this book, each suggesting a different way of maintaining poise in the midst of a churning, changing world. Uruguayan poet Mario Benedetti answers the resounding contemporary question of how there can still be joy in an age of powerful, easy injustice: "you will ask why we sing/we sing because . . ./ . . . we are the militants of life/and because we cannot and will not/allow our song to become ashes." The human spirit must prevail and be enriched by the powerful social transformations that can either overrun us or be run by us. To prevail, we have no choice but to sing of our sorrow.

The late Urdu master Faiz Ahmed Faiz asks the world for support. Speaking from Pakistan, he has seen much trouble befall his land. With so many wounds still open, he turns to face us and speaks in our direction: "Now tell us what we should do/*you* tell us how to heal these wounds." This might at first sound like some subservient plea for foreign aid, investment, and counsel, but it is anything but that. What Faiz is asking for is empathy. He wants culture and emotion, not commerce and trade, to cross international lines. He understands that the greatest hope the world has lies in putting on another's shoes and walking around in them for a while. In our northern climes, we insulate ourselves from the struggles and tribulations of people in nations we have long taken advantage of.

What is good for business may often be worse for human beings. We will learn more compassion if we take in more stories, if we reach beyond safety to the real and terrible beauty of suffering, if we understand, as Nuha al Radi and Jasmina Tesanovic (two women from opposite worlds) do, the globalization of evil. To step outside our comfort zone is to acknowledge that we are unified in our pain and our anger. To find commonality in suffering is to seek out compassion. The horrors of the world push us closer together until, as Tesanovic explains, "an old Bosnian woman raped in war will tell you a story identical to that of a teenage American raped on a U.S. campus." As unlikely a place as any other, in these terrors we find our empathy, the harmony of human experience.

The culture of globalization, the easy and sudden mixing of styles, images, aesthetics, colors, people, and ideas, can be celebrated and also watched. Rarely does a mix of cultures occur on perfectly equal ground. Usually one side or the other has some advantage—more to gain from the encounter than the other. Local traditions are valuable, firm yet fragile, easy to break, especially when bartered with images of Western convenience and attainable wealth. Fast cars, global brands, flashy clothes that unravel at the touch hide the fingers that ache from their making. For James Barilla, in his piece "Aliens in the Garden," there is a valid analogy between native plants being challenged by exotics and local quaintness being threatened by shallow aspirations. Of course, it is too easy to say that we should keep commerce local and controlled, ideas open and free. It's difficult to return to a concept so naive in a world gone global. Bill McKibben discovers what would do the most to improve the life of women in Bangladesh: give them control over the seeds they plant, a power taken away by foreign companies that sell their own product without knowing the specifics of each local situation. This will never happen until global capitalism learns when it must limit its desire for profit and control. Naomi Klein sees fences everywhere as the reminder that ownership and property are the prerequisites for admission into the club of capitalism and that most people have little to their name. Arundhati Roy shows how only the privileged trust the word of experts, who tell those in power exactly what they want to hear.

We do not want to cast the term *globalization* aside, like so many panaceas for world change whose meanings have been diluted to the point of being used up: green revolution, appropriate technology, and sustainable development, to name just a few. *Globalization,* like all those hopeful terms of the recent past, is a slippery word whose meaning can too easily be manipulated.

Choose the parts of globalization that most move you: the injustice, the inequity! The miraculously rapid transformations, the sudden fortunes and bankruptcies, the windfalls of money! Which one keeps you awake at night? Meanwhile, most of the Earth's 7 billion people struggle to get by, to secure the basics of food, shelter, clothing. Those who see furthest see tremendous challenges to resources and habitats, limits that will soon test the very abilities of our species to survive.

But the information is being dispersed, the stories and songs are spreading, the distance between humans is getting smaller every day. Let us mold globalization from danger into opportunity. Let us see our countries and our sensibilities as binding threads that stitch the world together. Let us be part of a culture of openness, interconnection, shared values, and linked wonder. No crime is an island, no language is untranslatable, no human experience is impossible to share.

Your earthquake, Alireza, is in our backyard. Last year's tsunami brought the whole world out to grieve and to care. The world's stories and troubles are all mixed up inside us, across our screens and in our thoughts. The voices that call to us from this anthology, seeking to be heard, attempting to teach us about other cultures, can better help us understand the place from which we originated. This country cannot exist without its connections to everywhere else. If we in the United States take the time to accept the rich ideas and thoughts of this whole diverse planet, to reflect on the voices of distant lands as well as the whispers at home, we might finally be able to earn a place at the global table. That's more important and more honorable than making the world American. The world is not our oyster but our teacher and our home.

Writing the World

Why We Sing (Por que cantamos)

Mario Benedetti

translated by D'Arcy Martin

If each hour brings its death
if time is a den of thieves
the breezes carry a scent of evil
and life is just a moving target

you will ask why we sing

if our finest people are shunned
our homeland is dying of sorrow
and the human heart is shattered
even before shame explodes

you will ask why we sing

if the trees and the sky remain
as far off as the horizon
some absence hovers over the evening
and disappointment colors the morning

you will ask why we sing

we sing because the river is humming
and when the river hums the river hums
we sing because cruelty has no name
but we can name its destiny
we sing because the child because everything
because in the future because the people
we sing because the survivors
and our dead want us to sing

we sing because shouting is not enough
nor is sorrow or anger
we sing because we believe in people
and we shall overcome these defeats

we sing because the sun recognizes us
and the fields smell of spring
and because in this stem and that fruit
every question has its answer

we sing because it is raining on the furrow
and we are the militants of life
and because we cannot and will not
allow our song to become ashes.

Uruguay, 1979

Arpita Singh, *For Anjum*, 2002

The Ladies Have Feelings, So . . . Shall We Leave It to the Experts?

Arundhati Roy

India lives in several centuries at the same time. Somehow we manage to progress and regress simultaneously. As a nation we age by pushing outward from the middle—adding a few centuries on to either end of our extraordinary c.v. We greaten like the maturing head of a hammerhead shark with eyes looking in diametrically opposite directions. I have no doubt that even here in North America you have heard that Germany is considering changing its immigration laws in order to import Indian software engineers. I have even less doubt that you've heard of the Naga Sadhu at the Kumbh Mela who towed the District Commissioner's car with his penis while the Commissioner sat in it solemnly with his wife and children.

As Indian citizens we subsist on a regular diet of caste massacres and nuclear tests, mosque breakings and fashion shows, church burnings and expanding cell phone networks, bonded labor and the digital revolution, female infanticide and the Nasdaq crash, husbands who continue to burn their wives for dowry and our delectable stockpile of Miss Worlds. I don't mean to put a simplistic value judgment on this peculiar form of "progress" by suggesting that Modern is Good and Traditional is Bad—or vice versa. What's hard to reconcile oneself to, both personally and politically, is the schizophrenic nature of it. That applies not just to the ancient/modern conundrum, but to the utter illogic of what appears to be the current national enterprise. In the lane behind my house, every night I walk past road gangs of emaciated laborers digging a trench to lay fiber-optic cables to speed up our digital revolution. In the bitter winter cold, they work by the light of a few candles.

It's as though the people of India have been rounded up and loaded onto two convoys of trucks (a huge big one and a tiny little one) that have set off resolutely in opposite directions. The tiny convoy is on its way to a glittering destination somewhere near the top of the world. The other convoy just melts into the darkness and disappears. A cursory survey that tallies the caste, class and religion of who gets to be on which convoy would make a good Lazy Person's Concise Guide to the History of India. For some of us, life in India is like being suspended between two of the trucks, one in each convoy, and being neatly dismembered as they move apart, not bodily, but emotionally and intellectually.

Of *course* India is a microcosm of the world. Of *course* versions of what happens there happen everywhere. Of *course,* if you're willing to look, the parallels are easy to find. The difference in India is only in the scale, the magnitude, and the sheer proximity of the disparity. In India your face is slammed right up against it. To address it, to deal with it, to not deal with it, to try and understand it, to insist on not understanding it, to simply survive it—on a daily, hourly basis—is a fine art in itself. Either an art or a form of insular, inward-looking insanity. Or both.

To be a writer—a supposedly "famous" writer—in a country where three hundred million people are illiterate is a dubious honor. To be a writer in a country that gave the world Mahatma Gandhi, that invented the concept of nonviolent resistance, and then, half a century later, followed that up with nuclear tests is a ferocious burden. (Though no more ferocious a burden, it has to be said, than being a writer in a country that has enough nuclear weapons to destroy the earth several times over.) To be a writer in a country where something akin to an undeclared civil war is being waged on its subjects in the name of "development" is an onerous responsibility. When it comes to writers and writing, I use words like "onerous" and "responsibility" with a heavy heart and not a small degree of sadness.

This is what I'm here to talk to you, to think aloud with you, about. What is the role of writers and artists in society? Do they have a definable role? Can it be fixed, described, characterized in any definite way? Should it be?

Personally, I can think of few things more terrifying than if writers and artists were charged with an immutable charter of duties and responsibilities that they had to live and work by. Imagine if there was this little black book—a sort of

Approved Guide to Good Writing—that said: All writers shall be politically con-
scious and sexually moral, or: All writers should believe in God, globalization, and
the joys of family life. . . .

Rule One for a writer, as far as I'm concerned, is There Are No Rules. And Rule
Two (since Rule One was made to be broken) is There Are No Excuses for Bad Art.
Painters, writers, singers, actors, dancers, filmmakers, musicians are meant to fly,
to push at the frontiers, to worry the edges of the human imagination, to conjure
beauty from the most unexpected things, to find magic in places where others
never thought to look. If you limit the trajectory of their flight, if you weight their
wings with society's existing notions of morality and responsibility, if you truss
them up with preconceived values, you subvert their endeavor.

A good or great writer may refuse to accept any responsibility or morality that
society wishes to impose on her. Yet the best and greatest of them know that if
they abuse this hard-won freedom, it can only lead to bad art. There is an intricate
web of morality, rigor, and responsibility that art, that writing itself, imposes on a
writer. It's singular, it's individual, but nevertheless it's there. At its best, it's an
exquisite bond between the artist and the medium. At its acceptable end, it's a
sort of sensible cooperation. At its worst, it's a relationship of disrespect and
exploitation.

The absence of external rules complicates things. There's a very thin line that
separates the strong, true, bright bird of the imagination from the synthetic, noisy
bauble. Where is that line? How do you recognize it? How do you know you've
crossed it? At the risk of sounding esoteric and arcane, I'm tempted to say that you
just know. The fact is that nobody—no reader, no reviewer, agent, publisher, col-
league, friend, or enemy—can tell for sure. A writer just has to ask herself that
question and answer it as honestly as possible. The thing about this "line" is that
once you learn to recognize it, once you see it, it's impossible to ignore. You have
no choice but to live with it, to follow it through. You have to bear with all its com-
plexities, contradictions, and demands. And that's not always easy. It doesn't
always lead to compliments and standing ovations. It can lead you to the strangest,
wildest places. In the midst of a bloody military coup, for instance, you could find
yourself fascinated by the mating rituals of a purple sunbird, or the secret life of
captive goldfish, or an old aunt's descent into madness. And nobody can say that
there isn't truth and art and beauty in that. Or, on the contrary, in the midst of
putative peace, you could, like me, be unfortunate enough to stumble on a silent

war. The trouble is that once you see it, you can't unsee it. And once you've seen it, keeping quiet, saying nothing, becomes as political an act as speaking out. There's no innocence. Either way, you're accountable.

Today, perhaps more so than in any other era in history, the writer's right to free speech is guarded and defended by the civil societies and state establishments of the most powerful countries in the world. Any overt attempt to silence or muffle a voice is met with furious opposition. The writer is embraced and protected. This is a wonderful thing. The writer, the actor, the musician, the filmmaker—they have become radiant jewels in the crown of modern civilization. The artist, I imagine, is finally as free as he or she will ever be. Never before have so many writers had their books published. (And now, of course, we have the Internet.) Never before have we been more commercially viable. We live and prosper in the heart of the marketplace. True, for every so-called success there are hundreds who "fail." True, there are myriad art forms, both folk and classical, myriad languages, myriad cultural and artistic traditions that are being crushed and cast aside in the stampede to the big bumper sale in Wonderland. Still, there have never been more writers, singers, actors, or painters who have become influential, wealthy superstars. And they, the successful ones, spawn a million imitators, they become the torchbearers, their work becomes the benchmark for what art is, or ought to be.

Nowadays in India the scene is almost farcical. Following the recent commercial success of some Indian authors, Western publishers are desperately prospecting for the next big Indo-Anglian work of fiction. They're doing everything short of interviewing English-speaking Indians for the post of "writer." Ambitious middle-class parents who, a few years ago, would only settle for a future in Engineering, Medicine, or Management for their children, now hopefully send them to creative writing schools. People like myself are constantly petitioned by computer companies, watch manufacturers, even media magnates to endorse their products. A boutique owner in Bombay once asked me if he could "display" my book *The God of Small Things* (as if it were an accessory, a bracelet or a pair of earrings) while he filmed me shopping for clothes! Jhumpa Lahiri, the American writer of Indian origin who won the Pulitzer Prize, came to India recently to have a traditional Bengali wedding. The wedding was reported on the front page of national newspapers.

Now where does all this lead us? Is it just harmless nonsense that's best ignored? How does all this ardent wooing affect our art? What kind of lenses does it put in our spectacles? How far does it remove us from the world around us?

There is very real danger that this neoteric seduction can shut us up far more effectively than violence and repression ever could. We have free speech. Maybe. But do we have Really Free Speech? If what we have to say doesn't "sell," will we still say it? Can we? Or is everybody looking for Things That Sell to say? Could writers end up playing the role of palace entertainers? Or the subtle twenty-first-century version of court eunuchs attending to the pleasures of our incumbent CEOs? You know—naughty, but nice. Risqué perhaps, but not risky.

It has been nearly four years now since my first, and so far only, novel, *The God of Small Things,* was published. In the early days, I used to be described—introduced—as the author of an almost freakishly "successful" (if I may use so vulgar a term) first book. Nowadays I'm introduced as something of a freak myself. I am, apparently, what is known in twenty-first-century vernacular as a "writer-activist." (Like a sofa-bed.)

Why am I called a "writer-activist" and why—even when it's used approvingly, admiringly—does that term make me flinch? I'm called a writer-activist because after writing *The God of Small Things* I wrote three political essays: "The End of the Imagination," about India's nuclear tests, "The Greater Common Good," about Big Dams and the "development" debate, and "Power Politics: The Reincarnation of Rumpelstiltskin," about the privatization and corporatization of essential infrastructure like water and electricity. Apart from the building of the temple in Ayodhya, these currently also happen to be the top priorities of the Indian government.

Now, I've been wondering why should it be that the person who wrote *The God of Small Things* is called a writer, and the person who wrote the political essays is called an activist? True, *The God of Small Things* is a work of fiction, but it's no less political than any of my essays. True, the essays are works of nonfiction, but since when did writers forgo the right to write nonfiction?

My thesis—my humble theory, as we say in India—is that I've been saddled with this double-barreled appellation, this awful professional label, not because my work is political, but because in my essays, which are about very contentious issues, I take sides. I take a position. I have a point of view. What's worse, I make it clear that I think it's right and moral to take that position, and what's even worse, I use everything in my power to flagrantly solicit support for that position. Now, for a writer of the twenty-first century, that's considered a pretty uncool, unsophisticated thing to do. It skates uncomfortably close to the territory occupied by political party ideologues—a breed of people that the world has learned (quiet rightly) to mistrust. I'm aware of this. I'm all for being circumspect. I'm all for discretion, prudence, tentativeness, subtlety, ambiguity, complexity. I love the unanswered question, the unresolved story, the unclimbed mountain, the tender shard of an incomplete dream. Most of the time.

But is it mandatory for a writer to be ambiguous about everything? Isn't it true that there have been fearful episodes in human history when prudence and discretion would have just been euphemisms for pusillanimity? When caution was actually cowardice? When sophistication was disguised decadence? When circumspection was really a kind of espousal?

Isn't it true, or at least theoretically possible, that there are times in the life of a people or a nation when the political climate demands that we—even the most sophisticated of us—overtly take sides? I believe that such times are upon us. And I believe that in the coming years intellectuals and artists in India will be called upon to take sides.

And this time, unlike the struggle for Independence, we won't have the luxury of fighting a colonizing "enemy." We'll be fighting ourselves.

We will be forced to ask ourselves some very uncomfortable questions about our values and traditions, our vision for the future, our responsibilities as citizens, the legitimacy of our "democratic institutions," the role of the state, the police, the army, the judiciary, and the intellectual community.

Fifty years after independence, India is still struggling with the legacy of colonialism, still flinching from the "cultural insult." As citizens we're still caught up in the business of "disproving" the white world's definition of us. Intellectually and emotionally, we have just begun to grapple with communal and caste politics that threaten to tear our society apart. But in the meanwhile, something new looms on our horizon.

It's not war, it's not genocide, it's not ethnic cleansing, it's not a famine or an epidemic. On the face of it, it's just ordinary, day-to-day business. It lacks the drama, the large-format, epic magnificence of war or genocide or famine. It's dull in comparison. It makes bad TV. It has to do with boring things like jobs, money, water supply, electricity, irrigation. But it also has to do with a process of barbaric dispossession on a scale that has few parallels in history. You may have guessed by now that I'm talking about the modern version of globalization.

What is globalization? Who is it for? What is it going to do to a country like India, in which social inequality has been institutionalized in the caste system for centuries? A country in which seven hundred million people live in rural areas. In which eighty percent of the landholdings are small farms. In which three hundred million people are illiterate.

Is the corporatization and globalization of agriculture, water supply, electricity, and essential commodities going to pull India out of the stagnant morass of poverty, illiteracy, and religious bigotry? Is the dismantling and auctioning off of elaborate public sector infrastructure, developed with public money over the last fifty years, really the way forward? Is globalization going to close the gap between the privileged and the underprivileged, between the upper castes and the lower castes, between the educated and the illiterate? Or is it going to give those who already have a centuries-old head start a friendly helping hand?

Is globalization about "eradication of world poverty," or is it a mutant variety of colonialism, remote controlled and digitally operated? These are huge, contentious questions. The answers vary depending on whether they come from the villages and fields of rural India, from the slums and shantytowns of urban India, from the living rooms of the burgeoning middle class, or from the boardrooms of the big business houses.

Today India produces more milk, more sugar, more food grain than ever before. This year government warehouses are overflowing with forty-two million tons of food grain. That's almost a quarter of the total annual food grain produce. Farmers with too much grain on their hands were driven to despair. In regions that wielded enough political clout, the government went on a buying spree, purchasing more grain than it could possibly store or use. While the grain rots in government warehouses, three hundred and fifty million Indian citizens live below the poverty line and do not have the means to eat a square meal a day. And yet, in March 2000, just before President Clinton's visit to India, the Indian government lifted import restrictions on one thousand four hundred commodities, including milk, grain, sugar, cotton, tea, coffee, and palm oil. This despite the fact that there was a glut of these products on the market.

From April 1—April Fool's Day—2001, according to the terms of its agreement with the World Trade Organization (WTO), the Indian government will have to drop its quantitative import restrictions. The Indian market is already flooded with cheap imports. Though India is technically free to export its agricultural produce, in practice most of it cannot be exported because it doesn't meet the first world's "environmental standards." (You don't eat bruised mangoes, or bananas with mosquito bites, or rice with a few weevils in it. Whereas we don't mind the odd mosquito and the occasional weevil.)

Developed countries like the United States, whose hugely subsidized farm industry engages only two to three percent of its total population, are using the WTO to pressure countries like India to drop agricultural subsidies in order to make the market "competitive." Huge, mechanized corporate enterprises working thousands of acres of farmland want to compete with impoverished subsistence farmers who own a couple of acres of land.

In effect, India's rural economy, which supports seven hundred million people, is being garroted. Farmers who produce too much are in distress, farmers who produce too little are in distress, and landless agricultural laborers are out of work as big estates and farms lay off their workers. They're all flocking to the cities in search of employment.

"Trade Not Aid" is the rallying cry of the headmen of the new Global Village headquartered in the shining offices of the WTO. Our British colonizers stepped onto our shores a few centuries ago disguised as traders. We all remember the East India Company. This time around, the colonizer doesn't even need a token white presence in the colonies. The CEOs and their men don't need to go to the trouble of tramping through the tropics, risking malaria, diarrhea, sunstroke, and an early death. They don't have to maintain an army or a police force, or worry about insurrections and mutinies. They can have their colonies and an easy conscience. "Creating a good investment climate" is the new euphemism for third world repression. Besides, the responsibility for implementation rests with the local administration.

In India, in order to clear the way for "development projects," the government is in the process of amending the present Land Acquisition Act (which, ironically, was drafted by the British in the nineteenth century) and making it more draconian than it already is. State governments are preparing to ratify "anti-terrorist" laws so that those who oppose development projects (in Madhya Pradesh, for example) will be counted as terrorists. They can be held without trial for three years. They can have their lands and cattle seized.

Recently, globalization has come in for some criticism. The protests in Seattle and Prague will go down in history. Each time the WTO or the World Economic Forum wants to have a meeting, ministers have to barricade themselves with thousands of heavily armed police. Still, all its admirers, from Bill Clinton, Kofi Annan, and A. B. Vajpayee (the Indian Prime Minister) to the cheering brokers in the stalls, continue to say the same lofty things. If we have the right institutions of governance in place—effective courts, good laws, honest politicians, participatory democracy, a transparent administration that respects human rights and gives people a say in decisions that affect their lives—then the globalization project will work for the poor, as well. They call this "globalization with a human face."

The point is, if all this were in place, almost *anything* would succeed: socialism, capitalism, you name it. Everything works in Paradise, a Communist State as well as a Military Dictatorship. But in an imperfect world, is it globalization that's going to bring us all this bounty? Is that what's happening in India now that it's on the fast track to the free market? Does any one thing on that lofty list apply to life in India today?

Are state institutions transparent? Have people had a say, have they even been informed—let alone consulted—about decisions that vitally affect their lives? And are Mr. Clinton (or now Mr. Bush) and Prime Minister Vajpayee doing everything in their power to see that the "right institutions of governance" are in place? Or are they involved in exactly the opposite enterprise? Do they mean something else altogether when they talk of the "right institutions of governance"?

On October 18, 2000, in one of the most extraordinary legal decisions in post-independence India, the Supreme Court permitted the construction of the Sardar Sarovar Dam on the Narmada River to proceed. The court did this despite indisputable evidence placed before it that the Sardar Sarovar Project did not have the mandatory environmental clearance from the central government. Despite the fact that no comprehensive studies have ever been done on the social and ecological impact of the dam. Despite the fact that in the last fifteen years not one single village has been resettled according to the project's own guidelines, and that there was no possibility of rehabilitating the four hundred thousand people who would be displaced by the project. In effect, the Supreme Court has virtually endorsed the violation of human rights to life and livelihood.

Big dams in India have displaced not hundreds, not thousands, but millions—more than thirty million people in the last fifty years. Almost half of them are Dalit and Adivasi, the poorest of the poor. Yet India is the only country in the world that refused permission to the World Commission on Dams to hold a public hearing. The government in Gujarat, the state in which the Sardar Sarovar Dam is being built, threatened members of the commission with arrest. The World Commission on Dams report was released by Nelson Mandela in November 2000. In February 2001, the Indian government formally rejected the report. Does this sound like a transparent, accountable, participatory democracy?

Recently the Supreme Court ordered the closure of seventy-seven thousand "polluting and nonconforming" industrial units in Delhi. The order could put five hundred thousand people out of work. What are these "industrial units"? Who are these people? They're the millions who have migrated from their villages, some voluntarily, others involuntarily, in search of work. They're the people who aren't supposed to exist, the "noncitizens" who survive in the folds and wrinkles, the cracks and fissures, of the "official" city. They exist just outside the net of the "official" urban infrastructure.

Close to forty percent of Delhi's population of twelve million—about five million people—live in slums and unauthorized colonies. Most of them are not serviced by municipal services—no electricity, no water, no sewage systems. About fifty thousand people are homeless and sleep on the streets. The "noncitizens" are employed in what economists rather stuffily call the "informal sector," the fragile but vibrant parallel economy. That both shocks and delights the imagination. They work as hawkers, rickshaw pullers, garbage recyclers, car battery rechargers, street tailors, transistor knob makers, buttonhole stitchers, paper bag makers, dyers, printers, barbers. These are the "industrial units" that have been targeted as nonconforming by the Supreme Court. (Fortunately I haven't heard *that* knock on my door yet, though I'm as nonconforming a unit as the rest of them.)

The trains that leave Delhi these days carry thousands of people who simply cannot survive in the city. They're returning to the villages they fled in the first place. Millions of others, because they're "illegal," have become easy meat for the rapacious, bribe-seeking police and predatory government officials. They haven't yet been driven out of the city but now must live in perpetual fear and anticipation of that happening.

In India the times are full of talk of the "free market," reforms, deregulation, and the dismantling of the "license raj"—all in the name of encouraging entrepreneurship and discouraging corruption. Yet when the state, supported by the judiciary, curbs freedom and obliterates a flourishing market, when it breaks the backs of numerous imaginative, resourceful, small-scale entrepreneurs, and delivers millions of others as fodder to the doorstep of the corruption industry, few comment on the irony.

No doubt it's true that the informal sector is polluting and, according to a colonial understanding of urban land use, "nonconforming." But then we don't live in a clean, perfect world. What about the fact that sixty-seven percent of Delhi's pollution comes from motor vehicles? Is it conceivable that the Supreme Court will come up with an act that bans private cars? The courts and the government have shown no great enthusiasm for closing down big factories run by major industrialists that have polluted rivers, denuded forests, depleted and poisoned ground water, and destroyed the livelihoods of hundreds of thousands of people who depend on these resources for a living. The Grasim factory in Kerala, the Orient Paper Mill in Madhya Pradesh, the "sunrise belt" industries in Gujarat. The uranium mines in Jadugoda, the aluminum plants in Orissa. And hundreds of others.

This is our in-house version of first world bullying in the global warming debate: i.e., We pollute, you pay.

In circumstances like these, the term "writer-activist" as a professional description of what I do makes me flinch doubly. First, because it is strategically positioned to diminish both writers and activists. It seeks to reduce the scope, the range, the sweep of what a writer is and can be. It suggests somehow that the writer by definition is too effete a being to come up with the clarity, the explicitness, the reasoning, the passion, the grit, the audacity, and, if necessary, the vulgarity to publicly take a political position. And, conversely, it suggests that the activist occupies the coarser, cruder end of the intellectual spectrum. That the activist is by profession a "position-taker" and therefore lacks complexity and intellectual sophistication, and is instead fueled by a crude, simple-minded, one-sided understanding of things. But the more fundamental problem I have with the term is that professionalizing the whole business of protest, putting a label on it, has the effect of containing the problem and suggesting that it's up to the professionals—activists and writer-activists—to deal with.

The fact is that what's happening in India today is not a *problem,* and the issues that some of us are raising are not *causes.* They are huge political and social upheavals that are convulsing the nation. One is not involved by virtue of being a writer or activist. One is involved because one is a human being. Writing about it just happens to be the most effective thing I can do. I think it's vital to de-professionalize the public debate on matters that vitally affect the lives of ordinary people. It's time to snatch our futures back from the "experts." Time to ask, in ordinary language, the public question and to demand, in ordinary language, the public answer.

Frankly, however trenchantly, however angrily, however combatively one puts forward one's case, at the end of the day, I'm only a citizen, one of many, who is demanding public information, asking for a public explanation. I have no axe to grind. I have no professional stakes to protect. I'm prepared to be persuaded. I'm prepared to change my mind. But instead of an argument, or an explanation, or a disputing of facts, one gets insults, invective, legal threats, and the Expert's Anthem: "You're too emotional. You don't understand, and it's too complicated to explain." The subtext, of course, is: Don't worry your little head about it. Go and play with your toys. Leave the real world to us.

It's the old Brahminical instinct. Colonize knowledge, build four walls around it, and use it to your advantage. The Manusmriti, the Vedic Hindu code of conduct, says that if a Dalit overhears a *shloka* or any part of the sacred text, he must have molten lead poured into his ear. It isn't a coincidence that while India is poised to take its place at the forefront of the Information Revolution, three hundred million of its citizens are illiterate. (It would be interesting, as an exercise, to find out how many "experts"—scholars, professionals, consultants—in India are actually Brahmins and upper castes.)

If you're one of the lucky people with a berth booked on the small convoy, then Leaving it to the Experts is, or can be, a mutually beneficial proposition for both the expert and yourself. It's a convenient way of shrugging off your own role in the circuitry. And it creates a huge professional market for all kinds of "expertise." There's a whole ugly universe waiting to be explored there. This is not at all to suggest that all consultants are racketeers or that expertise is unnecessary, but you've heard the saying—There's a lot of money in poverty. There are plenty of ethical questions to be asked of those who make a professional living off their expertise in poverty and despair.

For instance, at what point does a scholar stop being a scholar and become a parasite who feeds off despair and dispossession? Does the source of your funding compromise your scholarship? We know, after all, that World Bank studies are among the most quoted studies in the world. Is the World Bank a dispassionate observer of the global situation? Are the studies it funds entirely devoid of self-interest?

Take, for example, the international dam industry. It's worth thirty-two to forty-six billion U.S. dollars a year. It's bursting with experts and consultants. Given the number of studies, reports, books, PhDs, grants, loans, consultancies, EIAs—it's odd, wouldn't you say, that there is no really reliable estimate of how many people have been displaced by Big Dams in India? That there is no estimate for exactly what the contribution of Big Dams has been to overall food production in India? That there hasn't been an official audit, a comprehensive, honest, thoughtful, post-project evaluation of a single Big Dam to see whether or not it has achieved what it set out to achieve? Whether or not the costs were justified, or even what the costs actually were?

What *are* the experts up to?

If you manage to ignore the invective, shut out the din of the Expert's Anthem, and keep your eye on the ball, you'll find that a lot of dubious politics lurks inside the stables of "expertise." Probe further, and it all precipitates in a bilious rush of abuse, intimidation, and blind anger. The intellectual equivalent of a police baton charge. The advantage of provoking this kind of unconstrained, spontaneous rage is that it allows you to get a good look at the instincts of some of these normally cautious, supposedly "neutral" people, the pillars of democracy—judges, planners, academics. It becomes very clear that it's not really a question of experts versus laypersons or of knowledge versus ignorance. It's the pitting of one value system against another, one kind of political instinct against another. It's interesting to watch so many supposedly "rational" people turn into irrational, instinctive political beings. To see how they find reasons to support their views, and how, if those reasons are argued away, they continue to cling to their views anyway. Perhaps for this alone, provocation is important. In a crisis, it helps to clarify who's on which side.

A wonderful illustration of this is the Supreme Court's reaction to my essay "The Greater Common Good," which was published in May 1999. In July and August of that year, the monsoon waters rose in the Narmada and submerged villages. While villagers stood in their homes for days together in chest-deep water to protest against the dam, while their crops were submerged, and while the NBA— Narmada Bachao Andolan, the people's movement in the Narmada valley— pointed out (citing specific instances) that government officials had committed perjury by signing false affidavits claiming that resettlement had been carried out when it hadn't, the three-judge bench in the Supreme Court met over three sessions. The only subject they discussed was whether or not the dignity of the court had been undermined. To assist them in their deliberations, they appointed what is called an *amicus curiae* (friend of the court) to advise them about whether or not they should initiate criminal proceedings against the NBA and me for contempt of court. The thing to keep in mind is that, while the NBA was the petitioner, I was (and hopefully still am) an independent citizen. I wasn't present in court, but I was told that the three-judge bench ranted and raved and referred to me as "that woman." (I began to think of myself as the hooker who won the Booker.)

On October 15, 1999, they issued an elaborate order. Here's an extract:

> . . . Judicial process and institution cannot be permitted to be scandalised or subjected to contumacious violation in such a blatant manner in which it has been done by her [Arundhati Roy] . . . vicious stultification and vulgar debunking cannot be permitted to pollute the stream of justice . . . we are unhappy at the way in which the leaders of NBA and Ms. Arundhati Roy have attempted to undermine the dignity of the Court. We expected better behavior from them. . . . After giving this matter thoughtful consideration . . . we are not inclined to initiate contempt proceedings against the petitioners, its leaders or Arundhati Roy . . . after the 22nd of July 1999 . . . nothing has come to our notice which may show that Ms. Arundhati Roy has continued with the objectionable writings insofar as the judiciary is concerned. She may have by now realised her mistake . . .

What's dissent without a few good insults?

Anyway, eventually, as you can see, they let me off. And I continued with my Objectionable Writings. I hope I've managed to inspire at least some in this audience to embark on careers as Vicious Stultificators and Vulgar Debunkers. We could do with a few more of those.

On the whole, in India, the prognosis is—to put it mildly—Not Good. And yet one cannot help but marvel at the fantastic range and depth and wisdom of the hundreds of people's resistance movements all over the country. They're being beaten down, but they simply refuse to lie down and die.

Their political ideologies and battle strategies span the range. We have the maverick Malayali professor who petitions the president every day against the communalization of history texts, Sunderlal Bahugana, who risks his life on indefinite hunger strikes protesting the Tehri Dam, the Adivasis in Jadugoda protesting uranium mining on their land, the Koel Karo Sanghathan resisting a mega-dam project in Jharkhand, the awe-inspiring Chattisgarh Mukti Morcha, the relentlessly dogged Mazdoor Kisan Shakti Sangathan, the Beej Bachao Andolan in Tehri-Garhwal fighting to save biodiversity of seeds, and of course, the Narmada Bachao Andolan, the people's movement in the Narmada valley.

India's redemption lies in the inherent anarchy and factiousness of its people, and in the legendary inefficiency of the Indian state. Even our heel-clicking, boot-stamping Hindu fascists are undisciplined to the point of being chaotic. They can't bring themselves to agree with each other for more than five minutes at a time.

Corporatizing India is like trying to impose an iron grid on a heaving ocean and forcing it to behave.

My guess is that India will not behave. It cannot. It's too old and too clever to be made to jump through the hoops all over again. It's too diverse, too grand, too feral, and—eventually, I hope—too democratic to be lobotomized into believing in one single idea, which is, ultimately, what globalization really is: Life Is Profit.

What is happening to the world lies, at the moment, just outside the realm of common human understanding. It is the writers, the poets, the artists, the singers, the filmmakers who can make the connections, who can find ways of bringing it into the realm of common understanding. Who can translate cash-flow charts and scintillating boardroom speeches into real stories about real people with real lives. Stories about what it's like to lose your home, your land, your job, your dignity, your past, and your future to an invisible force. To someone or something you can't see. You can't hate. You can't even image.

It's a new space that's been offered to us today. A new kind of challenge. It offers opportunities for a new kind of art. An art which can make the impalpable palpable, make the intangible tangible, and the invisible visible. An art which can draw out the incorporeal adversary and make it real. Bring it to book.

Cynics say that real life is a choice between the failed revolution and the shabby deal. I don't know . . . maybe they're right. But even they should know that there's no limit to just how shabby that shabby deal can be. What we need to search for and find, what we need to hone and perfect into a magnificent, shining thing, is a new kind of politics. Not the politics of governance, but the politics of resistance. The politics of opposition. The politics of forcing accountability. The politics of slowing things down. The politics of joining hands across the world and preventing certain destruction. In the present circumstances, I'd say that the only thing worth globalizing is dissent. It's India's best export.

Adam Clayman, *Calcutta Office Foyer*

Systems

Tim Parks

"The sun shone, having no alternative, on the nothing new. Murphy sat out of it, as though he were free, in a mew in West Brompton."

So run the opening lines of Samuel Beckett's first novel, *Murphy*, written in the mid-1930s. In a single image, with fantastic dispatch, they posit both an eternal reality and a modern hubris: the solar system continues as it ever has and always must, no alternatives, nothing new; Murphy, the hero, the modern self, likes to think he can sit out of it, he can be free, his own man making his own decisions. The scene is set for comedy, the comedy of modern life. You think you engage with the world and its many systems on your own terms, you think you make decisions; in fact your identity, your very pattern of thought, may be no more than a casual expression of systems whose influence you haven't so much as guessed.

So, apart from the orbiting planets, what are the systems we all live in? Let's switch from experimental literature to true story. Thirty years ago, a small-time Italian entrepreneur—let's call him Giacomo—is running his own textiles business just outside Genoa. Giacomo is married with two small daughters. He and his family are perfectly integrated in an Italian society that recognizes in the one-man business the economic and moral backbone of the country. Giacomo is both *capo*, boss, and *capofamiglia*, head of the family. These are traditional roles. His wife, Laura, is a primary school teacher. Almost all primary school teachers in Italy are women. The job makes it easy to have children; having children keeps mothers-in-law happy. Again traditional expectations are satisfied. Both Giacomo and Laura go to church. Almost everybody in their small community goes to church. Both feel in control of their lives. They each have their plans, but plans that upset no apple carts. Nobody's going to lose out. The only difficulty is thinking of something to confess before receiving the host. But for that, there's the tradition of tax evasion.

Time to stop a moment here, maybe, and reflect that you are who you are only in relation to the people arranged around you. You can't be a son without a mother or a husband without a wife. You can't be a manufacturer without a market, or a member of a congregation without priest and prayer book. Any society is a complementary community of minds and roles, each making the other who they are: the boss, the secretary. But so long as everything is static, there is no need to take note. Giacomo certainly doesn't think that way. He believes he's an individual.

Then suddenly in the early seventies, economic circumstances change. On the edge of bankruptcy, Giacomo finds himself obliged to accept an offer of employment from the multinational that until now was his main customer. Very soon, his ambitions have metamorphosed. In this new environment, self-realization must come from promotion within the corporate system, not through survival in a world of cutthroat competition. Giacomo starts to learn English; in 1980 he is invited to run a new office opening in Finland.

Only when woken up do you become aware you were dreaming. Only when obliged to move do you realize how much of your state of mind depended on where you were. The first paragraph of *Murphy* continues thus: "Here [in West Brompton], for what might have been six months he [Murphy] had eaten, drunk, slept, and put his clothes on and off, in a medium-sized cage of northwestern aspect commanding an unbroken view of medium-sized cages of south-eastern aspect. Soon he would have to make other arrangements, for the mew had been condemned. Soon he would have to buckle to and start eating, drinking, sleeping, and putting his clothes on and off, in quite alien surroundings."

When the routine remains the same, you don't even know whether it's been six months or six years. Don't we often have that impression of our marriages, jobs, and houses? Deluding himself he's his own man, Murphy is in fact living in a cage, which turns out to be part of a complex system of cages. Even the language, with its balance of repetitions and opposites—medium size, northwestern, southeastern—seems to form a grid, another system that traps you in the rules of its syntax, the rhythms of its rhetoric ("commanding a view" indeed! From a cage!).

But here comes the irony: there's nothing worse than being bounced out of the cage—lodgings, language, or love affair—where you thought you were free.

Murphy's mew has been condemned. Beckett uses *mew* rather than *mews* because in sixteenth-century English, the word meant cage. Murphy isn't aware of the implications of the language he uses.

And more than anything else, it's the change of language that does it for Giacomo and Laura. They're in the suburbs of Helsinki. He is speaking English in corporate offices. No, he's not really speaking English. It's a code, a system of signs for getting on with business, for playing a power game. Leaving Italian behind, Giacomo enjoys a quite unexpected shiver of exhilaration. He is also leaving behind the catholic piety his mother tongue is drenched in, the in-laws who kept an eye on him, the weekly mass and unquestioned morals. English, for Giacomo and the German men and Finnish women who work with him, is just a tool for getting what you want. He wants his secretary.

All the more so because his wife has become miserable. Laura, whose mother was Calabrian, is slightly darker than Giacomo. This never seemed important in Italy, but in Finland it's noticed. She is treated badly. People call her gypsy. She has lost her job. She knows a few words of English, but hers is not the world of the corporate office. Shopkeepers and babysitters insist on Finnish. She cannot be who she is, or imagined she was, because the friends and the language that confirmed her identity are no longer there. She can't participate. Isolated and lonely, she puts huge demands on her husband, who is rarely around and helpless when he is. He begins to feel that the Italian culture he has left behind is a world of whining and chains, a mother tongue with mother's nagging. In bed with the charming Ilsa, and later Heike, and later Erika, he can't understand how he was ever happy there. In pidgin English, all the girls are turtledoves.

Eventually Laura is "saved" by the Jehovah's Witnesses. Like any close knit sect, these fine people stalk the lonely; they draw the depressed and insecure, those who have fallen out of a supporting system, into the cozy trap of their community. The Witnesses teach Laura Finnish; most of all, they teach her the Bible— their Bible in Finnish. She can now speak to shopkeepers and schoolteachers. She can speak to God, in Finnish. She takes her children to Jehovah's Witness meetings. She pulls them out of the international school and sends them to a Finnish school.

What a wonderful way of punishing Giacomo this is! Now when he is available, she is out delivering leaflets, attending meetings, earning salvation. What are the gains of a multinational's market share compared to a place in heaven? Her mind is locked into something else. She has a new identity. Irritated, Giacomo nevertheless senses that in this way, the crisis has been avoided. The Jehovah's Witnesses have bought him time. Who am I? he wonders, International playboy or wronged husband? The only thing that really annoys him is when Laura begins to speak to the children in Finnish.

Beckett's Murphy decides that if he can never be free in material terms, since one is always obliged to find food and shelter, he may at least be free in his mind. He recalls the old Homeric image of the sailor who is bound to travel east, because his ship is going that way, but is at least free to roam the deck at will. He opts for a life of meditation. But even this limited mental freedom soon proves illusory. Murphy falls in love: the mind is at the whim of biological imperatives. Then, even worse, he begins to suspect that his very thoughts are driven more by the English tongue than by his own intelligence. He is a pawn of his English heritage.

Giacomo gets off a long phone conversation in pidgin English. Laura, unable to follow, has been watching his animated face. "You've changed since we came here," she accuses him. "I could say the same about you," he objects. They are arguing. "Mummy, I don't understand," the younger daughter whines. They have been speaking Genoese dialect. Only her mother understands the girl's complaint, because she spoke in Finnish. Laura gets out her Bible to read to the children. Giacomo has to study a manual of network management software, in English.

Beckett became obsessed with the idea that rather than being an instrument for knowing the world, language, like any of the other systems in which we live, actually served to cloak and hide reality. You had an illusion of control and communication within a pattern of signs and sounds that were in fact a closed system, entirely detached from the world. If one couldn't do without language, he thought, at least one might do everything one could to show it up for what it was, "to bore holes in it."

But at the same time Beckett appreciated that such a project would not help anybody to live. Language, like any other habit, social, physical, mental, offered a way of getting through life. "There is no such thing as a bad habit," he paradoxically declared. Changing language to French in a desperate bid to gain control, he began to write a series of books in which decrepit characters cling pathetically, but wisely, to ancient overcoats, battered hats, the rags of their identity. One sleeps in a ditch, wrapping himself in the *Times Literary Supplement.*

After fifteen years, Giacomo and Laura move back to Italy. Everything has changed. The people who made them who they were have gone. Even the politics has changed. No more Communists and Christian Democrats. Dialect is dying out. Fortunately for Giacomo, it's been a long time since he lived in anything that could properly be called a geographical space at all, so he's not disturbed. He moves in a globalized world of airports, international hotels, videoconference rooms, hyperspace links. What is globalization but the vocation to create a world where at last everywhere will be the same and there will be no need to move out of one system into another. When all the races and gods and economies have been properly mixed and settle down together speaking bad English, then at last we may achieve the same security the ancient Greeks or Indians had in the closed systems of their myths. Everywhere CNN, everywhere the same multinational brand names, the same morals: a universal enchantment, the ultimate everlasting overcoat where, with no outside to fall into, I can at last feel sure I'm an "individual."

"You never look outside the narrowest, most sectarian, most bigoted bunch of ignoramuses," Giacomo accuses his wife. "Wake up!"

There is an international network of Witnesses. Laura didn't have to change her life greatly on return to Italy. Each group works in the same way with the same hierarchy, the same objectives.

"You worship a pure power drive in a treadmill of airports and hotels," she replies. This is a line she has recently read in *The Watchtower.* Why haven't they split up? Perhaps because each feels that at the deepest level, their fullest identity only exists by virtue of the other's reproach. The Witnesses are not quite enough. Network planning and occasional flings will not quite suffice. Maybe every system is tensed by the thought that it has rivals out there.

Until, catching them on a rare Saturday together, there comes a knock at the door. It's a tall blond boy in his late teens. Giacomo imagines he's a Witness. Their daughters have left home now, so it can't be a boyfriend. Laura assumes a salesman. But there is something familiar in the young man's eyes, the set of the nose. In broken English, he addresses himself to Giacomo: "I'm your son. Ilsa Saarinen is my mother. She said you refused to recognize me."

Perhaps rather than *system,* the word I should have used throughout this piece is *enchantment.* We have tried so hard and long to convince ourselves that knowledge is absolute, regardless of the observer or the medium of observation. Yet one only need change language, or culture, to appreciate that everything is known in a different way here, as though under a different light, with a different background noise, that changes the noise in our heads too. The language is a spell that makes thought possible; the systems of hyperspace are a bewitchment within which things can be known in new ways. But the ultimate sorcery is life itself, the fragment of quicksilver inside the head whose experience is that of being alone, while at the same time knowing it only can speak that thought to itself in a language learned from Mother. After nineteen years of resistance, Giacomo finally says: "Elias, Elias." This is the ultimate system of blood and generation, the trap of life itself. Without hesitation, Laura begins to speak to the boy in Finnish.

Ghost of a Full-Contact Commute

Mark Rudman

I'll go anywhere.
Preferably somewhere where you have to drive 50 miles to see a film,
250 miles for a repertory production of *Endgame*.
Anywhere, the more desolate and empty the better.
Where other people's lives are unimaginable.
What they do. Where they go.
And how, just how, they cultivate the simple life.
I'll go where the dawns are ratty and night lies wound inside the night.
Requirement one: that the streets be unlike these where I am.
And the thud of windshield wipers banned.
I'll go anywhere, anywhere but here.
I'll go where the fields are vast and the fences barely visible in the early morning
    haze.
I'll go where the possibilities are small,
The equation purged of infinity and choice
And the enemy known.
I'll go where the Number One communicable disease is conception
And no one conceives of acting on the impulse to deceive.
I'll go where phones have been replaced by interfacial voice activated "E"
And you can purchase a three bedroom ranch and an entire
Acre for what a studio apartment goes for.
I'll go where *cenotaphology* is a word and no one is subject
To a brute full-contact commute.
I'll go where the entire town lunches in one restaurant,
Every private conversation is public—though rarely does anyone press Record—
Roll is taken at events and absences
Noted. Just in case.
I'll go where the punishment for not showing up at events is exile:
(If you don't want to be here we'll help you to leave.)
I'll go where gum wrappers follow.
I'll go, if I have to, where there's never a line—
The populace has no time to kill.
And where, since there are no strangers, anyone
Can correct you in a lie, anytime.
I'll go where disobedient skies provoke shudders of inclemency
And where premonitory signs are removed from sight.

I'll go, if I must, where habit takes the edge out.
I didn't say the sacrifice was worth it, but it must be.
I won't be ruled by what I'm accustomed to.
I'll go where the batteries, duct tape, and plastic, are handed out upon arrival.
And if I have to, while I'm looking for a bungalow within walking distance of
    nothing,
I'll stay at the Amnesia Inn, "Vacancy Guaranteed."
I'll go where the one lane highway is a one lane highway in name only.
I'll go where every purchase is imperiled with a tracking device, invisible magnets
Instead of magnetized strips, just in case your car rolls over.
I wonder what fate led me to this intersection.

Carol Van Houten, *The Powerhouse, New Jersey*

We Better Collect the Birds' Nests before the Outsiders Get Here

Paul Spencer Sochaczewski

What could be more exciting than being with men who walk into the forest wearing faded basketball shorts, encumbered only with handmade bows and arrows, accompanied by just a couple of dogs, and return home an hour or two later with a deer? Where in the world are people still so independent and self-sufficient?

With my friend Mark van der Wal and a small team of researchers and support crew, I met two local men—Ely and Yos—in the tiny village of Jirlai on the island of Aru, just off the western coast of New Guinea.

I asked Ely and Yos how they made money. They explained that they sell birds of paradise, birds' nests, and deer jerky. Had they lived on the coast of this rarely visited island, their answer likely would have been sea turtles, sea cucumbers, mother of pearl, and sharks' fins. They rely on nature, and two of their main sources of cash—the birds of paradise and the swiftlets, which create birds' nests—are protected or vulnerable species.

Even in as isolated a place as Aru (a Puerto Rico–sized island some four times zones and five flights from the capital of Jakarta), people need *some* cash—to pay school fees, to buy kerosene and monosodium glutamate and beer and soap, to buy a T-shirt and a dress for the wife.

How ironic. *We* envy them for their simplicity. *They* envy us for our possessions. I thought of philosopher Thomas Berry's comment that the future belongs not to those who have the most but to those who need the least. I bet Ely and Yos wouldn't agree. They see only the present. And in the present, the one with the most toys wins. They're not unique—given half a chance, there are precious few societies in the world where people would not opt for electricity and TV, motorcycles and access to a town.

We asked whether they had noticed a reduction in birds or fish or big mammals.

"Yes. There are fewer birds' nests to collect now," the two men told me.

"But why?"

"We collect the nests three or four times a year, so there are fewer swiflets, of course."

"What if you collect nests only twice a year? What if you set up some kind of control system?" I asked.

"Yes! *Sasi*" they said, referring to a traditional control of harvesting natural resources. But they gave me looks that said it would never work. "The problem is, if we don't take them, someone else will."

"Who?"

"Outsiders."

Which shows that things haven't changed much since the Victorian explorer Alfred Russel Wallace was here in the middle of the nineteenth-century. "The trade carried on at Dobbo [now Dobo, still the only town in Aru] is very considerable," he wrote.

Then and now, the town of Dobo flourished because traders were raping and pillaging what Wallace called "natural productions." Dobo, where the majority of Aru's 63,000 people live, is in the running for the most miserable town in Indonesia, with stinking open drains, houses built over tidal flats reeking of sewage, muddy lanes, malarial mosquitoes, and surly, overfed Chinese traders. Half hidden away in the back of restaurants we saw rare parrots and cockatoos, available for a price. We ogled baskets of turd-like dried sea cucumbers, piles of dried sharks' fins. Merchants would happily sell you trinkets made from mother of pearl whose real price was never mentioned—the environmental cost and the fact that the untrained village lads who were paid by the piece sometimes got the bends because they dove too deep, came up too quickly, or used faulty equipment provided by the Chinese traders. Boats sailed from Dobo to Hong Kong restaurants with reef fish caught by dynamiting the coral beds. Other boats were loaded with live green sea turtles, as long as a man's leg, stacked on their backs like grotesque poker chips. In the Aru village of Sia, we saw where many of these creatures came from. Friendly kids offered to sell us cassowary eggs, crocodile skins, and dugong teeth. I admired a small green parrot that a young happy boy offered, only $5, a bargain, and protected by a law conceived in distant Jakarta. The boy had no concept this was an endangered species, a heritage of mankind, a treasure beyond words, a poster animal for the Western conservation movement. To him it was simply a product that could help him earn his school fees.

One day Mark and I wanted some vegetables to accompany the roast pork and fish we would be having for dinner, and in the forest of Aru asked Ely if there were any edible leaves growing nearby.

Ely disappeared for the afternoon. That night we were pleasantly surprised when he cooked up a potful of leaves, probably thinking it doesn't take much to keep two Europeans happy. The next day, while out walking, we came upon a tree, maybe 20 meters tall, about 30 centimeters in diameter, that had recently been chopped down. "What happened here?" we asked. "Yesterday you said you wanted vegetables," Ely answered, plucking some withering leaves from the fallen tree. We were incredulous. "Never mind," he said, allaying our unspoken doubts. "The deer like these leaves. We'll go hunting here tomorrow."

Around the fire we got to talking about abstractions.

"What's the most important thing to give to your children?"

"*Sayang*," Ely and Yos answered. Love and attention. "And education."

"Are your people more like the [Malay-race] Javanese or the [Negroid] Papuans?" I asked.

"Papuan," they agreed.

"I see lots of Javanese in the towns," I said, expecting to provoke an anti-Javanese response. "Javanese settlers move to Irian Jaya for transmigration. Javanese run the government."

"We need more education," Ely and Yos answered warily.

"Why don't you have better schools?" I asked, recognizing I was treading on sensitive ground.

"The Javanese want to keep us stupid," they eventually said.

"And the future? What about your son, Ely? Will he grow up to be an engineer, or governor of the province?"

Ely and Yos were silent. I pushed. Is there an Arunese equivalent of the American dream in which any child can grow up to be president?

"The boy will probably grow up to be like me," Ely finally admitted.

"And his world?"

"More people. Too many people fishing with nets. Fewer fish, fewer turtles. Fewer birds of paradise."

Ely and Yos then asked me what I thought would happen to nature.

I felt strangely close to these men. I told them how they face the same problems as other rural people in South America and Africa and all over Asia. How rich countries, like mine, could afford anything they wanted, and how less-rich countries, like theirs, survived by providing these luxuries. I told them about birds of paradise feathers being in demand a century ago for ladies' hats.

We talked about the need for a *Ratu Adil,* a just leader. How local people, like Ely and Yos, know full well how to maintain wildlife populations but don't have a chance because the global marketplace forces them into rapidly depleting their birds' nests. If Ely and Yos don't make money from nature, then an outsider will. To me it was clear. Don't give outsiders a chance to get rich, I said. They listened quietly.

I thought I should tell them about UNPO, the Dutch-based Unrepresented Nations and Peoples Organization that fights for statehood for Mohawks from Quebec, Kurds from Iraq, and Frisians from Holland. And if that doesn't work, well, get tough.

I sounded like Che Guevera. Like a college student of the late sixties. Rebel. Get control of your destiny. Peasants of the world arise. I was, God help me, paternalistic.

"Wouldn't you be happier being in control of your resources?" I asked. With each question, Ely became increasingly withdrawn. To me, the conversation was a mischievous intellectual exercise. To Ely, however, this talk was conspiratorial and not at all in the spirit of Indonesia's national feel-good philosophy of *pancasila.*

"Too bad we haven't seen birds of paradise," I said, changing the subject. Like many other visitors, we longed to see these rare birds, found only in Aru and New Guinea and surrounding islands. Besides being strikingly ornate, the birds come with a legend worthy of an epic poem. The early Portuguese and Dutch explorers, who were basically adventurous traders seeking wealth in the spice islands, then the only source of cloves and nutmeg as well as pepper and numerous other valuable commodities, were presented with curious brightly colored bird skins that had no feet. The locals had simply hacked off the appendages, perhaps deciding that a legless bird was more aesthetically pleasing. The Europeans, however, deduced that the creatures spent their entire lives in the air, using a depression in the female's back as an open-air nest, and dubbed them, in Portuguese, *Passaros de Sol,* or birds of the sun. The learned Dutchmen who followed the Portuguese dusted off their Latin schooling and named the creature *Avis paradiseus,* or paradise bird.

We accepted that we would never glimpse these rare creatures, so instead we explored the island's caves. In one cave, up to our knees in cold water, our flashlights caught glimpses of spooky white fish. We flailed around like schoolboys trying to catch some in our mist net, which was designed for nocturnal bats. Ely, seeing what we were after, borrowed one of our flashlights and disappeared into the depths of the grotto. He came back twenty minutes later with two small fish that he had speared. We were overjoyed, thinking that these *must* be new species. We were somewhat less amused when they arrived on our dinner plates a couple of hours later.

Finally, on our last morning, we saw a tree full of birds of paradise. There were well over a dozen, their calls somewhere between a squawk and a honk. One male was displaying his yellow and white tail feathers like a Portofino playboy cruising in his Ferrari. This was the great bird of paradise, one of just two bird of paradise species found on Aru.

Timo, a Javanese who seemed to have no clear job description in our small expedition, gazed up at the birds and said he wished that he had a gun. We thought this a bit odd, since Timo works for the Indonesian Department of Nature Conservation. We suggested that his department was supposed to conserve things. Our comments didn't seem to change his attitude, and he began making irritating popping noises.

But I wasn't about to let Timo shatter the moment. I gazed upward, as did Alfred Russel Wallace who exclaimed that "the bird of paradise really deserves its name, and must be ranked as one of the most beautiful and most wonderful of living things."

We watched the birds of paradise for half an hour. Mark and I remember this as a profound experience. Ely and Yos seemed to wait patiently until we had gazed our fill. Timo, realizing he couldn't shoot the birds in our presence, wandered about bored.

Funny, isn't it? Ely looked at the bird and saw a meal ticket, Alfred Russel Wallace wrote about the "ecstasy" of just seeing the creature, while Timo the game warden mentally calculated how much the birds would be worth stuffed and sold to a trader.

I tried, for a final time, to instigate Ely to revolt. "*You* should be controlling these birds of paradise." As soon as I said it, we both knew it was unlikely. Without saying a word, Ely and I looked at Timo and then looked back at each other in understanding. Timo, who was not-from-there, nevertheless had access to this forest and, via his government job, some authority that he could leverage into bribes in exchange for turning a blind eye to trading in birds of paradise. If push came to shove, it would be the Timos of the world who got control of the birds of paradise. I looked at Ely standing there in his shorts and carrying his bow and arrows and remembered our conversations about his needing money to send his kids to school. I then looked up at these valuable birds, true things of beauty. It's easy to paraphrase Keats, I thought, if you can afford to carry a Nikon around your neck.

In the West, we consider that the classic arrogance in Asia is white versus brown, the anthem of which is Kipling's famous "white man's burden," which he penned on the occasion of America's taking possession of the Philippines. He warned that when victory is near "watch sloth and heathen Folly / Bring your hope to nought."

While white-brown friction certainly hasn't disappeared, few outsiders realize that in today's Asia, brown-brown arrogance is much more prevalent and pernicious.

Take, for example, the message promoted by tourism boards throughout Asia, which encourage foreigners to experience "native cultures." This is an evolution of the African game park concept, but instead of judging the success of the holiday by whether the visitor sees elephants and lions, the cultural safari tourist will go home content having bagged an all-night rice-wine blast with sons of headhunters in Sarawak, one of the Malaysian states on the island of Borneo.

I sought out James Wong Kim Min for guidance. He was concurrently the Sarawak state minister of tourism and local government and one of the state's biggest timber tycoons, a combination that might befuddle a lesser man.

Although pasty of complexion, he was bursting with energy. "What do you want to talk about? Penans?" he asked, referring to the controversial group of several hundred hunter-gatherers who live in the interior of the state.

James Wong loves to talk with foreigners about the Penan, whom the foreign press has idealized as a group of innocent, downtrodden, blowpipe-wielding, loin-clothed people who are wise in the ways of the forest but hopelessly naive when faced with modern Malaysian politics.

At least no one can accuse James Wong of shrinking from a good debate. "I met with Bruno's Penans in the upper Limbang [River]," he said, referring to Swiss Bruno Manser who lived with the Penan for several years and allegedly encouraged them to blockade timber operations and fight for their rights. Manser disappeared in May 2000 in the middle of the Sarawak rain forest and is presumed dead. "I asked the Penan, 'Who will help you if you're sick? Bruno?' The Penans now realize they've been exploited. I tell them the government is there to help them. But I ask them, 'How can I see you if you've blocked the road that I've built for you?'"

I asked if he had a message for his critics.

"This is my message to the West. If they can do as well as we have done and enjoy life as much as we do, then they can criticize us. We run a model nation. We have twenty-five races and many different religions living side by side without killing each other. Compare that to Bosnia or Northern Ireland. We've achieved a form of nirvana, a utopia. Economic development, racial integration, and religious tolerance."

On that point James Wong is right. Leaving aside the downtrodden (but not yet annihilated) Penan for the moment, Sarawak *is*, in many ways, a model society. People's lives *are* improving. Education *is* important. Health services *are* common. It may be poor in spots, but in general Sarawak is one of the most harmonious places I've ever lived. You can walk anywhere in safety, and see smiles and eat good cheap food and buy whatever you need. Forgetting the forest destruction and related social and environmental dilemmas for a moment, it's a pretty good corner of the world.

I explained my experience with the Penans, who had been encouraged by generous government incentives to resettle into longhouses. How their natural environment had been hammered, how their faces were devoid of spirit and energy, how they had seemingly tumbled even further down the Sarawak social totem pole.

In reply, James Wong lectured me, as I have been lectured by numerous other Asian officials when I raised similar concerns. In effect, he said, "We just want our cousins the naked Penan to enjoy the same benefits we civilized folk enjoy."

"We are very unfairly criticized by the West," he added. "As early as 1980 I was concerned about the future of the Penans." To prove it he pointed out a poem he had written:

> O Penan—Jungle wanderers of the Tree
> What would the future hold for thee? . . .
>
> Perhaps to us you may appear deprived and poor
> But can Civilization offer anything better? . . .

And yet could Society in good conscience
View your plight with detached indifference
Especially now we are an independent Nation
Yet not lift a helping hand to our fellow brethren?
Instead allow him to subsist in Blowpipes and clothed in Chawats
    [loincloths]
An anthropological curiosity of Nature and Art?
Alas, ultimately your fate is your own decision
Remain as you are—or cross the Rubicon!

On a bluff at the entrance to the kingdom of Mustang, in the far north of the king-dom of Nepal, a sign warns wanderlustful trekkers: "Stop. You are now entering the restricted area of Upper Mustang."

Lured by the forbidden mystery, we gaze up the wide, graveled riverbed at a narrow track, accessible only by foot, pony, or yak, that connects the lowlands of India and Nepal with the isolated mountain plateaus of Tibet and Central Asia. Scattered villages, hours apart, and their patches of green barley, offer evidence of civilization in this otherwise arid landscape that is all ochres and browns and lunar. We have walked through a pass in the Himalayas and head north, along the ancient salt route that winds along the river's banks, toward Lo Manthang. This fabled walled city is the capital of Upper Mustang and site of the seldom seen Tiji festival, a three-day masked dance performed by monks that aims to rid the world of devils.

On top of the normal expense of hiring a trekking team of sherpas, porters, and cooks, visitors to the "forbidden kingdom" of Upper Mustang, which has been only open to foreigners since 1992, need a special trekking permit, which costs $700 for ten days. Additionally, you have to pay $400 for the services of a govern-ment liaison officer who's there to make sure you don't walk into Tibet.

The $700 fee, which buys a flimsy green trekking permit, has led to consider-able tension in Upper Mustang.

Mr. Purna Kunwar, the Jomson-based director of ACAP (Annapurna Conserva-tion Area Project), a powerful nongovernmental organization that runs many of the development projects in the Annapurna region, explained the situation.

"When the government opened up Mustang to tourists in 1992, they signed an agreement with ACAP promising that 60 percent of the fee would go for develop-ment in Upper Mustang," he says.

The potential profit gained from the 800 visitors who enter Upper Mustang annually would have been a nice sum.

In practice, Mr. Kunwar explained, the amount of money returned to Upper Mustang is just 8 percent, which doesn't go very far when shared by a dozen villages spread over 780 square miles.

In frustration at being deprived of income from high-rolling tourists, in 1998 the local Tiji organizing committee hit visitors with a hefty camera fee of $50 per day for a still camera and $150 per day for a video camera. Their rationale was that they needed the cash to maintain the costumes, instruments, and paintings used in the Tiji festival.

This fee was announced in a flier handed out to visitors when they first dug their Canons and Minoltas out of their backpacks. "Hearty welcome to Teeji Festival," it read. "Owing to our lenience toward clicking the festival in the preceding years its deep rooted religious festival gets diluted which in turn decreases the number of its attendants as it had before."

Pema Tsering, thirty, a shy, articulate teacher at the Great Sakyapa Monastic School and spokesman for the Tiji festival committee, explained: "We're embarrassed by this as well. But what can we do? Most of the little money that ACAP collects for Upper Mustang goes for community development. Almost nothing is allocated for cultural development. We use this income to maintain the Tiji costumes. We've asked the government for some money, but they ignore our request. If we don't take the initiative, the government certainly won't do it for us."

Most tourist groups nominated a designated photographer and bought one pass. One non-fee paying American doctor from Milwaukee, Wisconsin, had his video camera confiscated (it was returned to him when he left Lo Manthang) by Tiji camera spies, who busted him when he ignored the fine print in the festival's letter: "Severe action will be taken by the committee for those who are seen clicking without permits and who violate this rule in any unfair and tricky means."

The ethnic-Nepali people who run things in the distant capital of Kathmandu have no great love for the ethnic-Tibetan people of Upper Mustang. To the Nepali people in the relative sophistication of Kathmandu, the folks of Upper Mustang are a modest resource, the opportunity to earn a few thousand dollars a year. It's the same arrogant dynamic you see between the lowland Javanese disdain for the likes of Ely and Yos in Aru; similar to the paternalism of sophisticated coastal Chinese like James Wong, for the loin-clothed Penan who live far away from the city centers. The mentality seems to be: "We lowlanders run things." The never verbalized argument seems to go: "We're smart, educated, and civilized, and we grow wet rice." The rural people are none of the above, and if they grow rice at all, they are more likely to grow less sophisticated hill paddy rice using a slash-and-burn technique. Mix this arrogance with control over "natural productions" that fetch a high price on the global economy and the result is an invidious eco-paternalism that says, "We're more equal than you are, and nature be damned."

The us vs. them attitude has been at the root of nature destruction since societies were created. Look at the conquering of the American West, and you'll see a similar dynamic.

Perhaps this arrogance stems from man's like-fear relationship with nature.

On the one hand, we come from nature; we are part of nature. Our early ancestors groveled with other animals, fought them for carrion, found shelter in the forests, opportunity in the plains. Don't believe it? Why does the presence of green scenery lower our blood pressure and relieve stress? Why do people working in bleak, anonymous offices nurture a houseplant to brighten things up? Why do people recovering from operations improve faster when their window has a view of a park? Even having a photograph of nature speeds healing compared to a barren wall.

Yet what about the fear? Well, we define ourselves partly by what we are not. We are no longer "savages" who coexist with animals; we are beyond that. Eventually our ancestors learned to use plants for medicine, build complex shelters, and—after much trial and error—master nature by growing crops and domesticating other animals. We have civilization, language, Michelangelo and Michael Jackson and Michael Jordan. We have plows and guns. And above all, many of us have been imprinted by one of the three strict, paternalistic, monotheistic desert religions that put a lot more emphasis on us having "dominion" over nature than on, say, the Buddhist approach of living in "harmony" with nature. We don't like undisciplined nature too close to us. That's why we garden. That's why we work like hell to have a crabgrass-free lawn and a neat flowerbed. That's why the Balinese file the teeth of their preadolescent children—so that the child does not have pointy, animal-like cuspids. That's why most first- and second-generation urban people, like those you'll find in Jakarta, will look at you askance when you explain that you're going into the deep forests. You're likely to get a response like: "Ugh, full of snakes!" or "No electricity" or "Go shopping in Singapore instead." It's all a way of saying, "The forest is alien, it's dangerous, it's filled with people having strange animistic pre-Christian/Muslim/Jewish beliefs who worship spirits that reside in the trees and streams and volcanoes." There are creatures in the deep wilderness (think yeti) that will tear off your head. We're afraid of looking too deeply into the mirror and seeing our wild side.

Take this to its logical extension, and you arrive at the "big dick" approach to nature. Oil in Alaska? Well, it's our right, it's our obligation to drill for it, regardless of what damage such exploration might do. Pollution? Well, that's the price of progress. This is a mantra often heard when Westerners try to convince developing countries to conserve nature. Their argument: "But you built *your* civilization by cutting down your forests and civilizing your savages and creating great polluting cities. We just want the same opportunity to develop. You can't deny us that basic right."

This is near the core of our schizophrenic relationship with nature. We want nature but we fear it. We're part of nature but we want to dissociate ourselves from anything too wild. And we're likely to maintain this right brain-left brain view of our position on nature. On one side, we have what could be termed a female approach to nature: we are part of the global scheme of things, the interwoven tapestry of life that manifests itself as yang: mysterious, complex, sharing, questioning, fertile. On the other hand, we are very yin: logical, goal driven, protective of our own, confident, potent.

We park the car along the side of a rutted dirt road in the middle of an acacia tree plantation five times as large as Singapore. Lani anak Taneh points out a metal sign, the size of a paperback book, pounded into the ground at ankle height, which announces that the land we are about to enter belongs to his longhouse, Rumah Nor. We start walking through a desolate landscape that is all too common in the Malaysian state of Sarawak on the island of Borneo. What once had been ancient rain forest owned by a local community has been grabbed by big business and destroyed in the name of development.

Rumah Nor, some 60 kilometers southeast of Bintulu, site of the world's largest natural gas complex, is ground zero in a land rights battle in which Sarawak's indigenous people are fighting government and industrial powers.

Lani, thirty-three, was one of four plaintiffs in a legal battle that one conservationist has called "a major victory for the indigenous tribal people of Borneo—as important as the 1954 anti-segregation decision *Brown* v. *The Board of Education* was in the States."

Lani's Iban tribal longhouse community of some seventy families successfully sued to regain 672 hectares of land that the court decided had been illegally acquired by Borneo Pulp and Paper and the Sarawak state government.

"This case will open the floodgate to other suits," predicts Baru Bian, Rumah Nor's lawyer. "Anyone can now sue the government based on this precedent." He estimates there are more than twenty similar cases now pending in Sarawak against companies involved in oil palm, logging, pulp and paper, and mining.

We walk for several hours, first through cool natural rain forest where we can hear birds, then through a recent acacia plantation where few animals live, and finally along dirt tracks under the midday sun. When the forest was cleared, the thin layer of topsoil washed away, leaving sand and clay that eroded into curious cream-colored spires. We walk for an hour; the landscape has a desiccated lunar quality. "This is our *pulau menoa*," Lani explains, referring to a core area protected by traditional law. He realizes the paradox: "This is our rain forest," he says, gazing at the barren land. "This is what we won back."

I first lived in Sarawak in 1969 when it was largely covered in forests and people traveled to isolated longhouses by boat.

Today logging roads crisscross much of the state, three times as large as Switzerland, making it all too easy to see that some 70 percent of the forest has been destroyed or damaged.

Today, when I ask Sarawak government officials about the situation, they bridle at outside criticism, and argue that the timber business brings in needed revenue and that development will benefit local people.

Lani counters, "We are not against progress, only against injustice."

Government officials tell me that the United States built its wealth by using its natural resources, so why shouldn't they do the same?

Nevertheless, some people are unhappy enough in this utopia to blockade timber operations and sue the government, which I suppose is a healthier alternative to killing each other.

Sidi Munan, an Iban who is on the supreme council of the Parti Bansa Dayak Sarawak and former deputy chairman of the Sarawak Land Consolidation and Rehabilitation Authority, says, "Up to now, we have been free of the kind of hatred that we see in neighboring Indonesian Kalimantan," referring to the rampage of beheadings that took place earlier this year. On the surface, those 500 gruesome murders appeared ethnically based. Beneath the race issue, however, was the fact that indigenous Dayaks were fed up with arrogant Madurese immigrants coming in and taking away their land. The core of the fight was over who owns the land.

I thought of Euripides' statement that "there is no greater sadness on earth than the loss of one's native land," and how easily sadness can evolve into fury. It can get confusing out there for people caught in the middle of a globalization sandwich.

When the fundamentalist Baptist missionaries in the isolated Minyambou valley in Irian Jaya asked for contributions to build a new church, Zakarias chipped in with the most valuable thing he could find: a bird of paradise.

The irony of buying his way into heaven with a bird that represented holy salvation to the early Portuguese and Dutch explorers did not occur to Zakarias. What he does recognize is that everyone, it seems, is after his soul.

Zakarias showed me chunky grey caterpillars that nature conservationists encourage him to raise. These will become gaudy yellow and black swallow-tailed butterflies, and when sold to collectors will earn him a welcome few dollars each. Zakarias, I suppose, calls it a modest business that only recently has begun to pay off. For a couple of years, he had undertaken the extra work strictly as an act of faith—he had received promises of a payback, but no guarantees.

Conservationists like this kind of project, arguing that local people will conserve their rainforests only when they get some tangible benefits in return. The quid pro quo in this case is that Zakarias agrees to help manage and protect the Arfak Mountains Strict Nature Reserve in the "bird's head" corner of the Indonesian half of the island of New Guinea.

Call it what you will: an act of faith, a new way of saving nature, an example of "sustainable development." I call it a religion. In effect, the conservationists have, more or less, convinced Zakarias to change his behavior in return for a possible future reward. "Do not clear land for farms in the nature reserve," the conservation commandments say. "Respect the national park boundaries and enter not therein except to hunt deer with a bow and arrow. And don't even think about killing that bird of paradise."

The conservationists are among the most benign of the new religionists. The Javanese who run the country from distant Jakarta want to "Indonesianize" Zakarias by encouraging him to speak Bahasa Indonesia, to follow the civic principles of Pancasila, the national social-political philosophy, and to ignore the free-Irian movement simmering many miles and many languages to the east.

Fundamentalist Protestant preachers want to Christianize him, and by doing so add his tenor voice to the Sunday choir.

Tycoons who manufacture shampoo and jogging shoes want to consumerize him, by making him feel the desire for things his people have not needed for millennia previously.

And conservationists want to "empower" him, to give him a voice in saving nature, as long as it coincides with the way the experts think it works best.

And make no mistake, the four "religions" of church, nationalism, business, and conservation have achieved some significant results.

For example, some Christian missionaries in Irian Jaya, notably the Catholics, have helped stop cannibalism and infanticide, have established schools and clinics, and have initiated community development projects like water systems and gardens. But the conversions are not necessarily deep. While many people profess to be Christian of one form or another, it is not uncommon for Irianese to believe that sitting in church will result in immunity from sickness and that forgetting to shut one's eyes during prayers will lead to blindness.

"Trust us," the foreign preachers seem to say. "We're from the government/ church/business/nature conservation movement. We're here to help you. Believe in us—even though we give you no guarantee—and your life will be improved"— not dissimilar to the "we know better than you do and anyway God is on our side" arrogance of many modern cults, terrorist groups, and political parties. Napoleon said, "God is on the side of the heavy artillery." Today a cynic could add, "God is also cheering for the folks with the biggest bank account." Size matters.

And lots of people want a piece of that largesse. In Irian Jaya, many folks are retrograde cargo cultists. Sometimes it feels like the *koreri* cargo cult is back—a widespread Melanesian belief spawned during World War II when mysterious foreigners spoke into a metal box and hours later a giant noisy flying bird would drop boxes of treasures. All you need to do is perform the correct rites and the benevolent ancestors in the other world will bestow good health, food, and material goods. I guess it's like buying a lottery ticket every week. Material goods and Western values come through strange channels, and it's worth covering your bets despite the fact that the good Hatam people of Minyambou raise their voices to Jesus every Sunday before depositing a sweet potato in the collection box.

I was told this perhaps apocryphal story. An American missionary had a disciple, a young locally born man whom he had hoped would go off and undertake God's work in another isolated, wet, tuberculosis-ridden valley. The American missionary and his American wife and two kids lived in a prefab house that someone (surely not them) had somehow lugged up into the mountains. Although he had known the Irianese would-be missionary for several years, the American Bible thumper had lived aloof from the community and had never invited the acolyte into his house. Finally the American felt the local lad had passed all the hurdles but one. He suggested the young man join the family for a Coke, whereupon he asked him: "How will you know that you are the best Christian you can be?" The local man, who had grown up in a village without running water or access to medical care, where enough pigs could buy a wife or hire mercenaries to fight the tribe in the next valley, gazed around the inner sanctum, taking in the sight of a television and VCR, a radio-phone, a microwave, a refrigerator, a boom box, all powered by electricity generated by a tiny hydroelectric system the missionary had asked the local people to construct on the stream behind the village. The young man pondered the question, because it was important for him to get it right. When would he be an ideal Christian? Finally he replied: "When I have all the things you have."

Clearly the soul is a complicated organ. The day I was leaving Minyambou, I sought out Zakarias to say goodbye. He admired my watch. Seeing that I wasn't about to give it to him, he offered me a trade: my Casio for a bird of paradise skin.

I said a prayer for all of us.

The Aliens in the Garden

James Barilla

After the rains come in January, the seeds begin to sprout. Wherever the soil is bare, the milk thistle unfolds its prickly, white-veined hands. Where it is hard and packed with gravel, the Russian thistle swells into a bed of spiky tendrils, like a coral reef, while yellow-star thistle raises its luminous, succulent stems in the midst of dead grass. Evidence of their dominion is everywhere—phalanxes of last year's spike–tipped spears rattling in the wind, skeletons like giant porcupines caught in the fences, insidious tiny blades waiting for a passing thigh to embed themselves like fishhooks.

My job as manager of this sixty-acre expanse of former crop fields now slowly transforming into marsh and oak savanna is to kill them off. My initial delusion, that ecological restoration was exclusively a nurturing practice, ended with the first rains, when my boss told me that the thistles had emerged and it was time to spray—time to learn the ropes. The Californian Central Valley skies were full of yellow planes rolling loops and cutting the throttle to drift down like dragonflies, expelling white plumes of herbicide over the fields.

I didn't like the idea of handling the chemicals, even the ones that were supposedly harmless to humans, and I didn't want to ask volunteers to work where we'd sprayed. There was something dissonant, even hypocritical, in the picture of myself, someone who buys organic produce in the supermarket, dousing fields with weed killer. What bothered me most was the idea that we would remedy previous abuse with violence of our own.

The notion that people and species belong in certain places and not in others underlies such convoluted notions as homelands, exotic species, naturalized citizens, and permanent resident aliens, and despite our growing attention to the forces of globalization, it remains a primary source of violent conflict in the world. While it is tempting to escape this tension by separating the realm of science from the messy one of politics, when it comes to ecological restoration the two are inseparable, since restoration is the practical expression of a cultural ideal. When we plant button willow and pull out tamarisk, the stream bank becomes in part our creation, reflecting how we view ourselves—our desires, anxieties, and goals. Thus, the local prairie can become a flash point in the debate over globalization, the place where we find ourselves confronting difficult questions about what it means to be native and exotic in the midst of transcontinental communication and consumption. This is the place where our anxieties over homeland security and the threat of terrorist invasion, both of which pose uncomfortable questions for our democracy, are translated into local and less unsettling terms. Yet what motivates the restorationist is not xenophobia itself but the threat of extinction, the loss of global diversity that globalization brings. Globalization has placed the ecologist in the role of the police officer, an uncomfortable place for most of us to be. Balancing distaste for intolerance with the fear of extinction is the paradigmatic experience of globalization, leaving us in an ethical quandary from which there is no easy escape. The restored ecosystem is truly, as the writer and restoration ecologist William Jordan calls it, a "landscape of ambiguity," and it is also a landscape of ambivalence.

The practice of ecological restoration, I've discovered, means becoming intimate with the life cycles of globalizing species, perhaps even more so than with the natives we plant. Once we have chosen and planted the natives, we tend to step back as much as possible, to let them become more independent of us and therefore more "natural." Invasive species, in contrast, demand attention, disrupting our vision of natural harmony. They take over. In swarms, encrustations, blankets, and herds, they threaten to take control of the landscape away from us. To control them, we need to know their secrets—when they germinate, bloom, and set seed; how they disperse; whether fire will turn them to ash or spread their offspring in profusion. We learn more about them with every season because they always come back, forcing us to look again, to look more closely at the land.

When the milk thistle flowers, I buy a sickle from the hardware store and begin my quixotic attempts at manual control. As I stand before plants that were once the size of my fingernail and are now taller than me, it becomes immediately clear why the prevailing metaphors for biological invasions are militaristic. The plants, in a dense and uniform formation and armed to the teeth with spines, resemble nothing so much as the legions of an invading army.

Ugly species are easier to demonize. We often anthropomorphize these species into the creatures of our nightmares. The northern snakehead found lurking recently in a Maryland pond was not only voracious but hideous—a half-snake, half-fish poster child for the evils of hybridity. Similarly, the brown tree snake calls up all kinds of venomous and diabolical associations, making its tendency to fly the skies in airplane wheel wells, its strange attraction to electric power lines, and its assault on just about every creature it can lay its jaws on, all the more fiendish. Yet many of the invaders arrive because we bring them along for their beauty or usefulness. The fennel thatching the California roadsides once thrived in the garden, as did the forget-me-nots carpeting the state's shady groves. Milk thistle is a well-known European medicinal, used in treating the liver and pancreas. It is not a garden plant, but like Scotch broom or purple loosestrife, it could be. The plants bloom in June when all the grasses are withering in California, and like constellations of lavender sea anemones clinging to some brown expanse of rock, they seem to glow, glistening with nectar and intoxicating bees. It's easier to focus on the thorns, however, if you plan to cut them down.

There is something satisfying in the prospect of taking action against weeds with your own hands, a rectitude that harkens back to the Calvinist work ethic and Jefferson's notion of the independent yeoman farmer. Prairie restorationists often describe controlled burning, their preferred method for keeping invasive plants at bay, as a cathartic experience, when the tension that rises with the flames is finally released, and destruction balances cultivation in a ritual of renewal. I feel myself anticipating a visceral discharge of pent-up frustration as I swing at the thistles. I pick out a target, taller than its neighbors. Aphids cluster over its buds, tended by tiny ants, stalked by the ferocious-jawed larvae of ladybugs, by hoverflies that resemble bees, and by something akin to a stinkbug with a mouth like a hypodermic needle. The bugs are mostly exotics too, an entire community of nonnatives colonizing this colony of thistles.

Since I'm not familiar with the proper form for wielding a sickle, I settle into a baseball hitter's stance and swing for the fences.

Whack!

The tug of war that ensues is nothing like baseball. With the blade stuck fast in the grip of its fibrous stem, I have to wrestle the thistle for control of the weapon. Finally I wrench it away and level another blow, higher this time and not quite so hard.

Whack!

The plant goes down, but instead of catharsis, I can feel the aggravation growing. There is no sense of completion and renewal in what feels like hand-to-hand combat. After I have swung twice more, felt the recoil shiver up through my wrists, and struggled to free the blade, only two stalks have fallen back into the arms of their fellows, chopped off at the knees. I begin to wonder if an ax might be a more appropriate tool.

As the hours pass, thwarted honeybees swarm around my head, and pollen permeates my clothes. My gloves turn green. Behind me is a swath of decimation, stems like haggard and broken limbs, leaves wilting in the sun. Yet surrounding me on all sides are thousands more. Wherever a tire or a boot has scuffed the soil, wherever a ground squirrel has burrowed, the thistles rise in a thicket, blooming, buzzing, making plans for next year.

The debate over invasive alien species, and globalization more generally, is really a struggle over the question of "how newness enters the world," to use the novelist Salman Rushdie's phrase. One side, the side on which most restorationists find themselves, is concerned with maintaining uniqueness in the world. This side values categories, marks of uniqueness, characteristics that distinguish one object or person from another. It offers a sense of newness as the result of process of isolation. Speciation, the hallmark of the new and unique, occurs over a long period of separation, as two populations of the same species develop distinct behaviors and physiognomies in response to different environments. The classic example, Darwin's Galapagos finches, suggests that a profusion of unique species and behaviors corresponds to the number of isolated island habitats in an area. Newness, then, increases with the degree of isolation and the length of time without outside interaction, creating in turn a sense of global diversity. The richness of individual communities may be low, but at the global level, they provide another irreplaceable thread in a complex and plentiful tapestry of species and communities.

Invasive species disrupt this narrative on several fronts. The movement of people and species across borders and geological boundaries makes isolation difficult to maintain. This surging across boundaries also results in the introduction of the enemies of uniqueness—the snakehead, the tree snake, the invasive aliens. Strange dislocations and redistributions occur as a result, as species that are endangered in their place of origin become ubiquitous invaders elsewhere. I recall the shock I received while working for a native plant nursery in England, for example, when I found myself nurturing purple loosestrife specimens for sale to local gardeners. The same plant whose luminous blooms blanket the swamps of my home town, where local groups organize workdays to pull it up, was here a delicate, displaced rarity needing human help to retain its place in the landscape.

Ultimately, what is lost is not necessarily local diversity, since the diversity of the local community may actually increase as a result of invasions, but global diversity. The interloper takes over, turning an undersea rain forest into a monotony of invasive seaweed or zebra mussels. The natives can't compete, and vanish into extinction, leaving a hole in the increasingly tattered global tapestry.

This pervasive anxiety over the loss of uniqueness is not shared by many cultural critics, who celebrate the creative forces of synthesis and mutability and question the legitimacy of efforts to hinder movement across borders. From their perspective, it makes sense to harness the creative energy of genes, to mix things up, to break categories, or to find examples of "species" that vary across the landscape and prove the fallacy of discrete categories. Consider a different interpretation of the Galapagos finch story. One ancestral species of finch arrives, through migration or displacement by stormy weather, in the island chain, setting off a chain reaction of speciation through isolation. Those who seek to maintain uniqueness point to the isolation of the islands as the key factor. Those who view newness as arising in interaction, however, would point to the moment when the finch arrives in this new location as the moment of newness entering the world. Suddenly a new relationship between bird and place has come into being, generating a proliferation of new species. Without this invasion of the ancestral finch, there would be no Galapagos finches.

It is this kind of newness, this fecund dynamism, that I find arrayed against me in the field. Given the ache in my back and the quiver in my arms, I don't need further proof of what makes herbicides appealing, but a quick inspection of my work the next day reinforces the appeal nevertheless. Where yesterday the thistles lay withered, a colony of stumps left for dead, new buds and side shoots have already emerged, conspiring with the sun for a renewed march. They are shorter now, but tougher, like fists embedded in the ground, and the sickle is no longer a match for them. Looking around at my little patch of thwarted labor and the end-less host bristling for another fight, I find myself imagining what a relief it would be to spray. I see myself with a plastic jug strapped to my back and a wand in my hand, sprinkling these survivors with poison and walking away. No mixture of sweat and pollen burning my eyes, no blisters on my thumbs, no shiver of pain in my arms, just a casual stroll through the fields.

There is one more power I can summon before I succumb to the temptation of chemicals. The following week, I climb aboard an enormous tractor whose metal teeth churn and devour plant life and spit forth wads of masticated green. I have misgivings, of course. I no longer have to worry about an immediate impact on my own health, but from an environmental standpoint, how can I justify the plume of diesel drifting in my wake? The connection is a bit less direct, but by bringing the petrochemical industry into the field, I've implicated myself in a global system of resource extraction and pollution nevertheless.

From my perch, I watch the plants shudder and disappear while the remaining wedge gets thinner and thinner. The last row is full of life—fence lizards and voles, shrews, mice, snakes, crickets, grasshoppers, all manner of leaping and crawling life scrambling into the final stand of invasives. And then I come around for the last pass and mow them down.

The mowing seems to work. The fields remain barren, dusty expanses of soil and thatch, but in the wake of all this destruction I remain troubled. I wonder whether there is an ecologically appropriate method for controlling invasive spe-cies. And I find myself mulling over the more fundamental question of why we should attempt to control them at all.

Attempting to negotiate between a celebration of dynamic change, on the one hand, and the preservation of uniqueness, on the other, restoration ecologists can find themselves caught up in a moral quandary that borders on paralysis. The only way out of this paralysis, I've found, is to use the threat of extinction as our justifi-cation for action and to rely on the wildness of invasive species to ensure that we never achieve complete success. I can justify the use of violence only through my role as a mediator between native and exotic species, not as an exterminator. To prevent the extermination of one species or population by another, I intervene, in a limited fashion.

Anyone who has tried to deal with invasive species knows that control, not era-sure, is the only pragmatic goal. It should be the ideological goal as well. Without such controls, the process of liberation from geographical boundaries becomes a process of colonization and extinction. But neither biological nor cultural diversity is well served by extermination campaigns. The tale of biological invasions, for example, is replete with examples of species that are threatened or endangered in their native range, and an invasive pest where they have been introduced. In many cases, such an approach would lead to a reduction of the territory enjoyed exclusively by an invasive species without getting rid of it entirely, thereby increasing local diversity without decreasing global diversity. These ironies of displacement, hybridity, and the blurring of categories are likely to become the rule of a globalized environment rather than the exception, while isolation is not likely to continue as a source of uniqueness, either culturally or biologically, without intensified policing of the borders.

To acknowledge that we are imposing limits on movement is to acknowledge as well that we are in the business of controlling the wild according to our own aesthetic principles, not preserving the wild for its own sake. Extermination, suppression, and control—these are the strategies that have been used against native people, flora, and fauna throughout the history of colonization, whenever their interests have not served our own. We should note that the way cosmopolitan weeds, and even transgenic superweeds, turn the tables on their creators and burst out of containment is in fact an expression of wildness. The wild is the brown tree snake curled in the wheel well of the jumbo jet, more than the carefully tended native shrub. Their persistence may keep us from repeating past mistakes, but we should conduct our reclamation campaigns with a degree of trepidation and with great attention to the scope and methodology of the campaign.

What would these controls look like? Much like those limitations imposed on the organic agriculture movement, at least under some regimes. Unlike the blanket herbicide strategy of many restoration projects, organic agriculture employs methods to reduce the presence of pests that damage crops with the knowledge that the controls are imperfect and will never succeed in extermination. The growers are engaged in an ongoing process of interaction with invasive weeds and insect pests while fostering symbiotic relationships with other species that help produce crops—some native, some introduced. The intensity of their efforts is governed by the vulnerability of the crop to competition, but the parameters of control are human—keeping weeds in check often means pulling them by hand.

The result would be a mosaic of biological habitats, some with more native species, some dominated by exotics, but very few of them "pure" examples of pre-globalization habitats. There is little question that the scale of what one might term "industrial restoration" would be reduced, and the restoration of habitat would be limited in size to the commitment of those in the community willing to put in the time necessary to manage a restoration site without the assistance of weed killer.

To live with exotic plants requires an accommodation, an acknowledgment that things will never be tidy. Without herbicides, we've had to come to a point of acceptance in our fields, and to the untidy mingling of native and exotic that results. We cut some down—others elude us. We try not to disturb the soil, but the ground squirrels and jackrabbits don't abide by our rules. In the winter, the gales blow in across the valley and the Russian thistles take flight, tumbling across our acres until they strike the fence and are pinioned there in a mound, as if the rigid bars of the fence have suddenly grown a scruffy beard. Darting among the tumbleweeds, migrating flocks of golden-crowned sparrows and white-crowned sparrows take shelter from the wind, making a new habitat out of last year's weeds.

Bird, Billboard and Fountain, Roma, 2002 © Richard Robinson

Furbi

Edie Meidav

Furbi *is the single Italian quality which allows one to cheat not only time, but also progress and even mortality.* Furbi *in its deepest sense means cunning. To be gifted with* furbi *means you will arrive at your destination, whether it be your fate or your will's end, much more quickly, outpacing other mortals. In this sense, therefore,* furbi *becomes a form of hubris.*
—Emmanuel Messidoro

Early on Tonio must have thought that he could quietly marry the tall English girl and nonetheless be spared the ire you'd usually get for choosing a foreigner. Because he believed he was smitten with the English girl who came every summer, he believed the force of his feeling would spare him the world's slights. But what, after all, did Tonio know about being smitten?

Six years before Tonio would wed her, he had first spotted his bride across a field flanking the east of his small village not far from Assisi. He'd just finished celebrating his sixteenth birthday, having downed six and a half bottles of wine with his best friend. A few words about Tonio's best friend: many thought him a sophisticated boy, one who showed a marked taste for only the best vintages. Depending on your perspective, to his credit or detriment, this friend had a self-esteem far too grandiose for his peasant class. But this disparity never had deterred Tonio's friend: rather, it had spurred him on to much greater fantasies. He made no secret of the fact that he wanted to be a gentleman hunter, as well as a casual writer of stories, one fit to carry on the legacy of di Lampedusa.

The two of them, Tonio and his grandiose friend, therefore began sunrise of Tonio's seventeenth year on the fertile earth in a manner romantic enough for their adolescent hearts—spitting out the last of their bellies' linings, ignoring their respective headaches, grumbling. Amid this sport, both had laid eyes on the English girl, one boy no sooner than the other: she strode toward them out of the early morning mist.

"What's *that?*" Tonio changed the subject, his question as crude as if the girl had emerged from a rare family of wildebeest. Not just her appearance but her stride marked her as being of a different species from the local girls. For one thing, a firmness weighted down the dead center of her long flanks, a calm eye from which her gait motored forward. The two boys would soon hear it said by the locals that she resembled, somewhat, Lady Diana, whose even-keeled bearing they could imagine, a lady whose face they could quite easily graft upon the English girl, what with both sharing the same flaxen hair, long nose, and somewhat horsey face. Tonio, to his rue, would one day find himself secretly pleased by this comparison of his future bride to an English princess.

Of course, whether or not she resembled Lady Di, six years later the local café talkers and backgammon players would come to a consensus about Tonio's willfulness. Because Tonio felt he had to go beyond merely *bedding* the English girl: he had to go and *marry* her, a distinction of quality as much as degree. This was during the time when Tonio had returned to the valley after his university studies—which were, please note, not in oenology or even medicine, subjects that might have helped the valley. No, Tonio had chosen to study *computer sciences.*

It's *practical,* he'd justified to his best friend.

In at least a couple of ways, therefore, Tonio—who arose from at least seven generations of valley men—had managed to betray his heritage, and for this probably deserved all that came later, as his valley was no ordinary valley, and bore no small amount of pride. Most of the families, all possessors of a certain small, squashed nose, had lived in the same site (as peasants, one had to admit) since, allegedly, before the time of Hannibal's great march with the elephants. When people inquired too peckingly about Tonio's intermarriage—couldn't he have found a girl from a village some fifty kilometers away? had university life given him such exotic tastes?—Tonio justified his trespass by exaggerating it into a great joke. I'm getting into the ranks of the enemy, he'd say, the better to defeat it.

His loyal best friend was the only one who sniggered at this. Everyone else thought Tonio's new attempt at humor was suspect. They could understand what the enemy was: change, never a laughing matter. Yet before Tonio had married her, when he'd been merely *dating* the English girlfriend, the valley dwellers thought she had something of a respectable foreign glamour: plus, she showed commitment, arriving at their valley dutifully at the beginning of June every year. Perhaps this complexity had bewitched the young man, making him ignore the life his ancestors had pulled from the stubborn earth, deafening him to their disapproving clucks. Again, only Tonio's best friend stood by him in his hour of scrutiny: he, you'll begin to note, was not Tonio's best friend for nothing.

The friend early on informed Tonio that it was fine if the girl of his fancy was a year older; that Tonio wouldn't suffer if his girlfriend seemed to belong more to the adult world. After all, wasn't Tonio mature enough to date an *aristocrat?* His friend didn't egg Tonio on; he was just in the business of encouraging. Tonio armored himself with his friend's words. On their first date, to her endless gratitude, he had half-teasingly called the British girl an aristocrat.

"Your English is good," she had said, reciprocating the compliment.

And, flashing her the smile his friends called the *ladykiller,* Tonio had felt guilty for speaking an English he'd learned from watching too many television programs. With his friend he happened to have seen all the specials on Lady Di, a woman who seemed beloved in her own country for having filled the outdated monarchy with the *spirit of the future that maintained connection with the past.* Though Tonio couldn't quite digest this idea, it appealed to him as a kind of reconciliation, seeming profound enough that he repeated it not just to his friend but to his future wife.

"You have a head on those shoulders," she'd answered, in her flattering, understated way. The game was practically over; Tonio's insides both thrilled and shrank at the accolade.

Whenever anyone complimented Tonio, he dwindled away from his exterior, so much so that he practically imploded. You could say Tonio had been indentured into a life in which compliments had been his daily air and water: hence, they fulfilled his expectation while also making him suspicious. He'd been unduly coddled by his mother, for one thing, as he was the *unogenito,* an only child. Like every other mother of the village, Tonio's had thought herself not only correct in how she'd raised her son but unimpeachable, raising her young Tonio to have what appeared to any outsider as an excess of self-confidence. Why *excess?*

Charming as he could be, Tonio would let on that he did not differ with the opinion that one might rank him among the world's most beautiful men as well as among the geniuses of Italian history. Yet to look at him, his small cherubic features seemingly at odds with his great height, his small accomplishments at odds with the esteem in which others in the village held him, one had to question the self-diagnosis.

Admittedly, Tonio did have more than his share of charisma, which had to do with the bristle along his skin. Those closest to him knew this came mainly from his secret rage, an extraordinary rage, simultaneously running toward his surface and hurtling back inside. If one were psychologically minded, one could say Tonio's heat may have come from his father's having abandoned his family, though if one were biologically minded, one could say it was merely that Tonio's hindbrain happened to be exceptionally well developed. Whatever the case, this vitalistic energy vibrated Tonio's entire being, so that, to his friend's annoyance, from a young age, Tonio did appear charismatic. Because of this, the valley people had always called Tonio *little prince;* they'd always treated him with more respect than was his due.

It may help to underline here how great was the panic afoot especially among the peasantry: they feared the countryside around Assisi would soon change. Until recently, they'd been able to spare themselves the onslaught of the masses trooping up the mountain to walk in the footsteps of Saint Francis and Sister Claire, preventing this merely by virtue of their village's being located in one of the hotter parts of the valley, boasting little more than a soda shop at which tourist buses could spew noxious fumes and refill their coffers. Via luck, therefore, the villagers had been spared the fate of towns just a bit south, where so many foreigners had moved in. Nearby you'd find Germans and English and Americans, all the old war powers, rushing in to buy up crumbling villas and acres of land, as well as the great unseen aspect of their mortgages, writ in invisible ink—endless disputes with their native neighbors. These mortgages were being signed at the same point that there was talk of the European Union starting to command Italians—from Belgium!—to the point of telling Italy exactly which kind of brick ovens they'd need for cooking pizza.

Pizza from Belgium? Clearly, everything was going to hell far more quickly than it usually did. The locals felt their cherished region had become a shattered crystal vase, about to fly apart. Most of the old-timers were fatalistic, believing no magic glue could hold it all together, knowing that most of what they loved was about to be broken off, turned into a standard. They lived in fear, but all they could muster was a shrug at the impending wedding of one of their boys, one more sign of doom, what could one do? The regulation of pizza was inevitable, as were all kinds of loss no one could even fathom yet. Hannibal had invaded the valley with his elephants, but eventually he'd been vanquished by the Romans. These days, the old-timers couldn't begin to imagine how they could vanquish their new threats.

Tonio would soon have occasion to wonder at his choice of bride. How much had he himself made the choice? How much had the taste for the foreigner acted through him? Truth was, even when he'd been sixteen—sixteen, drinking bottles of pilfered wine with his best friend, who fancied himself such a gentleman that he would grow up to keep his guns well oiled, able to avoid doing a lick of work around his own house—even back when Tonio was sixteen, long before his friend's guns and the prospect of weddings, Tonio had found none of the local girls attractive. Some of the girls had raw peasant hands and hints of moustaches; or else they dressed like sluts, as did the barista, her chest heaving up like mounds of foam out of her famously flowered blouses. Others presented themselves as young buttoned-up nuns, tending to linger in the detergent aisles of the tiny market, their fantasies far too cloistered to crack.

But betrayal? Tonio did not view his betrothal this way. He thought the villagers were small-minded people, capable only of seeing his connubial preference through such a narrow lens that some actually called him traitor to his face. The morning that he found a dead raven on the doorstep of his wife's house, a sign of doom left by the villagers, he chose to take a new track: self-delusion. He told his friend the bird must have dropped out of one of the overstuffed dovecotes, that it had fallen on the doormat of its own natural accord.

"Natural?" his friend had asked, hiding a snigger.

Yet though Tonio might sniff at the villagers' superstitions and ruffled pride, there would soon come the worst blow he'd ever known. After the first year of married life, just after his wife had given birth to their first girl (whose Italian face he was still trying to locate somewhere within all her invasively Nordic looks), Tonio learned his own mother was planning to sell off their villa to one of the annual Englishmen. For Tonio, this was the equivalent of a thousand dead birds delivered in one fell swoop.

On hearing the news, which his wife relayed in her cold English (an ugly language in its monotony!), Tonio dilated with a rage impossible to contain. Veins on fire, he suspected his mother had decided to sell for ludicrous reasons: perhaps she wished to head off on a cruise around the world where she'd lack all dignity and, he thought, find herself a younger man.

The whole thing was a nightmare. And yet Tonio knew his mother was prone to romantic fancy: she'd spent much of life engaged to various serial teledramas. Yet that she would so readily give up their legacy, their link to the grand valley, one which had helped shelter some of Hannibal's soldiers on his march, all for the flimsy hope of some mashing and snookering of bodies on an air-conditioned boat—well, this surpassed anything he might have predicted. Could he see some swain's nose buried deep in his mother's newly exposed cleavage? The thought was abhorrent. The future had arrived on his doorstep, hidden within the Trojan horse body of his own mother.

Not that he didn't try to change his lot, storming his mother's midnight kitchen, petulant in the way he knew usually worked best on her sympathies. He pressed into the cause a loquacious village elder with strong views on the obligation owed by parents to their children. Tonio, alone or with village help, could drone out an endless wave of reproach. He had no need to remind mother, did he, that he was her only son, the last of the legacy of his father (though the house had been her mother's, and her mother's mother's, going back many bitter generations, all the women born in its drafty interior). How could she so readily dispatch the past?

But all this while she stayed pure and unchangeable. One morning, however, something clicked. She would take no more, wiping her hands—not on the apron she used to wear but on a crisp pantsuit—and sighing. "The past is a pigeon," she said, fully cryptic. Having turned sixty and having attended the wedding of her son to an English girl, all in one year, must have been the events that had wreaked a great change in her personality. It was clear she no longer worshiped her only child.

When Tonio was calmer, he thought it was as if she'd given up the future he'd once held out for her: love and legacy. Perhaps he'd disappointed her more than he'd known. "You let the past seize you as much as you want," she'd continued. "Either you don't move so you won't frighten the pigeon, or you make your way and let pigeons settle where they will."

This made no sense, though she'd said it portentously, as if it had been one of the many solaces she'd used after her husband had died. Tonio in fact felt quite befuddled by her manner and her words: he was, for all the esteem in which others tended to hold him, no great genius in matters of the heart or the head. All he knew was that her words stung.

So what Tonio did was interpret his mother's choice as being a slap in his face for having married the English girl. His mother would have liked a more dependent-minded bride, he decided, one from a neighboring valley, one whom his mother could have bossed around more easily. "What will you do with the money?" he asked his mother.

"Go on a cruise," she said, predictably, as unable to hide her glee as he was unable to hide his sullenness. "Want to come?" But he refused her this consolation, as it had the stink of afterthought. Only a few months later she would leave for her cruise. On a tropical island she would meet not only a younger man, but a man who'd once starred in one of the teledramas she'd loved so much, as she wrote Tonio in the first foreign postcard he'd ever had to receive from her.

At the time of his mother's departure, his wife had gone and gotten herself pregnant again, soon to pop forth their second girl, their first having turned out to be something of a grasping Nordic monster who already, at such an early age, bore an unfortunate resemblance to Tonio's mother-in-law. Unfortunate, yes. Especially after his own mother had left for her tropical idyll, Tonio began to know what people meant when they spoke of mother-in-law trouble.

Sometimes the thought visited him that he ought to feel more grateful to this mother-in-law, whose squat body had squirted forth into the world his tall English wife, the bearer of his children, a wife who at sunset could look like Lady Di. However, toward the older English lady, he couldn't feel much more than repulsion, and this was a sensation that started to consume not only his feelings for his mother-in-law but also, miserably, for his own wife. Her entire nation of nervous, fluted-nose people was repulsive! Though the mother-in-law, Hulda, was an especially strange specimen.

Witness: Hulda's own mother had left her at the London zoo when the girl was six, merely because she'd found Hulda uncontrollable—she, like Tonio, didn't know how to handle such wildness. Now some sixty-odd years old, Hulda's face had turned into one great androgynous splotch of crimson from the minor sea of wine she had imbibed. Though the doctor had warned Hulda away from eating rich foods, Hulda always sought excuses to cook in excess, crafting bestial platters of food, inviting gaggles of guests. Whenever Hulda's intestines started to protest, as they often did, she'd send for the kindly Italian neighbor, a seventh-generation doctor, asking him to survey, as she said, the boils on her bum, just to make sure they'd not gotten too serious.

As it happened, a friend of this mother-in-law, Jane, an Englishwoman confined to a wheelchair, had bequeathed her Tuscan house to Hulda's *daughter* (Jane rightly considered the daughter to be more responsible than the mother). Yet Jane had ensured Hulda would always have shelter within the house and freedom to ride her dappled horse, whom she loved and whom she was training her older grand-daughter, the wild grasping one, to love as well.

So there existed among mother-in-law, son-in-law, daughter, grandchildren, and horse a certain modus vivendi, wrought by the distant Jane: an uneasy arrange-ment. The responsible daughter and Tonio, along with their one and a half chil-dren, lived in the lower half of the house, while the mother, with her bum boils and her habit of inviting over big-boned nostalgic English or German or French friends, lived upstairs. Jane, the older friend who had bequeathed them The House, continued to check in only occasionally on how responsibly Hulda's daughter Mary managed what would one day be *her* legacy.

Tonio, however, found many things amiss within the arrangement. He would, for example, fly into a rage whenever his mother-in-law, in organizing one of her big parties, needed to use his kitchen. Once his own mother had sold his inheritance and left for her cruise, once he had no purchase on any land but the house that had been brought by his mother-in-law's charm and his wife's evident sense of duty, his biggest peeve was that his mother-in-law left all his knives dull.

Increasingly, squat Hulda stank of the rotten bargain he'd made. Yes, he'd sold his soul to the future! he complained to his best friend. He should've just married a simple Italian barista, some sexy girl with a more straightforward inheritance!

And his best friend concurred, his friend who lived with his own English-woman, one he never planned on marrying, as she was neither tall enough nor intimately enough connected to her rich parents.

"You have too many Englishwomen involved in your dwelling place!" he'd tell Tonio, and by this Tonio would feel goaded.

He sighed to his friend. It was especially his pink-skinned mother-in-law who reminded him of the loss of all the good old things. Craftsmanship and knowledge! Pure foods! Green olive oil cloudy with ancient know-how! Because above all, Tonio hated his mother-in-law's English accent and her cooking, mixing bits and pieces from here and there without respect for region or history.

"Virgin with nonvirgin, continental with English, *niente con niente*," Tonio's friend agreed soberly. Nothing with nothing. A man has to assert his place, a man has to take action.

For what it was worth, Tonio didn't have to be around his mother-in-law all that much. He'd salved both pride and the family finances by finding an important job in Milan, for which he had to commute every Sunday night, staying all week in a rented flat shared with three other fellows. He was not a terrible fellow, Tonio. You see, he did mean to be a provider. As time went on, he did have a pang of regret about missing special moments of his children's upbringing: the first step, the first word, the first birthday. *The first* generally seemed to him to swallow up so much of what came later: the first always remained the most important. Was this the insight his absconded mother, now crisscrossing the ocean, had meant when she'd said the past was a pigeon? He still didn't understand her.

And yet he had to admit that he also loved moving away from the valley. Every step away from his claustrophobic origins, with its Hannibal-worshipping stories, made him feel clean (why *would* those crazed villagers worship Hannibal when Hannibal had been one of the first invaders?). Tonio claimed to his best friend that he never felt quite so clean as when he was on the commuter train, heading toward Milan, important next to other important commuters, *people needed in two places,* all of them whizzing by quiet farms and towns.

His existence continued in this mode for a couple of years, peaceable or not, in which he took the speedy train back on weekends so he could sit with his wife at the white garden table while she hurriedly tried to slice Genovese salami with one of the dulled knives. Seeing the knife, he would rage back into the house, vociferous at his mother-in-law, cursing the lack of respect she showed for the old ways.

"My father would never have left such knives around the house!" he shouted, apocryphally: his father had, after all, merely left.

Only once did his wife, who tended to avoid confronting him, say, in her serious, fluted accent. "But your father wasn't around much, was he, even before he died?" a buried truth she'd learned indirectly, from a casual weekday gatepost conversation with Tonio's best friend, whom she thought brought out the best in Tonio.

Secretly, or not so secretly, Tonio wanted the squat horse trainer to go back to England: this was an idea his sympathetic friend had discussed with him, one night over a good peasant vino rosso, how much Tonio'd like his mother-in-law to leave him roaming rights to the upstairs. Underneath that, however, lay the idea that his wife might also one day leave Tonio—but this thought Tonio barely allowed into his joking sessions with his friend. After all, he and his English Mary still shared, occasionally, the delights of the conjugal bed, however diminished in frequency or quality. But his friend pushed Tonio to articulate the secret fantasy: if Tonio's wife did depart, unconscionable as it was to consider this, then Tonio could be all alone. Tonio alone could charm the invalid who'd already partially bequeathed the Englishwomen the house. He'd be left with his legacy, one a monster child, one more beatific, both however possessing infinite potential—potential Italian women of the valley who nonetheless would understand the greater world.

Tonio's confessions most often circulated around the fantasy of a departing mother-in-law. It had a certain cleanliness, one not unlike that which Tonio felt on the commuter train, shining with the perfect craftsmanship of old Italy. Mother-in-law gone, there'd at least exist the possibility of the past flowing back into the house. Slowly the fact of the house not being of Tonio's own patrilineage would be erased. He'd put up a few pictures of his severe great-grandfather, who'd accrued a military honor; the pictures would stare down those who doubted his uniformed dignity.

Some grandeur was due to Tonio, wasn't it? Some redemption of his modern insignificance. Hadn't Tonio been kicked out by *change* long enough? His mother, sucked off by the drama of television, had surrendered all natural motherly instincts. And now foreigners were starting to march in, buying up huge abandoned villas near their valley, finally encroaching on Assisi, where purity had always been taken for granted.

Some, like the local fruit seller Vanno, said the truth was that the valley had sunk into a financial depression not long ago; change, a certain amount of foreigners coming in, would never hurt anyone so terribly. According to Vanno, the people who butchered Italian made it possible for many peasants to go on eking out a living in their childhood places. In other words, the foreigners brought in enough money to let true Italians *stay* true. Foreigners valued the rustic far more than the natives who'd fled for the cities, the bourgeoisie who'd abandoned rotting ancestral manors to weasels and real estate agents, often a combination of the two.

Vanno's was one viewpoint; the other stated that it would take much more than foreigners, tourists, or villa buyers to save their village from becoming one more part of the sprawl creeping out from cities like Milan and even Florence.

Weeknights, when Tonio had commuted to work, living with the three other computer engineers in a strange flat, he often had the thought that he was to blame for everything. He'd started things off by having been drawn to the wrong Maria, the wrong wife.

But Tonio thought he could make up for it with various penances. In Milan he worked as a graceless computer slave in order to maintain the semblance of a life, the kids and the wife, the upkeep of the giant house that slowly had started to seem less like an eccentric gift to the mother and daughter by a handicapped Englishwoman and more like a valid part of his own legacy, dating back to Hannibal. Yet Tonio's life in Milan was nothing if not untraditional, premised as it was on speed, on quick meals in places barely qualifying as trattorias. Conventionally or not, he even let himself have affairs with the passing-through businesswomen and young aspiring models whom the city chewed up and spat out.

When Tonio spoke with these ladies, as he thought of them, ladies fleeting through his arms, he could not give up a certain habit: he had to inflate the importance of his job and his Milanese neighborhood. He also could not keep himself from blowing some of his hard-earned salary, the whole reason for his being estranged from kith and kin, on a certain hotel room in a certain part of town, where he believed he satisfied the ladies almost as much as they satisfied him.

As he told his best friend, little could soothe the aching beast in Tonio's belly, a yearning that had more to do with the life his region had bred him to expect.

"You have more right to be in that house than any of those Englishwomen," his childhood friend had told him recently. "Those people probably only understand war."

"War?" Tonio had asked.

"*Aren't there many kinds?*" his friend had asked, smiling broadly enough to reassure Tonio that all would resolve itself soon.

On his final Friday evening, on the train speeding toward Assisi, Tonio had suffered an argument. It had to do with the building codes recently enacted to keep the valley pure. An acquaintance, one of the men who shared the flat with Tonio, a man sworn to stay mum on the subject of those comely models, was not for the building codes.

He had just called Tonio a nostalgist, a man who'd like to see Italy forever turned toward the Renaissance, and not toward what could be the country's true rebirth. "We are stuck in the past," he chided Tonio. "That's your problem."

What spoke to Tonio was not so much the man's words, but the crispness of his collar, the hydraulic, modern nature of the greased hair pressed close to his ears. He was a possessor of some greatly modern cunning, one far beyond Tonio.

Though he had his own share of vanity, Tonio felt he was getting relegated to a crumbling crypt, one he'd chosen but which would also bury him alive. He'd not made the right choices in life, he'd chosen to learn computer engineering out of a lack of imagination, and soon whatever he'd learned would be relegated to the dustbins. There would be other Tonios soon breathing down his neck. And he had done terrible things in the pursuit of what had seemed to him the only way to survive: he had been lonely many nights in Milan, trying to service an old value, and so, in a chain of consequence, had passed on a modern venereal disease to his wife. Then he could not explain to her why she was beset with terrible symptoms every once in awhile. But this was the least of so many things he could not explain, least of all to himself: his mother, endlessly orbiting the world on its waters. And he himself, stuck in a back-and-forth between a valley (near the birthplace of one of the greatest saints) and Milan (one of the world's most modern cities). Stuck on a commuter train, he argued with some inconsequential computer engineer about whether Italy should move forward or stay in its transfixed regard toward the past.

By the time he'd arrived home that late Friday afternoon, he was in a fine rage. Everything seemed plotted on some terrible axis of new and old: his mother-in-law's bric-a-brac (new), the photos of his half-English, half-Italian children who some weekends barely remembered to call him Papa (new), the villa's crumbling foundation (old), his knives, sharply gleaming (old, a legacy from the disappeared father).

Unfortunately, when he arrived home, the only person in his kitchen was his mother-in-law, Hulda, whose bad sense of timing had her preparing a torte for one of her feasts the next day.

"Tonio," she said. "You came early today. I'll just get out of your way—" said in her bad Italian (new).

"I will not accept this," he said, more quietly than she had ever heard him speak.

"Accept? Can you just give me a hand with this, dear?"—oblivious, and, worse, in English, which set him off, as she must have known it would. English in his dominion!

Penetrated with a fury beyond any he'd ever known, he recognized the mother's face was that of an old eggplant. It was then that he took out two knives, brandishing them without understanding how the moment would play out. And, as if in answer, the afternoon shadows mocked him, dancing on the cream and carbonara of the kitchen's interior.

"You dulled my knives," he ended up saying more to the knives than to her. "You destroy everything."

Her purple splotch of a face turned up at him, stammering something in bad Italian.

It was only then that he felt he understood what the villagers meant when they praised *furbi,* a sense of cunning. He had no connection to the great men of his historical moment, he had demonstrated no cunning, he had lost out, had lost the battle and might soon lose the war. Whatever he'd once held precious, whatever he or his friends had believed in—hunting, cultivating, living like grand men on their estates, knowing opera and wine, or else just being heir to di Lampedusa— would soon not be available to them any longer. All was going, and it had to do with the upturned, quizzical, cheery blotch of his mother-in-law.

"Don't be upset, love," she said, turning back to her work. "I'll be out of your way in a moment."

"*Certo,*" said Tonio, sarcastic.

The next morning, gloomy and having chosen to sleep in the children's room rather than with his wife, he found himself confiding to his best friend. They were sitting in comradely fashion on the bench near the cabana, on the terrace overlooking the bluish valley veined with olive trees, along which the growers, old men with knees as knobby as their trees, burnt refuse from that year's pruning.

"Like they're sending up flares begging for help," said Tonio's friend. "They need someone to save them."

"I just hate that *Hulda's* about to have another party," said Tonio.

His friend considered this for a deep moment, a moment full of old Italy, when insects happy among the flowers only heighten life's gravity. Tonio's childhood friend leaned forward suddenly.

"I know," he said, with feeling. "This is my advice. When the guests come, you have a duty."

Tonio waited. His friend had a flair for dramatic pauses, and Tonio appreciated this. They each finished their glasses of wine and refilled them within the largesse of that suspended moment.

"Show who belongs here," his friend said at last.

Tonio shrugged. "How do you show anything to blind women?"

His friend looked around and considered. "With bigger gestures."

"Bigger?"

In answer, his friend pointed to the lawn mower waiting under the eaves of the cabana, unused since last season. It was a machine Tonio had bought for the handsomeness of its design rather than its constancy, and it appeared to sparkle at its mention.

"Couldn't you make some kind of ruckus?" asked Tonio's friend. "C'mon, I'm drinking you under the table. Have more wine. You drink too slowly today."

"I'm savoring it," said Tonio.

When actually it was this new idea that Tonio savored. As soon as his friend had mentioned the lawn mower, Tonio saw immediately the plan's beauty: it appealed to the mania for order Tonio felt whenever he was most upset.

Once they'd finished the bottle, they rose, Tonio thanking his friend from the bottom of his heart. As Tonio hugged him goodbye, he felt the broad slope of his friend's shoulders and in it the contours of unvanquishable Italy, the Italy that had been a light unto the world.

"You're the only one who understands me," Tonio then told him. He waved warmly at him as he left. "*Avanti popolo!*" he shouted into the valley, as much at himself as at his friend. "Forward!"

Back in the house, he announced to his wife that it was time to clip the lawn. She seemed a little startled. "The party?" she asked, but could tell that Tonio was in *one of his moods* and not to be stopped. Tonio therefore got into the lawn mowing uniform he liked to wear, a custom of many Italians of his generation. Lacking a true war, and with all the old processionals dying out, they'd found that lawn mowing had become an activity that one should not take on casually. Lawn mowing required respect and respect required uniforms. It was therefore in a neatly tailored camouflage design that Tonio crossed the lawn, striding manfully out to the waiting machine. Already Tonio could feel a restoration of Italian pride. He enjoyed, further, the way his breath fumed over the interior of his camouflage visor and gas mask: it was in this strange elephant-nosed guise that he began his work, the giant engine's thrum a solace.

Though he should have been more pacified, he could not help what happened when he saw the first guests: a strange urge filled his hands. The foreign ladies were starting to arrive in twos and threes, crossing the lawn in their British and German youthful summer whites. He saw through the ladies as easily as he was meant to see through their dresses. These were women gazing at one another in a manner he'd call *sympathetical,* the whole nation now overrun with their comradely but secretly competitive looks. In Italy the ladies reinvented themselves; they'd go from being Marge with a flat in Hampstead to Margareta still capable of flirting with Italian men.

To Tonio, through the veil of his gas mask, the women in their whites were big women, bigger than sails, growing bigger as they approached him and his machine. His hands gripped the handle and he turned away from them, trying to keep his eyes fixed on his job. The uniform helped immeasurably. As his friend had said, Tonio should show these foreigners who ran this valley. His uniform showed them. Yet unfortunately, he'd hit a rock, and his handsome if inconstant machine started to sputter, which seemed to make a few ladies laugh.

This was the moment in which he saw his own wife near the house, out of the corner of his vision, raising a hand to her mouth to hide either shame or a titter. So perhaps it was this which made him behave as he did, turning toward a group of three, feeling the paradox of being well hidden behind the loud roar of his lawn mower's engine. Now, this group of three happened to include his own squat mother-in-law, who was just then removing her apron and embracing the waists of two of her taller friends. Remember that Tonio's view must have been smoky, but no smoke could swerve Tonio from his intention.

In the split second in which an army can realize its defeat, Tonio switched the lawn mower to its highest power and then turned toward the ladies. To its credit, his machine had come back to itself, sucking up grass at a furious rate. It was heading toward ending the party, ending the visitors, ending the constant onslaught of change.

From behind, he could hear the fluted tones of his wife, who slipped into English whenever she was most upset. "You're crazy!" she shouted. "What do you think you're doing?" The diagnosis, long time in coming, made him thankful: in a second he perceived that it was perhaps the first time in their long union that she'd bothered speaking the truth to him. "You're going to hurt people," she was shouting.

Her abysmal language, so cut and dried. You could say it was her words, or the words of his friend earlier, or his derangement after he'd been disowned, which made any damage he might wreak feel justified. Damage has its tributaries. Just for a second, he had to turn back toward his mother-in-law; for a second, and then he was on a rampage, heading toward those who would make an incursion on his land.

"What do you think you're doing?" a tall German woman cried, her hands up, a thing in his wake, a tall Aryan reed ready to be mowed down.

He just waved the gas mask's nozzle at her, feeling better than a giant elephant, his mower heading straight ahead. What was Tonio thinking? Perhaps that he was the conqueror, that he could vanquish them all, that he was the soul and emperor of movement. An illusion that he had mastered change! In one fell action, he thought he might call upon generations of *furbi,* pressing it into what he thought was the greatest cunning of all: action.

But action, finally, is not synonymous with *furbi*. And finally I, his best friend, his longtime childhood friend, destined soon enough to leave my own English girl-friend, to continue to hunt, to be a polite friend and visit Tonio in the prison's visiting room (during the correct hours), would be someone who would wish him well and congratulate him on whatever he had managed to accomplish amid the vagaries of prison life, his correspondence degrees, his new-found love of whittling. I could congratulate him easily because I had won, all hands down. Because it was I who ended up living in the house he had so desired, enjoying his walnut trees as my own, his knives as mine, yes, even his conjugal bed now mine, his wife twining her long flanks between mine. Even his mother-in-law had been vanquished (though we'd always got on amicably), as she'd chosen to decamp to Versailles for part of the year. But the children were left, and of their own accord (and with a small bit of bribery) they chose soon enough to call me *papa,* which helped, as certain men in my own line had been called infertile. Thus, I found myself blessed by them as well as with the wife, one who chose to brighten whenever I returned home in the evening with my guns and whatever I'd found in the diminishing forests—truffles, berries, the like. In other words, for the most part, I was a free gentleman, hunting the day away.

You might wonder what exactly Tonio had lacked. Because there was a lack, clearly; otherwise he wouldn't have been slotted for prison. As far as I could see, he'd failed at square one: he'd never understood our old tales, say, the one about lazy Rozella, blessed by both her greed and cunning, winning the rich merchant as reward for her vast hungers and *furbi*. He'd barely listened at all, too involved in self-love to know that real self-love requires a good set of ears. Because we Tuscans (I include Vanno the old fruit seller) understand what it means to listen. We forever cock our ears at the horizon for elephant heels, for news of oncoming tricksters, for signs of our mortality: this goes beyond cleverness or ambition. You can say that whatever Tonio was made of, he lacked our valley's talent: listening well enough to change to make it your very own obedient slave.

Civilizations

Inna Mattei

New civilizations emerge
in the estuaries of highways.
They swing like gigantic flowers
with invisible roots.
Histograms of skyscrapers
are establishing new statistics
of claustrophobic phantoms
crowded in cozy wombs.

I can almost hear a key of doubt
turning inside me,
fascination precipitating down
at the city in swoon,
where wondering lights
that emerge in the night
try to swallow the Tylenol Moon.

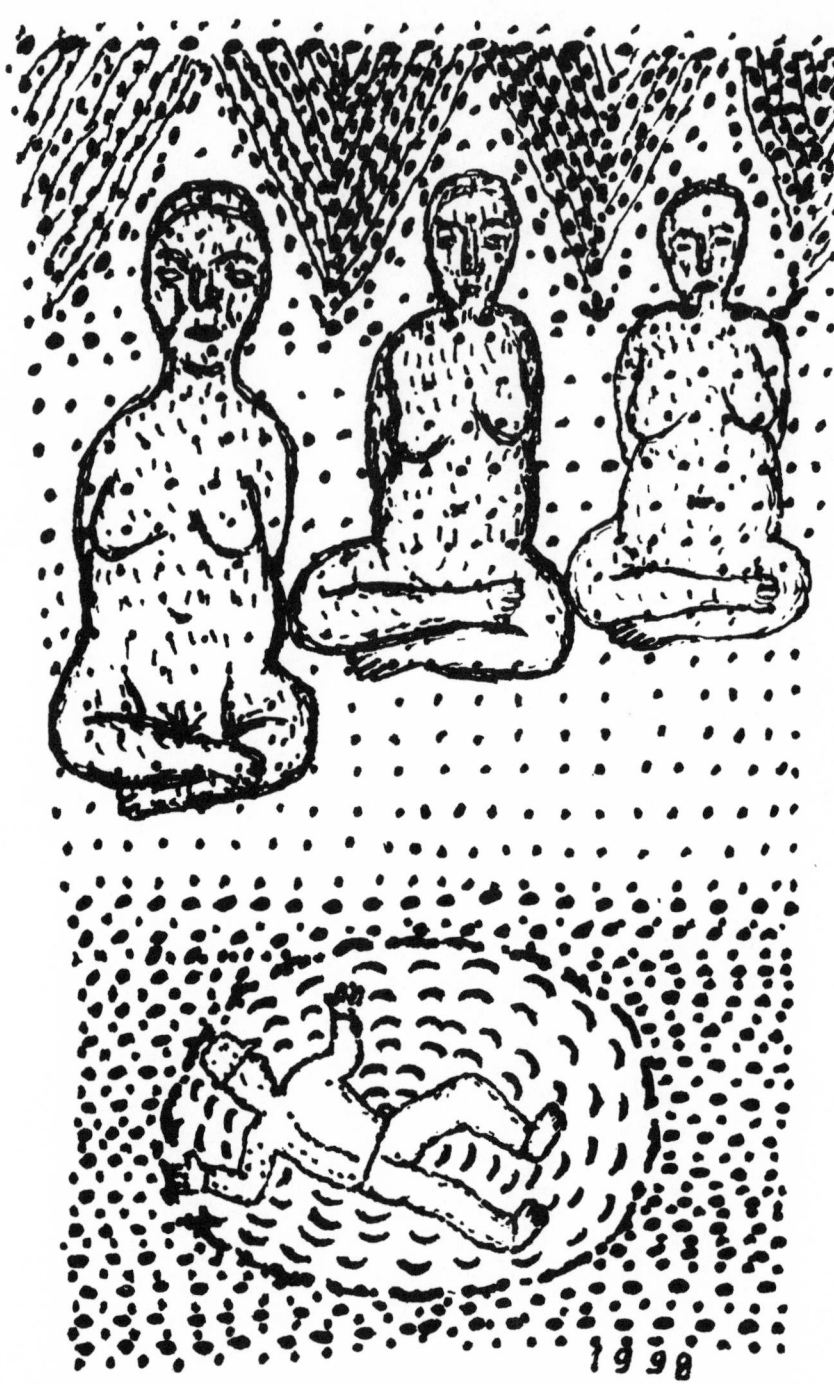

Arpita Singh, *For Anjum*, 2002

The Engagement

Daniel E. Weinbaum

From the corner of his eye, Ethan noticed the small group gathered outside the window of Barnaby Leather watching them work on the display. It was almost as though he and Setsuko were in a movie or on stage. But they were like props on a set, not characters with their own stories. He turned his attention back to Setsuko, who knelt on the floor, her feet pressed beneath her. She pinned a coiled belt below black Italian leather gloves, creating a cascade of expensive leather goods that snaked down the velvet-covered panel. As he observed her work, he was mesmerized once again by her gift for making meaning out of merchandise. The certainty with which she placed each item made him feel as though there was a hidden order to the world, and it only took someone like Setsuko to make it apparent. He wanted to be part of that order, or maybe just have some of it rub off on him. But as Setsuko's nimble fingers hid a pin in the stitched seam of a wallet so that it appeared to float unsupported on velvet, the spell was broken. Was every display a trick? Maybe there was no hidden order, only merchandise that promised magic, which was no more than the manipulation of desire.

The bright November sun angled through the window, settling on Setsuko's long hair, one moment a dense black, the next as she tilted her head to see her work from another angle, shimmering on her shoulders like a lake whose depths remained impenetrable. She seemed oblivious to the spectators, and although Ethan was standing only a few feet away, she seemed equally unaware of him. The ability to focus her attention on one thing excluding all else was part of her gift.

Now as he watched her, he thought of a conversation they had in bed over the weekend. It still made no sense to him.

"I'm stupid," she had admitted to him like a long-held secret.

"No you're not."

"Yes, I'm stupid," she said, her pale cheeks flushing red.

"No way. I think it's amazing how you set up windows."

"That's not smart."

"Sure it is," he said taking her in his arms. "At least you've got something you're good at. If you're stupid, then I'm in serious trouble."

"No," she said snorting a laugh. "You're smart."

"Hey, maybe we're both stupid, and that's why we belong together."

Setsuko punched him softly on the shoulder. "I'm serious," she said.

"Look, I don't know what we are, but I know one thing I'm good at." He rolled on top of her, his thin, sinewy body covering hers, shoulder blades hunched as he poised above her. In the months since they began their relationship, he had gained a whole new understanding of sex. In college, before he had dropped out, he had sex a couple times, but it had been tentative, fumbling, inadvertently selfish. Setsuko had been patient with him, and each time they made love, it was like discovering a secret life, and he could not get enough of it. He stared into her eyes framed by her black hair fanned out on the pillow, her full lips slightly parted, ripe in the half darkness. Although he had begun to understand the curves and crevices of her body, she still looked naked to him without her black oval glasses. She stared back into his hazel eyes, blinking, for without her glasses she was quite nearsighted. His angular but pleasing face floated above hers, olive skin illuminated by a street lamp outside the bedroom window, a small scar on his chin from a childhood fall. As he lay on top of her, Setsuko's admission and the shamed look on her face lingered between them; it struck him as a sad thing to say about oneself. He took one of her small breasts in his mouth and reached his hand down into the soft folds of her vagina, already wet from the sex they had earlier that night. She raised her legs. Slowly he slid back inside her, and their conversation was lost in the motion of their bodies.

"Pass me the ball," she said, interrupting his thoughts. He handed her a large-scale version of a Christmas ornament big as a human head, which he had spray-painted a speckled red, gold, and black. She positioned it at just the right angle against some briefcases, effortlessly haphazard but with an underlying symmetry.

When the window was finished, they stepped into the store and walked over to Leo, the Manager. Normally their boss, Takami, might be there for a final once over, but Barnaby Leather, Takami Studio's most recent and biggest client, was planning to open new stores in a number of cities across the United States and Japan, and Takami had flown to Tokyo for a design consultation. The company had recently moved production to Asia, and the resulting cuts in the cost of labor would allow them to manufacture a cheaper line and expand their customer base. Takami had been called in to help refashion the company's image to market Barnaby Leather to the middle class without undercutting its aura of wealth and exclusivity.

"Leosan, we finished," Setsuko said bowing slightly at the waist. Leo and Setsuko went outside to look at the window while Ethan stayed in the store, admiring some of the items in a glass display case.

"Wonderful, guys," Leo said clapping his hands together as they came back in a minute later. He faced Setsuko and made a deep bow, his own outsized version of what she had just done. Ethan liked Leo, but thought he appeared absurd in his pleated dress pants and black pointy cowboy boots, a look fashionable in the early eighties, and already a relic as the decade came to a close.

"I guess being engaged makes for fabulous windows," Leo said, glancing back and forth between Ethan and Setsuko with a big grin curling the corners of his goatee. Ethan gave Setsuko a questioning look. He had asked her to marry him only two weeks ago, and they hadn't yet broken the news to Takami.

"It's okay. Your secret's safe with me," Leo said, resting a hand on his arm. "It's not her fault. I pried it out of her. I saw you two hold hands when you left the store last month."

"Aha."

"How long have you been keeping this affair a secret?"

"I don't know," Ethan said.

"Four months, I think," Setsuko added.

"Boy, you work fast," Leo said, winking at Ethan, the corners of his mouth turning down, impressed. "Well, I think it's great. You've got yourself a gorgeous older woman who can teach you about love, and Setsuko's got herself a nice young Jewish boy to look after her and keep her busy, if you know what I mean. What more could a girl want?"

Ethan smiled uncomfortably. "How do you know I'm Jewish?"

"Oh, please. I'm right, aren't I?" Ethan didn't say anything.

"Don't be offended. No, I don't think you have a big nose. You've got that sensitive nice Jewish boy look. You're not fooling me with that spiky hair cut."

Ethan's eyes narrowed, and he gave Leo a sideways glance.

"My God, you are sensitive. It's a good thing. My mother, Peaches, and all the other yentas on Ocean Parkway would just eat you up."

Setsuko stood there smiling. Even though she didn't really understand what Leo was talking about, she was amused by the way he said things.

"We gonna get married at city hall next Saturday. After the ceremony, we gonna have a party at my apartment. Why don't you come," she said. Leo noticed a customer at the cash register.

"Call me at the store, give me the info, and I'm as good as there. Look, anything you two lovebirds want from the store is yours with the employee discount. I mean that," he said walking away. Ethan and Setsuko carried their toolbox and leftover props out of the store and onto Madison Avenue, where they hailed a cab. They loaded their stuff into the trunk and jumped in. He draped his arm over her shoulder as the cab sped off. When they stopped at a red light, she turned toward him.

"Are you really Jewish?"

He stared out the window as if he hadn't heard the question. Just as she was about to repeat it, he shifted in his seat.

"I guess you could say I'm Jewish."

"You don't know?"

"Well my mother wasn't at all religious. I mean, every year we had a Christmas tree—you know a fake one because it's hard to get the real ones in Los Angeles. Sometimes my mom left it up right through spring, and every year it got more beat up." Ethan paused and shifted again in his seat. "But by birth you could say I'm Jewish. At least my grandparents were."

"One of my roommates—he's Jewish—last year I give him a Christmas present and he told me Jewish people don't like Christmas. Why your family celebrate?"

"I don't know. I never asked why."

"Oh," Setsuko said and they sat in silence for a moment. Ethan still had one hand resting on her shoulder, and with the fingers of his other he began to tap on the armrest of the cab door.

"Yeah," he said as if answering a question. "If it wasn't for the camps, I'd probably never think about being Jewish at all."

"What do you mean?"

"You know, if it wasn't for the concentration camps."

She wrinkled her brow, and he stopped drumming his fingers.

"I have a great uncle who survived one of them. Sometimes it makes me think. If I had lived back then, I'd have been put in a camp too whether I said I was Jewish or not. I wonder if I would have survived."

"Survived what?"

"I don't remember the name. I only met my great uncle once, and it was a long time ago."

"You saying you don't remember your uncle's name?"

"No. I thought you were asking me the name of the camp."

"Right. I want to know what is the camp."

"You don't know about the camps?" Ethan said, taking his arm from around her shoulder and turning toward her. Her brows knitted together behind her oval glasses, and she stared up at the roof of the cab trying to remember.

"You're kidding me, right?"

Her eyes remained on the roof.

"I don't know," she finally said facing him.

"Do you know about Hitler and World War II?" he asked hesitantly, afraid to hear the answer.

"Yes, of course I know Hitler and the war. My grandfather was officer in the Japanese Army."

"But you don't know about concentration camps?"

"I don't think so. Maybe I don't know the word in English."

"How do I explain this?" he said pausing. Almost every day they came across words in English that Setsuko did not know, for she had moved to New York only a year ago. Ethan would try to explain them, and then she'd tell him how to say the word in Japanese. While her vocabulary had steadily grown, his Japanese was still limited to *hello,* the names of his favorite sushi, and the Japanese word for *pussy* that Setsuko had taught him the first night they slept together.

"How do I explain this? Well, Hitler built these big camps. The Nazis gathered up Jews from all over Europe and put them there. Then the Nazis murdered them."

"That's so terrible," she said frowning.

"You mean they never taught you in school about how the Nazis killed the Jews?"

"I don't think so. I don't like history, but I think we learned Japanese history of the war: Japan fighting America, Hiroshima, and what happened after the war." She ran her fingers through her hair. "My grandfather talk about the war all the time. When I was a girl, he showed me his medals. I remember one day when he was old like a child, he put on his uniform and walked around shouting at every-body. *Do this, do that.* It was crazy," she said, rolling her eyes.

"Man," he said, shaking his head.

"It was funny at first. Then we could not shut him up."

"I can't believe you don't know that stuff."

She shrugged her shoulders.

"I thought everyone knew that."

"It's not my fault I don't know."

"I didn't say it was." He glanced at her from the corner of his eye.

"Then why you looking at me like that?"

"I'm not looking at you like anything."

For the first time, both of them seemed to become aware of the driver, a motion-less round bald spot on the back of his head held at an angle that made it impos-sible to tell if he had been listening. The sound of the accelerating engine filled the cab. They stared out opposite windows as the car made its way downtown.

"It's a long time ago," Setsuko said after a while.

"I guess so."

"Anyway, you don't know if you really Jewish. What does it matter for us? Right?"

He nodded his head, his eyes unfocused. She put her hand on his knee and kissed his cheek. His hand, the nails speckled with Christmas-colored spray paint, covered hers.

The cab pulled up at East Third Street in front of Takami Studio, located on the ground floor of an old red brick building crisscrossed by a rusty fire escape. Inside, they found that Takami's other assistant, Yoshi, was at lunch. They set their bags down, and Ethan put the taxi bill in the receipt box by the door. Setsuko called out a loud *moshi mosh,* to make sure they were alone.

"Come here," she said, leaning into Ethan and brushing her lips against his neck. He stepped backward, bumping into a battered work table. Since a fight in the early days of the relationship in which they had nearly split up, they had never been physically intimate at the studio. Once, with Yoshi and Takami gone for the day, Ethan begged Setsuko to have sex until finally she slammed the door of Takami's office in his face and bolted the latch.

"Maybe you don't care for me, only sex," she said through the door.

"That's not true."

"I thought you were different type of man. But you the same as him."

"The same as who?"

"From now on we work together. Nothing more."

"What are you saying?"

"You don't speak English?"

"Are you saying you don't want me anymore?" He leaned in closer to the door. "Setsuko."

No answer. The speed with which things had fallen apart dazed him. He turned and slid with his back to the door until he sat with his pointy knees near his chin, head in his hands, spiky hair sticking up between his fingers. He started crying, quietly at first and then like a child—in big sobs that shook his body against the door.

A moment later the office opened.

"Stop crying. Takami will come," she said severely, but this only made him cry harder.

"Stop crying. It's okay."

Still he shook. He looked so pitiable and upset that she put her hand on his shoulder.

"I didn't mean anything bad . . . I love you. Don't leave me . . . don't leave me, don't leave me," he said between sobs.

She put her arm around his shoulder, and he buried his face in her hair. His tears were contagious, and drops slid down her cheeks beneath her glasses as she held his head against her.

Now as she covered his neck with kisses, he gripped the edge of the work table and raised his chin above her head. From across the studio, a gray mannequin with no arms watched them.

"What are you doing?"

"Kissing," she said, not stopping.

"What happened to no sex at the studio?"

"No sex. Just kissing."

He reached down under her chin and lifted her head upward. She looked at him and made a move to kiss him on the lips, but he pulled his head back and took her cheeks between his hands.

"It doesn't feel good?"

"No, I mean yes. It's just that . . ."

"What's the matter?"

"I'm worried Takami will walk in on us. It's distracting."

"Takami's in Japan. Remember?" she said tilting her head to the side.

"I mean Yoshi."

"We gonna tell him soon anyway. He's not gonna care."

"Later," he said.

They strolled arm in arm through Soho, Setsuko wrapped in her faux leopard skin coat that she managed to make hip and chic. Ethan couldn't explain how she did it, but everything she put on looked as if it could be worn in no other way. Ethan had on a gray cashmere-lined overcoat that Setsuko had picked out for him the previous weekend, the same day they bought his wedding suit. It was only the second suit he had ever owned.

"It's cold. You need a coat to go with the suit," she had said.

"I'll wear my leather jacket."

"You funny," she said holding her hand over her mouth suppressing a laugh, and without saying another word she selected his coat. It was the most expensive piece of clothing he had ever owned, and he was still not sure how he felt about it or, more precisely, how he felt in it.

They headed toward De Medici, where Setsuko's closest friend from Japan had gotten a job. Like other companies, De Medici was cashing in on the Japanese economic boom. They had opened a store in Tokyo, and Midori, who spoke fluent English and some Italian, was part of their marketing team. She had told Setsuko to meet her at the store, to see if there was a pair of shoes she liked for the wedding.

Post-Thanksgiving holiday shoppers clogged the street, laden with shiny paper bags—lava red, royal blue, matte gold—emblazoned with different names and logos. The couple threaded their way along, remaining arm and arm until they reached De Medici's window, where a handful of women's shoes were displayed atop white marble columns of different heights. A single shoe was poised atop every column like a bust in an art gallery. Long sprigs of mistletoe emerged from several clear glass vases on the floor, and red berries and dark twisted branches stood out against the variegated white marble. The shoes were uncomplicated by ornamentation; the supple leather, the careful stitching, and pleasing lines arrested the eye. Setsuko pointed to a pair, and as she stood admiring, Midori spied them from inside the store. She waved her hand high as if she were in a crowded train station even though there were only a few customers inside. As they came through the door, Midori rushed over to give them a hug. She wore a tight pencil skirt and a pair of De Medici heels that limited the length of her stride. Above her thin immaculate eyebrows, her hair was pulled back in a tight bun that seemed to be the only thing restraining her from jumping up and down with excitement. Ethan had met Midori several times, and she was always animated, talking a blue streak. The prospect of shopping for a wedding seemed to propel her into a new stratosphere.

"You look so cute together. I like your coat. Is everything ready for the party? I can't wait for the wedding. He's gonna look so handsome," she said to Setsuko as if Ethan wasn't there. "Nakamura would be so jealous."

"Who's Nakamura?" Ethan asked.

Setsuko cut in speaking Japanese. Midori covered her mouth, then pulled her hand away.

"What are you talking about?"

"Girl talk," Midori said.

"Who's Nakamura?"

Setsuko looked toward Midori.

"Setsuko's high school boyfriend. A jerk who broke her heart a long time ago. He would be jealous now, you're so handsome. So what shoes do you like? I love these," Midori said taking Setsuko by the hand and pulling her in a half trot of excitement toward a pillar on which was displayed a pair of red pumps. Ethan was left standing by the door. Nakamura, the high school boyfriend. Midori's explanation made some sense, but Setsuko's reaction did not. Why did she interrupt Midori in Japanese? Setsuko was thirty-three, high school a memory. Maybe it was just a story from the past, and that's why Midori said it. If Nakamura was Setsuko's lover now, he doubted that Midori would say anything. That made sense, and he tried to leave it at that.

The two women had wandered farther into the store, looking at more shoes, speaking in Japanese. Ethan remained where he was, eyes wandering, taking in the low Italian leather benches, the step down to the rear of the store as if it were a sunken living room and the clients were friends coming to socialize rather than to buy shoes. He became aware of the unfamiliar sensation of the soft cashmere lining of the overcoat touching his wrists, and in that moment the coat felt absurd, like a costume having nothing to do with him. The store seemed a world cold, incomprehensible, a kind of lie that mocked him for not being part of it. A wave of panic washed over him, and he felt like a child who had wandered away from his parents and all of sudden discovered he had been left behind. If he went outside the store, he could find his way again, calm down, but this need itself embarrassed him, and he remained where he was.

"What do you think?" Setsuko said, holding out a foot and pointing her toes to display a pair of cream-colored pumps with chestnut piping and a delicate heel.

"They're going to look so good with your dress," Midori chimed in.

He stared at the shoes.

"You don't like them?" Setsuko asked.

"No, no."

"Why don't you like them?"

"I mean yes. I like them. Great shoes. Great."

"Are you okay?"

"Sure I'm okay. Why wouldn't I be?"

"I don't know."

Setsuko paid for the shoes at a discounted rate, and Midori, bubbling over with excitement for the wedding festivities, saw them out of the store. Back on West Broadway, they were swept along by the river of shoppers and carried down the street.

The next week was a blur of activity. Ethan hardly had a moment to think. He moved about in a daze, as if it were someone else's life. He watched himself haul boxes of wine and beer from the liquor store, shop with Setsuko for all the hors d'oeuvres. There he was paying a visit to the jeweler to have the white gold wedding band she picked out for him sized, another afternoon at the barber getting his hair cut.

They had made a mutual decision to leave family out of the wedding, so that, at least, was not an immediate worry. Ethan's mother had been enraged with him when he dropped out of college, and even angrier after hearing of his decision to move to New York. She refused to accompany him to the airport, and they had hardly spoken since. As for Setsuko, she said that New York was a new life free from Japan, and she wanted her wedding to be also. Furthermore, she told Ethan, it served her mother right not to be invited after torturing her for so many years about becoming an old maid. The wedding was going to be about them, their future together in New York. In time, they would tell their families.

Midweek, the morning of Takami's return from Japan, Ethan and Setsuko came into his office and stood by his desk. Ethan felt like a kid visiting the principal.

Takami was a short man with a crewcut, his body a compressed spring taut with energy, so that he seemed to be everywhere at once. As usual, he wore sneakers, expensive sweat pants, and a T-shirt. Even when he met clients, he never wore anything more formal than a sweater or button-down shirt. Creativity such as his did not need to follow the rules of the business world.

"I can't believe this. Why didn't you tell me sooner?" Takami said after they had delivered the news.

"We didn't know how you would react," Ethan said.

"You're adults. It's your business. I'm shocked, but of course I'm happy for you. Love at Takami Studio," he said shaking his head with disbelief. "Maybe I'm blind, or you two are good actors. How long have you kept this wedding a secret?"

"Ethan proposed last month."

"Do your parents know?"

"We didn't tell them yet," she said.

"Yeah, we wanted the wedding to be ours."

"Then I'll be the father of the bride and the groom. Us parents are always the last to know," Takami said, letting out one of his cackling laughs.

As the week evaporated, the wedding seemed to take on a life independent of them, like a car rolling downhill. When Setsuko returned to her apartment Friday evening, she found Ethan sitting on her bed looking abstractedly out the window. It felt as if they hadn't seen each other in a while, even though they had spent the whole day working at the studio. She closed the door behind her and dropped her purse on the bed.

"No kiss," she said kneeling on the bed behind him. "Are you okay?"

"I don't know," he said, still gazing out the window.

"What happened?"

"Nothing."

"Then why you look so upset?" She got up, walked around the bed, and sat beside him. "Really what's the matter?" she said, putting her arm around him.

"Who is Nakamura?"

"That's why you worried? Midori told you. A boyfriend from school. I don't know why she talk about him."

"I don't believe you," he said, turning to look her in the eye.

"Why you don't believe me?" she countered, taking her arm from his shoulder.

"How come you never told me about him?"

"It's a long time ago. Do you tell me every girlfriend you have?"

"No."

"Why should I tell you?"

"After Midori said his name, you spoke to her in Japanese so I couldn't understand, and then she covered her mouth like she said something wrong. How do you explain that if Nakamura was just a boy from a long time ago?"

She looked down at her hands, her lips pressed together.

"Tell me the truth, Setsuko. Are you in love with someone else?"

"I love you."

"Then why are you lying to me about this?"

"I'm not lying. Midori said he was my school boyfriend, not me. I didn't lie about anything."

"Then who the fuck is he?" Ethan got up and stood over her.

"It's my business. I don't know why Midori said something. She has a big mouth sometimes."

"Well it's too late. Now it's my business."

"I didn't want to tell you."

"Why?"

"It's my shame. I'm stupid woman." She looked as if she was going to cry.

"What are you talking about?" he said holding his fists against his eyes.

"When I come from Japan, I left that behind. It's not my life now."

"If it's not your life now, then why can't you tell me?"

Setsuko sighed and kept looking at her hands.

"It's my shame."

He sat down next to her again and covered her hand with his.

"Whatever it is, it's okay. You don't have to be ashamed."

She lifted her other hand, brushed the hair from her forehead and held it against the back of her neck.

"Your love is a kind of . . ." She paused. "It's a kind of . . ." She said something in Japanese that he did not understand. "I don't know the English word. Like a children who don't know bad things in life."

"You're saying I'm a child."

"No. I wish you could speak Japanese. Your love is like a child who doesn't know bad things about life."

"You mean innocent."

"A type of pure."

"Innocent."

"Maybe that's it. Your love is innocent."

"How do you know?"

"I know."

Her hand tightened around her hair at the back of her neck as if she were about to pull it.

"I don't understand why you won't tell me."

"I said it's the past. Not my life now."

He leaned forward, resting his chin on his fists so that he could not see her.

"I don't know," he said.

"I love you, not someone else," she said, reaching out and touching his back.

He stood up and stared at a vague reflection of himself in the window glass.

She joined him, and he saw her outline in the window like a silhouette.

"Maybe we don't really know each other."

His words hung in the air. The faint sound of laughter drifted up from the street below.

"Everybody gets scared before they get married. It's natural," she said, her voice soft. She stepped in front of him now, and reached up to hold his face between her hands.

"I know I love you and you love me."

He looked away from her, but she lifted his face and found his eyes.

"Tell me you don't love me, and we don't get married."

"I do love you."

"Then the past doesn't matter. It's nothing. Just our life now."

She leaned in toward him, and he met her lips, tentatively at first, and then taking her lower lip between his teeth, her flesh in his. He held her there, afraid to let go.

Roadblocks and Bridges

Roberta Levitow

It's a long plane ride from Los Angeles International Airport to Nairobi—twenty-four hours in the air, and you get there two days after you started. I arrived with a couple of extra boxes containing books—theater books of all kinds, textbooks, and play scripts. On the label I had boldly printed their destination: Ford Foundation East Africa Office, Rahimtulla Tower, Nairobi, Kenya. Perhaps because of this address—either that or the literature—I was able to pass through customs without paying the duty for which Kenyan Customs is notorious. Officially charged at their original value, these books should have cost me an additional $1,000. I was, in effect, carrying contraband.

The participants of the September 2001 East African Theatre Workshop were fourteen artists from Kenya, Uganda, and Tanzania. They were leading artists in their countries—playwrights, directors, actors, producers, ranging from nineteen to fifty-four years old, eleven men and four women. In Nairobi, we worked every day for four weeks, from nine to five with a short lunch break. Local Kenyan women delivered home-cooked meals in plastic containers, alternating country-appropriate starchy dishes: *ugali* for the Kenyans, *matoke* for the Ugandans, rice and hot sauce on everything for the Tanzanians. Evenings we went to theater events or watched performance tapes that I'd brought from home.

On the first day of our workshop, I laid the books out on the small stage floor. Suddenly all fourteen participants, without speaking, walked up and stood silently, flipping through book after book, as if I had set out a sidewalk sale. A "lending library" was spontaneously constructed. Days later, deals were cut when one book became necessary to one individual or another, and upon my departure, the rest of the books were consigned to the Ford Foundation East Africa Office, where they could be lent out to those interested. Nowhere else was safe. Books would be stolen, I was told.

I was housed at the Fairview, a hotel well known to missionaries, nongovernmental organization aid workers, and old Africa hands. Like every other enclave housing foreigners and wealthy locals in Nairobi, a guarded gate surrounded the property. Inside, everything was elegant, wood-paneled, flowered, and clean, with a bar and several restaurants and even a pool under construction. Outside, until the last days of my stay, I saw the city only from behind glass as my driver, Joseph Maiyo, and I shuttled to various appointments across a sea of human poverty. I was told not to walk the streets of the neighborhood alone, my white face announcing dollars in my pocket to the thousands of residents drawn to the city, desperately searching for their next meal. At the end, to say my good-byes, I asked a young Kenyan visual artist, who had joined me for lunch at the hotel, if he would do me the honor of walking me around the block.

The Fairview was located directly across the street from the Israeli embassy, a building surrounded by fences, barbed wire, surveillance cameras, and armed guards. While we drove past that military fortress several times every day, the American embassy was nowhere to be found. It was being rebuilt, after the infamous bombing in 1998, several miles outside Nairobi proper—purposely far from the constant foot traffic that carries Nairobi's people from place to place. Even the trails of human beings that one sees leading into and out of the city could barely reach this new location, now also fortified into a virtual military base. In place of the old embassy downtown, a park has been built. How lovely, I thought, until I discovered that it was locked and that Nairobi citizens are charged 25 Kenyan shillings to enter and sit under the shade of a precious American tree— 25 shillings in a country where $1 a day is fine wages and millions of people starve in the Kibera slums.

Each day, I would order the "lunch box" option from my hotel and set it up as a communal snack box for the rest of the group. The soon famous "lunch boxie" (always nice to place a vowel at the end of an English word to give it the Swahili lilt) contained a protein-rich feast: fried chicken, an egg, cheese sandwiches, fruit, crackers, juice, cookies, and a chocolate bar. Over the weeks, my colleagues developed an unnamed ritual for parceling out each item. Silently it was determined who would take the egg, who the chicken, who the chocolate. The *Muzungu* (European/white person) food was apparently shared among all.

The space for our workshop was very good by Nairobi Standards—an abandoned private school near Daniel Arap Moi's presidential palace. The old cracked swimming pool was now home to thick algae, fish, and frogs. The floor of the auditorium where we chose to work was built out of good dark wood, dangerous only in the few spots where tropical rains had poured through the roof. But the toilets flushed. The lights turned on. I discovered that few performing spaces of better quality could be found anywhere in the city.

There were several: The French Cultural Center, located in downtown Nairobi, was where we went regularly to see performances, work in pleasant rehearsal rooms, get French-language books from the library, drink good coffee, sit in the secluded shady garden, meet each other, find a quiet respite from the noise and dirt on the streets—all of this provided gratis to anyone who entered. The British Cultural Center, also downtown, had, among other things, screening rooms for training Kenyans on how to write soap operas for the UN—also free. The German Cultural Center/Goethe Institute, around the corner, was not as well equipped with rehearsal or performance spaces, but its facilities could still be engaged, and it offered classes and an interesting film series at night for free.

"Where is the American Cultural Center?" I asked innocently. Long gone, was the answer. "They used to have a free library, but now they've moved out of the city center off the bus routes, and they charge for use." My colleagues politely noted these changes without additional comment.

Our group communicated through two common languages, English and Swahili. The Ugandans, Kenyans, and I used English, and the Tanzanians and Kenyans used Swahili (Kiswahili). The individual participants represented over ten mother tongues or tribal languages.

How did we communicate? We found ways. Physical action was essential. Songs spoke to us even when we didn't understand the words. Similarly, characters and narratives seemed to express themselves beyond language. We began to play with different languages and discovered, in improvisation, new ways to speak. If the need was strong enough, someone in the group could always translate thoughts that begged more nuance and complexity.

We spent our days in a kind of dream. They, because they had never before been given the opportunity to do nothing but be creative for four weeks, living in pleasant surroundings, working in quiet and peace, and receiving generous per diems. I, because I was Alice in Wonderland, surrounded by a sensory collage, a social vibrancy and human connection of an abundance and intensity far beyond my expectation.

My colleagues, I thought, were like desert plants starved for water. Every book I brought with me, every videotape and CD, every kind word, every cup of tea, every day we could spend together allowed us to experience the exhilaration and engagement of theatrical collaboration. I often thought of southern California's Anza-Borrego desert—barren until the spring rains ignite a profusion of yellow and scarlet wildflowers bursting out of prickly pear and beaver tail cactus.

They spoke of the rare privilege of working with each other. It was harder for a Kenyan to arrange to work with a Ugandan than with a European. Travel between the three East African countries is dangerous, difficult, and expensive. They longed to discover the similarities and differences, not with America and Europe but rather among themselves—subtleties that I could barely perceive but that bespoke thousands of years of shared history. As I came to understand, East Africa is a universe unto itself, with a past and a culture as dense and as rich as any. The notion of expressing an East African aesthetic and identity became the central focus of the project.

The daily exercises eventually evolved toward a "presentation," which we were asked to share at the Bagamoyo Arts College annual festival. Bagamoyo is a small Muslim village on the coast of Tanzania, just across the Indian Ocean from more famous Zanzibar. But Bagamoyo has an infamy of its own. In its tragic history, it was the center of the Arabic slave trade out of East Africa, and later Germans arrived to take over, building forts, still standing, for continuing slaving. The broad white beaches bordering a turquoise sea, although exquisite, carry echoes of dark times. During Tanzania's socialist period, Bagamoyo became home to an arts college supported by the People's Republic of China. The first public performances took place under the mango trees in a grove that still stands on the grounds. Later, the Swedish government built the performing arts facility that held 1,000 people a night on one side and sheltered 500 people from the midday sun for indoor performances on the other. (Sadly, I've been told that the year after our presentation, the festival was forced to perform once again under the mango trees, since a fire destroyed the thatched roof of the theater.)

At festival time, it seemed as if the entire town of Bagamoyo showed up in their finery. Over a thousand barefoot and sandaled Muslim villagers, wrapped in colorful fabric, carrying home-cooked dinners, young and old, male and female, were crammed into every crevice of the concrete amphitheater. Over four days, they sat for five or six bum-numbing hours (sunset to midnight) as performers from all over Tanzania (and beyond) sang, danced, and enacted in an ever changing variety show. Boos alternated with cheers as the work ranged from clumsy amateur troupes to chanted Swahili poetry, from European-trained dance companies to an acrobatic percussion group from a Burundi refuge camp. Thankfully, our presentation rated one of the more rousing responses, just as the workshop participants had assured me it would.

Seeing the presence of so many other nations actively involved in providing support to the East Africans, I kept asking myself where exactly my fellow countrymen were hiding. Where was America in the midst of all this diversity? Yes, we were there in recognizable businesses and pharmaceuticals and Coca-Cola and fancy hotels and, of course, in expensive safari trips. We were there in Starbucks coffee beans bought at agonizingly cheap rates from the coffee farmers, who cannot partake in leveraging the price since the Kenyan government controls all the processing. We were there in privileged jobs and elegant restaurants and fabulous house compounds in exclusive neighborhoods on the way to the International (American) School.

One day earlier in the workshop, in preparation for our upcoming presentation in Tanzania, our group caravanned out from our home base in central Nairobi, deep into the suburbs, past the gated armed guards protecting sprawling tropical gardens on quiet landscaped streets, and down the bumpy country road that lead to the International School of Kenya. We'd been invited to perform our piece for the American and international students. Although I'd been advised by a workshop member whose husband taught drama at the school, I was not prepared for the quality of the facility we found: a brand-new performing arts complex; shiny wooden floors; comfortable seats; air-conditioning; hundreds of lighting instruments; up-to-date sound equipment. We did a brief warm-up with the students, and then the actors gave a fine performance, and the passionate, curious, and sympathetic young people rose for a standing ovation. Most of the Africans had never seen a theater space like this, let alone performed in one. The National Theatre of Kenya, which seats 700 people in broken chairs surrounded by ravaged walls and a torn curtain, has five stage lights. And yet this world-class performance space, for the benefit of "international" high school students, was only a thirty-five-minute drive from downtown Nairobi.

As we gathered in the parking lot afterward, preparing to drive back to our dilapidated old school grounds, we said nothing about the obvious discrepancy. It seemed from their silence on the matter that such a thing was to be expected. Americans are known to take care of their own.

I found that America is not "on the ground" in East Africa. In fact, we are seldom to be seen at all, and when we are viewed, it's in "dumped" television programming, donated clothing resold on the streets, and violent action films. Or East Africans hear about our latest military adventure on *BBC World News*. And they know we've been propping up their corrupt governments. How long was Daniel Arap Moi protected by American and international business?

Toward the end of my stay, Joseph, my driver and impromptu Swahili teacher, picked me up as usual at the Hillcrest School to take me back to the hotel. Joseph had taught me to count in Swahili from one to ten with the tenderness that he must have used with his own children. As I got into the car, he said quietly, "A bad thing has happened in your country." I saw him look back at me through the rearview mirror. We both sat very still. He could not find any words. He started the car and turned on the radio, tuning in to the BBC, and I heard the reporter describing explosions as airplanes flew into the World Trade Center. The rest of our journey was traveled in the silence.

Dropping me off at the Fairview, Joseph, usually so robust and sociable, seemed to sag into his seat. I walked into the lobby and saw that someone had moved a large TV set into one of the meeting areas. I joined people from all over the world, black and white, who sat quietly watching the *BBC World News*. We were shown footage of the towers falling, the people running, the people jumping. Several of the hotel workers whom I had come to know during my weeks in residence came up to me to say, "So sorry." I thought of the U.S. embassy bombing in Nairobi, 200 Kenyans killed along with 12 Americans. Of course, they understood. I ordered food and went to my room to continue watching the news. I called my husband in Los Angeles and futilely tried to plan tomorrow's rehearsal.

Africans are a stoic people. They suffer immeasurably and carry their suffering with silent dignity. I was not so sure I was the same.

The next morning, I arrived at the school early. As each participant arrived, they walked over to me and shook my hand to greet me. They each looked me in the eye and said, "I'm so sorry what has happened in your country."

"Thank you," I said. And I wondered about their political beliefs. I wondered about the suffering they had personally seen. I had heard their stories about Idi

Amin, political exile, death threats, imprisonment, disease, and hunger. Could I be as brave as they had already shown themselves to be?

Once we were convened, we gathered in a circle and took each other's hands. I put on our warm-up CD—joyous African music—and we danced.

After the success of the East African Theatre Workshop, our sponsoring organization, the Center for International Theatre Development (based in Baltimore, Maryland), organized a second phase. In May 2002, a workshop had already been scheduled for graduate students at Towson University and young theater students at Warsaw's historic Akademia Teatralna im. Aleksandra Zelwerowicza w Warszawie (Warsaw Theater Academy). Philip Arnoult, the center director, invited me to lead the workshop and bring along three of the younger East African participants. We would form The Three Continents Workshop, working first at Towson in the United States and then traveling together to Poland for further work and a final presentation at the academy's first International Student Theatre Festival.

A surprising roadblock appeared when the U.S. embassy in Uganda denied a visa for one of the African workshop participants. I soon learned that the current U.S. Immigration and Naturalization Service position is to summarily reject all visa applications from certain countries unless the petitioner can demonstrate family, financial, or job-related motivation to return to his or her home country. U.S. embassies regularly refuse applications by artists who are not married, do not have children, big bank accounts, or full-time jobs. In that spirit of hospitality and in spite of letters of support from the Ford Foundation East Africa Office, our Ugandan participant was refused three times. We soon found ourselves in a pitch battle. It was only after appeals from my congressman's office, a personal letter to the U.S. ambassador to Uganda, and my threat to file a grievance with the State Department's Bureau of African Affairs that the embassy in Kampala reversed its decision.

Visas in hand, the Africans and Poles arrived safely at BWI Airport, and we held our first meeting gathered around a world map taped to a blackboard in the Studio Theatre at Towson University. In spite of linguistic obstacles, once together, we did manage to engage productively with one another, carefully trudging though various unexpected cultural differences. The Africans explored the mysteries of the thermostat and garbage disposal in the modern American apartments where we were housed in Maryland. The Poles got the firsthand experience of being white faces in an urban African American slum when they took an innocent walking tour of South Baltimore.

Swahili, Polish, and English were all spoken daily but not with any shared proficiency. So, at least within the workshop, we turned to physical, musical, and nonverbal conversation. Our Africanized renditions of Polish children's songs and Anglo-Saxon romantic ballads led us into hours of spontaneous singing and dancing. Eventually improvisations formed into narratives.

We all learned to do African tribal dances, then Polish-style ballet, and finally, an American kick-line, but we were unable to arrive at a common theme around which to build our Three Continents presentation—not nationalism, or love, or ecology, or globalization, or family. Each group seemed to feel and think too specifically about each of those topics. We ended up building three short stories that seemed to revolve around notions of death, loss, and identity, told from three points of view and in three distinct styles. The African story involved sickness, death, the UN, government corruption, and the unfair distribution of funds. The Polish story was based on the legend of Princess Wanda, who committed suicide rather than marry a German prince and lose her national identity. It was told with subtle grace and a profound sense of history. The American story was abstract, cool, ironic, and alienated as it appropriated images from the first two stories and reassembled them, ending with the two young students staring blankly at a television set.

These stories incorporated the other cultures, at the will of the creators. That is, the Africans used a Polish Grotowski exercise for one sequence and incorporated the Robert Wilsonesque slow-motion walk that we had seen in a performance of *Eugene Onegin* at the Warsaw Opera. The Poles asked the Ugandan to sing one of her Banyankole children's songs to mark Wanda's retreat to the comfort of an old woman in the forest.

The American students' story dealt with the struggle for connection, an experience most Americans recognize—an attempt to relate to foreigners, which is fraught with guilt, fear, and even self-pity. Ironically, the same students who created this piece seemed to cling to each other during breaks and after rehearsals. They would generally go off to eat without asking fellow workshop participants to join them. Surrounded by people who were grateful for every given opportunity, I saw the Americans pick and choose their outside experiences, conveniently missing several that didn't spark their curiosity.

At the same time, they would enter passionately into rehearsal discussions, pouring out a wellspring of self-criticism, eager to castigate the American way of life as the perpetrator of vast global crimes. They readily acknowledged the suffering America has caused. They bemoaned their terrible sense of isolation.

The contradictory and conflicted behavior I was observing reminded me of my own inner struggles. Having grown up in an upper-middle-class southern California suburb, I experienced enormous anxiety the first time I ventured outside my comfort zone. The angst of my young American students was all too understandable, and as the weeks progressed, I looked for opportunities to speak to them privately. Finally, confronting them one afternoon, I said, "This isolation and helplessness you feel, is it real? Who and what do you fear? The people in this workshop feel enormous affection and curiosity toward you. They are waiting for you to offer your hand."

On that day, the American participants were quiet, but the next morning they joined the other students for the hotel breakfast in Warsaw.

What were they afraid of?

Perhaps the same things we all are. We fear that we will not be comfortable—physically, mentally, and emotionally. We fear that our daily American lives, with antibacterial soaps, prescription medications, washable wool blankets, frozen waffles, new Nikes, and café lattes, will evaporate upon arrival in these strange places. We fear being shown our ignorance and feeling stupid. We fear defending our privileges on the basis of anything but luck. We come to believe that we can no longer explore new territory. So we stay home, where we are safe—and that fills us with unbearable loneliness. So we try to venture out. But even when we travel, we work hard to keep our comfortable cocoon intact.

Globalization is not only a business concept. Globalization is a cultural concept. We can't just send our money, our politicians, or our machines. We have to send our bodies, our selves.

I have no doubt that millions of Americans want to help make this world safer and better through means other than guns, soldiers, and tanks. To do so, other cultures must be allowed—encouraged—to speak, and we must be able to listen. Let us become a people who are unafraid to learn from others how to view a world that is different from our own.

On September 11, 2003, I silently commemorated the World Trade Center bombings by standing onstage as one of twelve honorees at the closing ceremony for the Fifteenth Cairo International Festival for Experimental Theatre. The Festival showcased over sixty productions from over forty European, Asian, African, and Arabic countries. In attendance were hundreds of artists from all over the globe, as well as several Americans. One was on the selection committee, one served on the jury, another presented a paper. There were three young Americans writing for various theater journals and one San Francisco theater director whose company specializes in work dealing with the Middle East. No American artists or companies performed.

I stood onstage on a day in which Cairo's 18 million people went about their business seemingly without noticing the anniversary of September 11. They certainly didn't speak of it onstage. Instead, we celebrated the efforts of artists from Palestine, Yemen, Saudi Arabia, Qatar, Bahrain, Kuwait, Algeria, Tunisia, Morocco, Libya, Jordan, Lebanon, Syria, Iraq, Oman, England, Switzerland, the Netherlands, Belgium, Rwanda, Cameroon, the Sudan, Kazakhstan, Uzbekistan, Kosova, Serbia, Albania, Bulgaria, Turkey, Cyprus, and, of course, Egypt. *Karma,* the evening's culminating performance, was a stunning dance theater piece by young artists from South Korea. Its exquisite execution and notable life-affirming themes of hope and continuity won Best Production and brought us all to our feet cheering.

As the names of the first honorees were read, artists from France, Scotland, Italy, and Spain, one by one, climbed the stairs onto the stage. This was the moment I had imagined in fearful daydreams—me, an American Jew in Cairo on September 11, standing alone in front of hundreds of strangers whose plays clearly exposed the dense fervid rage, hurt, and isolated madness now awake in the world. Then my name was called, and I heard applause as I started up the stairs, applause that continued as I was given a medallion inscribed in Arabic and featuring the ancient Egyptian god Toth, god of wisdom and learning, as I was warmly greeted by the Egyptian minister of culture and the president of the festival, as I crossed the stage and looked straight out at the assembled audience for the requisite photo, and as I returned to my seat next to my distinguished fellow honoree, Shakib Khoury, from the Lebanese American University in Beirut. In the audience was Gichora Mwangi, who now runs the Arts Centre in Nairobi, Kenya, and helped organize that first East African Theatre Workshop two years before.

On September 11, 2001, my people had been attacked, and I had been surrounded by the compassion of my African friends and colleagues, who taught me that in Africa when a member of a village is in mourning, the whole village cries. On September 11, 2003, I felt conspicuously alone. But I learned that I was welcome and that my presence was no mistake.

I had been afraid, but my colleagues were only waiting for me to reach out my hand. They caught my fear in their open arms.

Monika, before Reunification

Ingrid Wendt

Blue, blue eyes, and still she has wanted them bluer:
fluorescent blue lids above black
eyeliner, drawing
a zone between us that any other day I wouldn't have
bothered to cross, but here in Frankfurt I am
the guest, treated

after my lecture to green tortellini, red wine at noon
and my duty is still not over
So Dresden, I ask,

indeed was depressing? expecting something surely
kin to guilt if not guilt itself:
how can we

the victorious walk those streets and not see firebombs?
Not remember who dropped them?
And Monika here

with her British accent (that until I lived a month in Britain
always sounded too prim to be true)
leaping past

all my carefully hidden assumptions, revealing
her own, what she hadn't
expected:

the greyness; how much destruction has not been rebuilt: a reminder:
We have deceived ourselves once.
Monika whom I can

no longer ignore, telling us *How much more honest than here
in this colorful West, all of us thinking: We do
what we want to.*

*We buy. We spend. We set ourselves apart, choosing among
what is offered: visions we keep on
thinking are real.*

Monks' Portrait (White House), Washington, D.C., 1991 © Richard Robinson

El Halloween and the Día de Muertos

C. M. Mayo

> *Yet meet we shall, and part, and meet again*
> *Where dead men meet, on lips of living men.*
> —Samuel Butler

Wings

The first airplane arrived at San José del Cabo in 1931. The people couldn't believe it, that this thing could stay up above the earth, swoop over them without falling. The pilot's surname was Flores, but no one remembers his first name.

It is the town historian, Don Fernando Cota, who is telling me this story. It is late October, more than sixty years later. Most of the people who were there that day are dead.

They stood watching, Don Fernando tells me, on the stoops of their houses, at the edge of their citrus orchards, in their fishing boats: a machine with wings, its body glinting in the sun, engine droning across the pale desert sky. It had come from the other side of the Sea of Cortés; this must be so.

The dogs began to bark, mules and burros neighed and whinnied and stamped their hooves. Someone rang the bells of the church, and someone else ran to ring the bells at Municipal Hall. Everyone gathered on the beach.

It was not possible! This Flores, he started to climb and climb—Don Fernando raises his hand—and then *paf!* he would stall and dive. He did the loopy loopies! The people stood there on the beach and they clutched at their hearts because they thought he was going to die. Some of the ladies fainted, right on the sand.

The whole town, Don Fernando smiles, we were so grateful. We made Flores a party in Municipal Hall, a great ball, with dancing.

I am unlatching the wrought-iron gate of Don Fernando's house, leaving. He stands in the shade of leafy green plants in his patio and waves good-bye, having told me this last story. One of his caged parrots, plump and yellow, whistles like a bored child. Outside it is hot; there is no shade. A bus barrels by, a Coca-Cola truck.

Half an hour later, in downtown Cabo San Lucas, I find a swarm of black paper bats taped to the street-side walls of Planet Hollywood. Cardboard tombstones and pumpkin-headed scarecrows are propped below on the broiling-hot sidewalk. Soon it will be Halloween, and there will be a costume contest.

One in a chain of franchise restaurants from San Diego to New York City, Planet Hollywood has been open for less than a year, but it has already become the dominant feature of downtown Cabo San Lucas. At night its revolving red neon sign can be seen for miles. Tourists bunch up along the sidewalk in front, examining the plaster tiles at the entrance, casts of the handprints and shoe prints of celebrities: Sylvester Stallone, Bruce Willis, Whoopi Goldberg, Keanu Reeves, Jean Claude Van Damme. ("Look!" a little boy elbows his dad, "Steven Seagal!")

The rumor in Cabo San Lucas, avidly spread by bartenders, hotel clerks, touts and taxi drivers, is that Sylvester Stallone owns a house here in the Pedregal, the gated neighborhood that straddles the boulder-strewn mountain above town.

Later, Cecilia Avalos tells me, "It's not true," and she laughs. Cecilia is an old friend from Mexico City, married to Jacinto Avalos, an architect noted for, among other projects, several spectacular houses he has built in the Pedregral. Cecilia ought to know: Sylvester Stallone does not have a house here.

We are eating lunch at Mocambo, a Veracruz-style restaurant: seafood cocktails and fish, metal tables cluttered with bottles of hot sauce. Here is where the downtown begins to turn, no longer Planet Hollywood, Dairy Queen, KFC; the Cabo of *For Sale, Long Distance to the U.S. and Canada, $EXCHANGE*, but not yet the dirt-road Cabo of *se vende, farmacia, zapatería*. About half the patrons in Mocambo are tourists, half are local Mexicans. Cecilia recognizes a Mexican real estate agent whose office is across the street. The menus are bilingual, as are the waiters, reciting the day's specials in the rapid-fire clip of Mazatlán. We order tall soda glasses of shrimp in spicy tomato juice, chopped onion, cilantro, and lime.

Cecilia has spent the morning trying to find *calaveras*—the traditional sugar skulls for the *Día de Muertos,* the Day of the Dead—for her children. Her oldest boy is in boarding school in northern California, and he had wanted to make a *Día de Muertos* altar to show his classmates. She would have sent him some *calaveras* with his father, who will be flying to San Francisco on business. "But there is nothing of that here," Cecilia tells me. No *pan de muerto,* the sugar-dusted loaves of bread for the dead, either. "*Todo aquí es* Halloween," she says, shaking her head. Everything here is Halloween.

After lunch I'm back at this borrowed beach house, such a pretty little house, pastel-washed, with a swimming pool. I make my way down the flagstone path to the water, past the wall grown over now with masts and trailing vines of bougainvillea, sumptuous tresses of canary yellow, plum-purple, and crimson. Ten years ago, this was raw land on the edge of a hardscrabble cattle ranch named after the river Tule, a wide bed of dry sand except during the *chubasco,* or hurricane season. Behind the house and across the highway, the apron of land that spreads down from the Sierra de la Laguna is a sun-parched tan, fuzzed with cardón cacti and tangles of thorny bushes and mesquite. Below, the water is a blue so dazzling it hurts the eyes. At night the sky is awash with stars. Here at the end of the Baja California peninsula, the waters of the Sea of Cortés and the Pacific Ocean mingle. There is no land between this shore and the Antarctic.

A pair of pelicans skims by, fast and still, their wing tips centimeters above the water.

What Came from the Sky

"1907, 1918, oh much suffering; another one in 1927, many animals and fruit trees lost." The town historian counted the years of the great *chubascos* on one hand. We were sitting in his living room in San José del Cabo—I was on the sofa, Don Fernando settled like a Buddha in his rocking chair.

"And then"—Don Fernando placed his hands on his knees—"there was the *chubasco* of 1939. I was nineteen years old, already a teacher in High School Number 3. Some people rode in on horseback from Cabo San Lucas—it was impossible to cross El Tule in an automobile—and they told me when they passed by the school: Cabo San Lucas is gone! So we went there on horses. We sent some mules across El Tule first because they are more surefooted, and if they can cross, the horses follow. We rode and walked through the night, and we arrived at sun-up. From the sea to the foothills of the sierra"—Don Fernando swept his arm across the space between us—"there was nothing but broken pieces of cardón cactus. There were no references, everything had disappeared!"

And the people?

"Not many died, only five, because the *chubasco* came down in the daytime. Had it been at night, that would have been different. But they lost everything, their clothes, their dishes, their beds. Forty families! The governor, Lieutenant Colonel Rafael M. Pedrajo"—Don Fernando paused to spell out the name—"he delivered the material for forty houses! I don't know how he did it. The floors and walls were of wood, the roofs of corrugated iron. For forty families! Incredible, such a work. They should put his name on a street, or a monument, something."

I knew about the *chubascos,* the tropical hurricanes that hit the peninsula in late summer. A bad one hit the cape in 1993. The highway from San José to Cabo San Lucas, only recently inaugurated by President Salinas, was washed out at several points, and thousands of cardón cactuses were swept down from the sierra, clogging the road and the beaches. The ocean churned up a brown froth that lasted for days. In September 1995 more than a hundred shrimpers died when they were caught out in the Sea of Cortés. More recently, in a mild *chubasco,* a tourist from Nebraska and two of his children were swept out and drowned as they walked on the beach by their hotel.

For a moment I was speechless, contemplating the furor of that *chubasco* of 1939—and the poverty and isolation that made the delivery of boards and corrugated iron for forty shacks like the miracle of manna.

Wrote John Steinbeck, "It is a miserable little flea-bitten place, poor and smelly." He visited Cabo San Lucas with the marine biologist Ed Ricketts in 1940, the year after the great *chubasco.* They were making a collecting expedition on the *Western Flyer,* a sardine boat out of Monterey, California, and they would sail, after their stop in Cabo, deep into the Sea of Cortés.

Cabo San Lucas was smelly then because of the fish cannery, the ruins of which can still be seen at the end of the pier just past the marina. Offal was tossed onto the beach for the pigs and vultures. Steinbeck noted the skinny dogs ("without racial pride"), the road into town ("two wheel-ruts in the dust"), and a "mournful" cantina where "morose young men hung about," hopelessness in their eyes.

But San José del Cabo was always different. It was a town when Cabo San Lucas was but a territory through which Pericú Indians wandered, foraging for cactus fruits. Later, Cabo became known for the whaling supply station and cattle ranch run by an English sailor named Ritchie, then for the fish-canning factory and ramshackle settlement of forty families. And San José del Cabo is still a town when Cabo San Lucas is, well, something else.

Cabo San Lucas wears a smiling, sometimes leering face that bellows, always in English. "Good morning, amigos!" the touts call out. "Something fun to do! How-are-you-today! HELLO!" Moto-tours to the old lighthouse, fishing tours, glass-bottom boat tours, tours to see the seals and the pelicans and the arch, scuba-diving tours, snorkeling tours, sunset tours, cocktails included. "YES!" The humor is hearty and forced. The Tai Won On bar does not serve Thai food, Señor Sushi serves everything but. Rules are posted: "No talking to servers, No talking to invisible people, No Jimmy Buffet music." Advice is offered: "In case of emergency: 1. Panic; 2. Pay bill; 3. Jump out window; 4. Run like hell." "Avoid embarrassment," says the sign in El Squid Roe's T-shirt shop, "don't wear these clothes on nude beaches." At the Giggling Marlin: "If the food, drinks and service are not up to your standards, then lower your standards."

San José del Cabo, a half-hour drive around the curve of the cape, feels slower and sleepier. The tourists look older. There is a church built on the site of a Jesuit mission, and the Plaza Mijares, with its quaint little wrought-iron bandstand and benches, is heavily shaded with palms and jacaranda trees. The shops—jewelry, furniture, *zapatería, tintorería*—close for siesta.

But San José too wears a mask: postcard-pretty town, have your enchiladas and margaritas, take your photos, buy your souvenir straw hat. A nice place to retire, play golf, go fishin'. FONATUR, the development arm of the Mexican Ministry of Tourism, has been seeing to that for more than twenty years.

Not that the welcome was wholehearted.

In San José's main plaza there would be a contest for the best altar, announced *El Diario Peninsular:* "To rescue the Mexican tradition of the *Día de Muertos,* as well as to counteract foreign influences."

"Hopefully," sniffed the *Tribunal de los Cabos,* "this will leave in the trunk of forgotten things the ritual of the Americans: Halloween."

A Real One, with Linen and Flowers

"I don't have anything against the Americans," Alfonso Fisher said. "But it's changed." He sighed and crossed his arms over his chest. He'd lived in Cabo San Lucas since 1947, he said, except when he went away to school, first in Guadala-jara, then Mexico City. Although middle-aged, Alfonso was dressed like a teenager in shorts, flip-flops, and a loose avocado-green T-shirt. I had to strain to follow what he was saying; the rhythms of his Spanish were not what I was used to.

We were sitting in his restaurant in the Plaza Bonita mall, only a few steps from Planet Hollywood. The customers had not yet arrived; it was midmorning. A cleaning lady mopped the floor with languorous sploshes of sudsy water. Alfonso's was a small but upscale restaurant, with marble-top tables, good linen, an antique piano. A stone fountain burbled softly; overhead, a ceiling fan turned, slow as the second hand on a clock.

"My father was chief engineer of the fish cannery. You can see the ruins from here." Alfonso gestured toward the window and wrinkled his nose. "It smelled really bad."

The cannery closed in the early 1970s, to the relief of the handful of tourists who flew down for the sportfishing. In 1973, the Transpeninsular Highway was inaugurated, linking the cape with the rest of the peninsula for the first time. Two years later, Alfonso and his mother opened El Arco, Cabo's first trailer park.

"It was small," Alfonso said. "Thirty spaces. It had water, light, good services. The people who stayed there were very interesting. Good people, the people who go to the trailer parks. And so many! The children of King Humberto of Italy came in a gigantic motor home, Peter Fonda stayed with us. All kinds of people. Some of them came every Christmas, they'd bring their piñatas and all that. Very few were Mexicans, most were Americans. A few Italians. They could buy what they needed at a general store in Cabo run by a Chinese named Chong. There wasn't a supermarket." Alfonso sighed again. "Now I feel like a stranger here. When I was a kid, we were a little town of three hundred people."

I had thought Alfonso might be part American himself, despite his accent; his surname was Fisher. When, I wanted to know, did the Fishers arrive in Baja California?

"1827." He chuckled at my surprise. "William Fisher was a sailor. There are lots of Fishers in Baja California, we're a big family. You'll find many names like that here: Collins, Green, Kennedy, Ritchie."

When did he begin to feel like a stranger?

"The last ten years." But things began to change before that, he explained. The Hotel Palmilla was built in 1955, then the Hacienda in the late 1960s, and the Hotel Cabo San Lucas in the 1970s. After that came the deluge of the Finnisterra, Twin Dolphins, Solmar, Howard Johnson's, El Presidente, Melia, Plaza las Glorias, Marriot, Westin Regina . . . Not that Alfonso hadn't been able to take advantage of business opportunities. He ran El Arco trailer park, he opened Alfonso's, which was the first restaurant in Cabo San Lucas—"a real one, with linen and flowers"— and in 1980, he and his mother built the Marina del Sol condominiums.

"You know what they say?" He grinned like a magician about to pull something out of a hat. "The world is a supermarket! And Hong Kong is the cash register." He laid both hands flat on the table. "So I'm moving there. I'm going to open a Mexican restaurant in front of the Jockey Club, very elegant. I already have my apartment in Hong Kong, on the thirty-eighth floor."

I was so startled, the only thing that occurred me to ask was whether his apartment had a view.

"Yes." He twisted his neck to one side and screwed up his eyes like Quasimodo. "If I go like this."

It Will Be a Marvel

It was the day before Halloween, and my mother was arriving from San Francisco. Late in the afternoon, I went to pick her up at the airport. The airport! I couldn't help thinking of the pilot Flores and his flight, so daring and flamboyant. ("No one remembers his first name," Don Fernando had said. "He did the loopy loopies!") Suddenly Los Cabos International Airport with its staid, boxlike terminal and its asphalt parking lot seemed monstrous in its modernity.

I wanted X-ray vision, to see through the flesh of the present into the past. Don Fernando and Alfonso Fisher had helped me do that; now I wanted to examine a few bones on my own. As I explained to my mother, on the beach just east of the Cabo San Lucas marina was a slight sandy rise topped by the Hotel Melia. According to a nineteenth-century map, this would have been the site of the house of Thomas "Captain" Ritchie, an English cabin boy who jumped ship in the early 1800s and became, in the words of journalist J. Ross Browne, "one of the institutions of the country."

"Smuggling, stockraising, fishing, farming, and trading have been among his varied occupations," wrote Browne in an account of his travels through Baja California for *Harper's New Monthly Magazine*. "He now has a family of half-breeds around him, none of whom speak his native language. He has made and lost a dozen fortunes, chiefly by selling and drinking whiskey." Ritchie's hospitality was legendary. Browne tells us that his house was

> the home of adventurers from all parts of the world. Admirals, commodores, captains and mates inhabit it; pirates and freebooters take refuge in it; miners, traders, and cattledrovers make it their home. In short, the latch-string is never drawn in. All who have money pay if they choose; those who have

none he feeds and makes drunk from sheer love of fellowship and natural generosity of heart.

One of that multitude was the Hungarian-born János Xántus, a naturalist stationed at Cabo San Lucas to observe the tides for the U.S. Coastal Survey and collect specimens for the Smithsonian Institution. Xántus's letters to his patron were peppered with references to Ritchie, such as, "I send all my boxes . . . which are at present pele mele piled up on the floor in Mr Ritchie's house."

Browne sketched Ritchie's house as he found it in 1866, a two-storied wooden structure with a pitched roof and five large windows facing the water. This is not the house of a dupe, a drunken bumpkin; Captain Ritchie was a mogul of his time and place. He enjoyed a virtual monopoly on supplying the whalers who put in for water and fresh beef; he kept a herd of mules that he employed packing passengers and freight to the inland mines at El Triunfo and San Antonio; he ran a hotel (albeit of a casual sort); he was a moneylender. Ritchie may have been bullied by the Mexicans—at one point, Browne tells us, they confiscated his property and imprisoned him in Mazatlán, until an English man-of-war that happened to be in port threatened to bombard the city on his behalf. And if Ritchie was an alcoholic, he was robust. "The various injuries inflicted upon him would have destroyed any other man on earth," claimed Browne. "It will be a marvel if he ever dies."

And so, I invited my mother for a drink at the Hotel Melia, to toast Captain Ritchie, I told her. We sat in the bar by the beach, alone but for a waiter who stood off to the side staring at the water. An American yelled from the balcony outside his room, perhaps six or seven stories up; another answered, bellowing like a sick cow. They were laughing; they were drunk. The sun had fallen behind the arch at Land's End, and the lights of the hotels strung along the beach began to twinkle. Anchored off the arch was a cruise ship draped with lights as if there were a carnival aboard. The air was warm and smelled of the sea.

Pelicans and Turkey Buzzards

As for the naturalist János Xántus, his camp would have lain in the lee of the massive outcropping that ends in the arch and the tall islands of rock called Los Frailes (the Friars), somewhere on the neck of sand between the ruins of the fish cannery and the Hotel Solmar. The fish cannery overlooks the placid blue of the harbor; the Solmar, only a short walk up a hill of dunes, faces the Pacific. The Solmar's is a featureless beach: swath of sand, swath of pale, hot sky. The surf pounds in, hurling up riffs of spray.

Xántus spent two years here measuring the tides and catching, killing, and preserving whatever he could: pelicans, crabs, rattlesnakes, wasp nests, scorpions, starfish, wildflowers, even (I gulp to think of it) a coyote. When he arrived at Cabo San Lucas in 1859, virtually nothing was known of the peninsula's natural history. By the time he sailed back to San Francisco in 1861, as his biographer, Ann Zwinger, notes, he had discovered and shipped to Spencer Fullerton Baird at the Smithsonian Institution nearly three hundred species new to science. Almost forty of these—among them a hummingbird, a screech owl, a gecko, and a tiny red-tailed triggerfish—bear his name.

It was a painstaking task, but Xántus worked quickly, and boxes of specimens piled up in his tent and "pele mere" at Captain Ritchie's house. Whenever a whaler dropped in for provisions—"I pray all the time for one," he wrote Baird, "like the frogs for rain"—he would send his boxes on. "[We] must take our chances," he wrote, early in his stay, "and you shall not be surprised if you receive from me letters via the Japanese seas, or Feejee islands or by some New Bedford whaler! I wonder whether you received a dispatch from me . . . via Sandwich islands by a friendly Yankee whaler?"

His nearest neighbor was Captain Ritchie. Xántus relied on Ritchie, as his letters show, for storage, water, occasional shelter, mail deliveries, and loans of cash. Ritchie also gave him advice: about the waterbirds, gone, he said, to Socorro Island to breed; about the "quite different" birds to the north near Todos Santos; the dangers of a rabid skunk.

The work of setting up camp and the tide gauge, and collecting and preparing specimens absorbed Xántus for more than a year. His letters reveal glimpses of his life: a pointer dog named Jack he'd trained to dig for crabs; a visit from the governor who brought him "two beautiful magpies . . . alive in a cage . . . very funny pets"; "an old indian woman & her boy, who cook for me"; and "many presents, consisting of objects of natural history, mostly from ladies." He went hunting deer and dined "on a couple of roasted quails in a deep canyon near a spring"; another time, he was out with Jack when they came upon a mountain lion gnawing the carcass of a doe. A "very fine specimen," he boasted of the cat to Baird. "I took great pains with her, prepared very carefully, & dried well." And would Baird please "by first opportunity" send the mountain lion to the Hungarian National Museum, "also her skull, which you will find in a box."

But Xántus's ebullience began to fade. "I do not know how the world stands," he complained to Baird. "I wonder whether Empr Napoleon rules yet Europe, or somebody else?" Soon Xántus was in flat-out despair: "near my camp is at present a perfect desolation, I killed everything." His letters became fewer, brief. In his last field-book entry he wrote:

> I am quite sick indeed of this place, every day seems a long year, and every one with the same monotonous desolation around me, not affording the least pleasure, variety, or enjoyment of any kind. . . . I am now of Gods grace nearly two years perched on this sandbeach, a laughing stock probably of the Pelicans & Turkey buzzards, the only signs of life around me.

Xántus's camp would have been closer to the ruins of the fish-canning factory; but the Solmar Hotel would be close enough for my purposes. I drove up the path that wound through the dunes and parked in a lot walled by a mountain of granite. The hotel rose up out of the sand, bone-white and angular. I walked through the lobby to the Pacific Ocean. The wind billowed my shirt and whipped my hair against my face. Even with sunglasses on I had to squint and shade my eyes.

The beach was deserted. The guests gathered around the swimming pool, only partially sheltered by the mass of rock at Land's End. Most of them lay on plastic chaise longues reading paperbacks: Tom Clancy, John Grisham, *The Bridges of Madison County*.

How galled Xántus would have been. To think: people would actually *pay* to come here!

I took refuge in the palapa bar and ordered coffee. Another toast, of sorts: Xántus' was a tremendous contribution to science. Not only was the sheer number of specimens he sent to the Smithsonian Institution impressive, but the condition they arrived in was almost uniformly excellent—remarkable given that the specimens ranged from birds and mammals to fish, plants, and insects, and even more remarkable given the primitive conditions in which he had to work. "The wind blows too hard all the time," he wrote Baird, "and upsets every now & then my tent, as there is nothing but quick sand to fasten the pegs in. Besides it is so small & so we have to sleep on top of the boxes." The boxes—made of wood, a scarce commodity on this remote desert cape—he nailed together himself.

According to Steinbeck, Xántus left another legacy. The manager of the fish cannery had pointed to three little Indian children and said they were Xántus's great-grandchildren. "In the town there is a large family of Xántuses," he added, "and a few miles back in the hills you'll find a whole tribe of them." Perhaps Xántus had fancied one of the "ladies" who brought him presents (a branch of milkwort? a cactus wren's egg?), a simple girl with rough Spanish and calloused hands—someone he could abandon when he returned to Europe. I had looked for that "large family" in the encyclopedic *Guía Familiar de Baja California.* I found Ritchie and Fisher, but no Xántus. It was as though his name had been covered over by the sands themselves.

Everybody Wears One

And so where fisherfolk and farmers once gaped at their first airplane sprawls an international airport; on the site of Captain Ritchie's house, a TV screen shows RuPaul holding forth in his waxy yellow wig; and on the shifting sands where János Xántus pitched his humble tent in the roar of the wind, bleats of Muzak soothe vacationing office workers. The past lies behind the present, strange and necessary as bones are to flesh. But to reverse the analogy, the present laid over the past, they sometimes seem foreign to one another, yet as fitting as a fright mask to a face.

In the more recent past came the surfers, spearheading the first great wave of Americans to venture down the peninsula after the Transpeninsular Highway opened in 1973. As I write, hundreds are waiting for their "surf fax." It's a service—it costs some two dollars a minute—provided by a company that maintains buoys all across the Pacific. The buoys register swells from a storm, say, in New Zealand, and these predict the quality of surfing conditions in Baja California. When they're good, three or four hundred surfers from southern California alone will fly down to Cabo for the weekend. The planes will all be full, the car rental agencies sold out.

"Live to Surf, Surf to Live," as surf star Mike Doyle inscribed his autobiography to me.

Mike was making a living as a painter now, he told me when I met with him under the big top-size palapa of a seafood restaurant. He was a rangy, square-shouldered guy in shades and a sea blue-and-white Hawaiian shirt. His heyday as a surf star was back in the 1960s. His life since then had been peripatetic: Honolulu, Aspen, Jackson Hole, Idaho, Oregon. He'd sold granola, purple surfboard wax, suntan oil, beachwear, real estate. He'd invented the single ski, precursor to the wildly popular snowboard; he'd taken up sailboarding. He'd married twice, divorced twice, dated New Age minister Terry Cole-Whitakker, remarried. It wasn't until he was in his late forties that he began to recognize the patterns in his life. "Things didn't just fall apart," he wrote, "I tore them down on purpose to get what I really wanted, which was freedom and the sense of adventure that comes from starting all over again."

That bohemian impulse had drawn Mike to surfing back when he was a teenager, inspired by the likes of Tubesteak, a surfer who lived in a shack at Malibu, surviving on a diet of roasted hot dogs financed by collecting Coke bottles. It also drew Mike to Baja California. He'd ventured south of the border before on "surfaris" with his buddies from Los Angeles, but he didn't get down to Cabo until 1974, the year after the Transpeninsular opened. "They kept saying there was no surf here," Mike told me indignantly. "But it was great!" Cabo was a village of four hundred people then and the road to San José was unpaved. The only place to stay was Alfonso Fisher's trailer park. Mike bought a plot of land on the hill overlooking the half-moon of beach called Zippers—world famous now for its outstanding surfing—and began to construct his house. Not long after, when a legion of Americans followed Mike's lead, the area was dubbed Gringo Hill.

Mike moved down full-time in the mid-1980s. He sold real estate for a few years, but no longer. "The thrill," he told me, "is doing what you want to do. I'm really creating something. Being a salesman is not as exciting, it's not like putting color on a canvas." He was surprisingly soft-spoken. If I'd closed my eyes and just listened to his voice, I could have pictured someone in his early twenties.

Did he still surf?

"Surfing is first!" He'd looked at me as if I were insane.

Later, Mike met my mother and me at the gate of his house on Gringo Hill. The view from the patio was dark, but we could hear the rush and pull of the breakers against the beach below. His studio was a large white room lit with flood lamps placed on the floor. His canvases were big, loud, and colorful. Beach scenes predominated: a cluster of candy-colored skiffs under a lavender sky; a rim of surf, coconut palms bent in the breeze. The largest painting was of twin purple and lime-green trees rendered in strokes as broad and crude as a housepainter's. My mother admired *Squid Woman,* a red-and-yellow figure with flowing hair.

Today was a good day, Mike said. After surfing Zippers, he'd finished a six-paneled canvas of orange and fuchsia, yellow and lime-green masks, all wild and scribbly. Its title, scrawled across the bottom: *The King in Me.*

I liked the energy and playfulness of his work, and I appreciated the courage of his lifestyle. Painting was not a steady salary. "But you overcome that," Mike had told me. "You feel free again. What's the worst that could happen? I could go out surfing. I need to eat? I'll get my bag of brown rice."

But there was a pragmatic side to Mike, too. He traveled the circuit of surf trade shows, selling his book and a longboard called the Mike Doyle Waterman Special. He'd recently been commissioned to do the poster art for a surfing contest to benefit Scripps research on cancer. He himself—"surfing legend Mike Doyle," as last year's brochure touted—would participate.

Mike brought out one last painting, of a bare-chested man with a chalk-white face. The eyes were shaded with purple and turquoise, and delicate lines of scarlet scrolled around each cheek, like the war paint of the Maoris. The expression was at once watchful and amused. A self-portrait. Its title: *Everybody Wears One.*

He was going to a costume party tonight, Mike said as he began stacking the canvases against the wall. "As van Gogh—you know, tape over one ear and add ketchup."

El Halloween

The night was still young, and my mother was curious to see the new Planet Hollywood. Besides, the Halloween-costume contest might be fun to watch. We went in, up the sweep of carpeted stairs and past Charlie Sheen's tie, Geena Davis' bathing suit, Sylvester Stallone's shoes. The restaurant was dim, zebra-skinned, loud. It was also empty.

"Nah," my mom said, and we left.

We walked along the main avenue, by the restaurants and bars decked out for Halloween with black and orange streamers, fake cobwebs, paper cutout pumpkins and ghosts and skulls. The Bee Gees' "Stayin' Alive" blasted out the door of the Rio Grill. At the entrance, a peroxide blonde dressed as a dominatrix passed out candy to a group of Mexican children accompanied by their mother. The baby—wide-eyed in his stroller—was outfitted as a devil, with sequins pasted on his little red felt horns. "*El Halloween! El Halloween!*" the children cried, holding out plastic grocery bags.

The avenue was filling with children, and all along it the employees of restaurants, bars, real estate offices, and T-shirt shops were handing out candy. Several older American couples were also handing out sweets, fistfuls of little twist-wrapped licorice, strawberry chews, and Chiclets. Most of the children wore homemade witch or vampire costumes, their faces smeared with white and black greasepaint. A few sported fangs, and one tiny witch, perhaps four years old, carried an enormous plastic bone that she held like a baton. Some of the smaller children were mummies, wrapped with gauze or Ace bandages.

My mother and I decided that we too would hand out treats, and we stepped into the grocery store for a kilo bag of candies. Immediately on returning to the sidewalk we were surrounded by a crowd of children—some witches and vampires, but many without a costume—pushing their bags at us, crying "*El Halloween! El Halloween!*" and then, a few sweets dropped in, not a *gracias,* but a chorus of "thank you! thank you!"

As we worked our way down the avenue we met several small groups with their parents. From their accents I guessed the parents were the white-collar workers of Cabo, shop clerks and restaurant managers recently arrived from mainland cities such as Guadalajara, Obregón, or Guanajuato. For a couple of blocks this was an agreeable intercultural kind of thing—we delighted by the children and their costumes, they delighted with the candy, the parents beamingly polite, thanking us always in English.

And then, near the Giggling Marlin, we ran into that same crowd of unescorted children. They pressed up against my mother, crying, "*Dame el Halloween!*" Give me my Halloween!

"But you've already had your candy," my mother said, holding the bag closed against her chest.

"*El Halloween!*" they cried, "*El Halloween!*" A little ghoul with greasepaint circles around his eyes and a penciled scar that looked more like a centipede tugged at her blouse, his face an agony of hurt. I believe he'd already gotten candy from my mother twice.

Feeling somewhat put-upon, we moved off the street to the patio bar at the corner of Plaza Bonita, a good vantage point for watching the Americans who were beginning to file out of their hotels and houses to explore the costume parties along the avenue. There was a Batman, a woman in a Dodgers baseball uniform, a pirate with a stuffed fake-fur parrot Velcroed to his shoulder. A clique of girls in fright wigs and black leather miniskirts rated whistles from the waiters. One of the waiters crouched behind a potted bougainvillea and yelped like a coyote.

It was nearly nine o'clock when we headed back out to the avenue. The air was cooler and the bass bleat from the restaurants and bars-cum-discos louder, muddled. Most of the children were gone, or flagging. I spotted the devil asleep in his stroller. One little mummy, his unraveled bandages revealing an expanse of diaper, held his father's hand as he slowly scaled the steps of Pizza Hut.

The Día de Muertos

And so Halloween had passed, and the first day of November, All Saints'. On the second, I drove my mother back to the airport. The airport was filled with franchises: Domino's Pizza, Carnation Ice Cream, Mrs. Field's Cookies. Long lines snaked to the counters of Continental, Mexicana, Alaska Airlines. The bar was packed with Americans, all watching football on TV.

"Touchdown!" they shouted, raising their fists.

Today was the *Día de Muertos,* that tradition—the local pundits claimed—so in need of rescue from "foreign influences." A blend of European folk practice and pre-Hispanic ritual adapted to the Catholic All Souls', it is celebrated in mainland Mexico as a happy day. Families visit the graves of relatives, sweeping and then decorating them with flowers, candles, and offerings of food—tamales, chocolate, beans, and tortillas. In some parts of Mexico an altar with the offering is assembled inside the house, and may include photographs, favorite toys, musical instruments, and even clothing. Until recent years this celebration was an intimate one, the dead honored by those who knew and loved them. Now tourists, both Mexican and foreign, crowd into the mainland Indian towns of Mixquic and Pátzcuaro, jumbling through the narrow rows between the pretty graves, cameras clicking away. "Mexico has sold its cult of death," writes Mexican critic Carlos Monsiváis, "and the tourists smile, anthropologically satiated." Even the urban middle and upper classes—in generations past, at a careful remove from any taint of the indigenous—revel in their *mexicanidad,* assembling altars to no one in particular, loudly colorful constructions for the lobbies of museums, offices, shops and hotels, schools and universities, and town plazas.

On my way back from the airport I stopped in San José's. A hot afternoon. Trees thick with birds. An old man sat nodding on the steps of the church, which was a pretty little building, buff yellow and cream with twin bell towers flanking its entrance. In front of the ice cream stand, a tourist in a golf hat and cork-soled sandals fanned himself with a folded brochure. At the far side of the plaza, I found one *Día de Muertos* altar, half assembled in the shade of a lush, feathery palm.

Like all the many others I had seen, it looked impersonally attractive. A riot of color and pottery (from Puebla and Michoacán), it beckoned the camera, its chief purpose to win a competition.

I almost didn't notice that the little paper cutout skull taped above a bowl of apples and bananas read:

AMELIA WILKES

Water, Then Fire

At the mention of the name Amelia Wilkes, the town historian, Don Fernando Cota, rocked back in his chair. "*Ah, la profesora,*" the schoolteacher. He'd been stroking the dog, Solovino, behind the ears; now he laid both hands Buddha-like across his belly and closed his eyes for a moment before he began.

"Amelia Wilkes—Wilkes is a name like Ritchie or Fisher, from a sailor—was born in Cabo San Lucas in 1907 and died in 1989 at the age of eighty-two. She was a teacher and a community leader. She served as president of the electricity supply, she directed the water commission. This was around 1930, a long time before the *chubasco.* When they named Amelia Wilkes subdelegate for the territory, she became the first female authority in Baja California Sur. She was un *personaje,* a real character, very respected. They dedicated the plaza of Cabo San Lucas to her in 1976.

"I'll tell you a story that shows you what kind of person she was. She used to collect money from the townspeople in order to buy heating oil for the generator that produced the town's electricity. She would buy the oil and keep it in barrels in her house. Her house was made of wood. This was after the *chubasco;* it was one of those from the governor. She was also the director of the school, so she had all the savings of the students in her house, along with the barrels of heating oil. One night her sister knocked over a kerosene lamp, and the house caught fire. As fast as they could, so the house wouldn't explode, Amelia and her sister began rolling out the barrels of oil. And then she ran back into the house—the flames were everywhere!—and grabbed the children's savings. That was what she rescued, nothing of her own. She lost everything."

Just as in the *chubasco* of 1939.

When John Steinbeck and Ed Ricketts went ashore at Cabo San Lucas in 1940, Amelia Wilkes would have just moved into that wood house given to her by the governor. Like Janós Xántus, that unhappy Hungarian, Steinbeck and Ricketts had come to collect specimens; in their case, marine animals. To put it less nicely, they were there to kill things, and seal them in little bottles of formaldehyde and take them home. Ricketts, the author of a standard reference work on Pacific tide pools, owned a laboratory on Monterey's Cannery Row. Steinbeck had just published *The Grapes of Wrath*, which, on his return from Baja California, would be awarded the Pulitzer Prize.

Perhaps from her window *la profesora* saw the Americans in their yachting caps and sweaters swagger through her "sad little town"; perhaps she even saw them push through the doors to the "mournful" cantina. I like to think that Amelia was inside, one elbow on the bar—why not? The novelist's wife, Carol, was there, although she isn't once mentioned in his *Sea of Cortez*.

Lower

Only a quick three and a half-hour flight down from San Francisco—and an hour less than that from LAX—Los Cabos perches at the end of what fanciful mapmakers once drew as the Island of California. But we don't call it California, we call it Baja California. Baja, which means "lower": unfortunate adjective. At the end of the eighteenth century, the missionaries moved north into the more fertile and populous land of Alta, or Upper, California. The United States took that territory in 1848 and with it, the name California. The memory of that rankles in Mexico, like so much else. Halloween, for instance.

"*¿Qué significa el* Halloween?" What does it mean? a Mexican teenager asked me with a defensive cock of the chin, a sneer. He'd sauntered up to where I was sitting on the steps of Planet Hollywood. In the melting light of afternoon, we were surrounded by the decorations, the bats and pumpkins, the plaster tiles with their shadow-filled handprints and shoe prints of American movie stars. I answered his question. He'd had no idea that Halloween meant All Hallow Even, the eve of All Saints' Day, *Todos Santos*.

"*¿De veras?*" Really?

I nodded. His expression relaxed; the foreign was familiar, after all.

"You know what?" he said, pointing with his chin toward the rocky mountain of the Pedregal. "Sylvester Stallone has a house here."

William T. Ayton, *Depleted Human*, 2003

Is This What Democracy Looks Like?

Hannes Westberg

I've heard that a bullet has a soul of its own. A shot to the chest, fired from below, can travel back and forth in your body, ricocheting from side to side, only to emerge just below the waist. The one that hit me at a Reclaim the Street party during the European Union's 2001 top summit meeting was not so erratic. It exited through my back in a fairly straightforward way. My spleen and a kidney had to be removed, and my aorta repaired with Gore-Tex. Over twenty-five gallons of blood had to be pumped through my body.

People are drawn to guns for the power they promise. The gun presents a mirage, the illusion of control, but after awhile it's hard to know who controls who. When one is addicted to power, the only thing that matters is the accumulation of more. People sacrifice their own self-control and free will, frantically trying to preserve the position to which they've climbed. The more they attempt to combat their fears, the more fearful they become.

Here in Europe, we hear stories about Americans and the fear that poisons their daily life, about some man (they seem to be mostly male, right?) waking up in the middle of the night disturbed by some sound—an intruder in the home. Watching out for his belongings and family, the man fires into a pitch-black hallway and only too late realizes that he's shot his own son or daughter. These stories serve as a parable to society in a sometimes symbolic, but often all too literal, way. The strife to own is the strife to control, to subdue, and it takes its toll, especially if you happen to succeed. Every day it seems more obvious that the world is not ruled by sane men (they are mostly male, right?), nor could anyone be sane in a position of such great power.

In 2001, during three warm days in June, an immense collection of power gathered in my home town of Gothenburg, Sweden. The greatest rulers of the European continent were present. Inside the city's major conference center, they shook hands, smiled, and ate lobster. The area around the center was closed off, and people living inside the city were, in effect, under martial law for three weeks prior to the meeting. There were regular ID checks and body searches, and permits were required to receive mail.

United States President George W. Bush was to participate as well, giving an extra glow to the meeting. The CIA had been there for a long time and cooperated with the Swedish police force, which caused people to speculate on the importance of the president's attendance. It reminded me of what a Native American holy man once said to me—"I saw your president the other day. There were a lot of people with a lot of guns around him. . . . He must have hurt a lot of people." Simple, but true. The younger George landed Thursday at eleven o'clock, a minute before the police force raided a school used to house demonstrators and activists. The over 350 people staying in that school were all said to be suspected of "inciting riots"—and all this before the summit meeting, much less riots, had begun! They were arrested and taken away, only to be released without charges being pressed or apologies made. Later, the chief of the Swedish intelligence agency, Margareta Linderoth, stated that the Secret Service "thought the Swedes were very smart—first renting out the school to demonstrators and them locking them in! The Americans thought it was a good working method."

The raid led to some not-so-violent clashes between activists and police. If the aim of the police force was to divert attention from the actual meeting between Bush and Goran Persson, our prime minister, it was successful. More important, it started a chain of events leading up to the following Friday night when bullets were fired into a fleeing flock of people, myself being one of them. Exactly how many rounds were shot, we'll never know. The police apparently neglected to check the guns involved and never found any bullets. A journalist found one over two weeks later, but it was confiscated by the police and then "lost" in their archives. The very same thing happened to a roll of film containing the only picture taken in the moment I was shot, revealing the identity of the shooter. This is the reaction of a fearful system. With methods such as these, the image of Gothenburg 2001 was presented as one of chaos, destruction, and seemingly random acts of violence perpetrated by young, angry mobs.

It is truly a miracle that only three people were wounded and none were killed that day. It took seventeen doctors over fourteen hours of nonstop surgery, and a host of other specialists the following intense month, to save my life. And, yes, I remember the panic as I got colder. I thought I would surely die there, in the midst of camera flashes as journalists hung over me like vultures. Still, the image that stays with me is of what seemed to be a thousand hands reaching out to help, and with it comes a sense of hope.

The first days of the Gothenburg summit meeting, also known as GBG, excitement was in the air. Not only were politicians from the United States and Europe gathered together, but people from all over the world as well. There were farmers from the Landless Rural Workers' Movement (MST) in Brazil, indigenous people, leftist organizations from the Association for Taxation of Financial Transactions for the Aid of Citizens (ATTAC) to Anti-Fascist Action, churches and theater groups and musicians, each with its own story to tell. We spread through the city as the air grew thick with anticipation. The feeling of change not only being possible, but inevitable, was something I cherished deeply and found in the sheer tens of thousands of people. Pressing our bodies against the steel walls and armed guards, we knew that we were part of a greater context, a unity that crossed all borders, refusing to be confined. I have never felt more at home in Gothenburg than I did those days, surrounded by so many strangers—music everywhere, good food, movies, lectures, the city belonging to us, perhaps for the first time.

Culture should provide us with this sense of vitality. Far from merely belonging to a lucky few, art and inspiration should be present in everyday life for all of us. Culture should be a force that challenges and reshapes our political landscapes, opening our hearts to change and waking us to infinite possibilities. In order to understand the crimes of capitalism, it is important to feel a longing for life's many wonders.

As protesters gathered for the European Summit, I looked forward to the Reclaim the Street party (RTS), where techno is the music of choice, combining high-technological aspects of today with the most primitive expression of life on this planet—the repetitious drum. Through the past ten years, RTS protests have had some impact. (A warning to any shamans out there: don't bang your drum in

London!) The rapid growth of techno culture and free parties have given the United Kingdom its most outrageous law to date. The law makes it illegal to play "music made of repetitious rhythms" in public spaces.

Many of us dwell too deeply in the present miserable state of things to understand the true potential of spontaneity and creativity. The doors they open are enough in themselves to have a tremendous impact on our shaky and unstable world. Techno is my example, but there are countless others. Did you know that even Bill Haley and the Comets' "Rock around the Clock" created riots for days in numerous cities when first played? One should not underestimate the power of music or any other cultural expression. Therein lies the sudden surfacing of consciousness, the protest of the soul that is always waiting for a release. Take jazz, or gospels, and their role in the "surprising" black uprisings in the United States. Many of the first hip-hop jams were attacked by the police, and so were raves and, I'm sure, jazz clubs in their day. The energy that music has when it's new and raw shakes the foundations of the system and, as always, the state makes whatever it cannot understand illegal (until, that is, they find a way to make money off it). Those who are not able to be consumers in this society are forced to become creative in their own lives. Unfettered creativity offers a taste of freedom, which is why it is potentially harmful to power structures. Participants of cultural movements suffer persecution because the notion of a new culture, created by the people, for the people, could contain the seed of (r)evolutionary change.

If only we could realize this as fully as those in power do. We should not look to the number of voters in elections or active members of unions to understand the potential for change. Things are already changing. What happened in Gothenburg is a good example. Not everyone on the streets was a convinced socialist, yet all it takes is a spark, and the anger and resolve of thousands become evident. We cannot be happy if our brother or sister is not. We all suffer the inhuman consequences of capitalism. It could be starvation or anorexia—we die from malnutrition all the same. All the top meetings—be it WTO, IMF, or EU—see the same vibrant display of resistance. It is a dangerous resistance, and it doesn't matter whether you're a theorist, artist, or anarchist. It is not the methods you use. It's that you use them. Protesters are arrested, registered, beat up, and even shot in ways that until recently were thought impossible in a democracy. It comes as no surprise that the WTO now prefers that dictatorships such as Qatar host their meetings. The protest against the IMF in Papua, New Guinea, for example, left up to ten people dead, though I'm sure you never heard about it. But now that similar events are happening in "civilized" countries, they're getting harder to ignore.

The leaders of the world are afraid, and consequently fear is now running the day with warnings of terrorist attacks, reports on the war in Iraq, images of bombs, and supervillains. We are encouraged to lock our doors, watch *Cops* and the nightly news, and be afraid—be very afraid. The Swedish police force embodies this type of fear. During the Gothenburg Summit meetings, they despised demonstrators and did so long before any riots had taken place. I don't see the police as my enemy, and have never called them such, though I've been called much worse by them. What I wish to destroy is the system that imprinted fear and hatred on their faces. As it has often been said, the world shrank down to Gothenburg's size on those days. Like good art, the most inspiring and important aspect of Gothenburg's summit protests was that they reflected the whole in minute detail. Listening to police radio communications from those three days will tell you all you need to know about the society in which we live. Peaceful demonstrators were termed bitches, communist cunts, niggers, and scum. During the protests, there was not a single derogatory term that wasn't used, displaying the hierarchies that tear the world apart in splendid verbal technicolor. Police officers dragging sixteen- and seventeen-year-old girls by their hair, shouting profanities into their faces, explaining how they weren't even worth raping. Cops pulled foreigners with dark complexions through dog food and then threw them to their dogs. They threatened activists with guns and beat them up behind closed doors.

It is a common misconception that the police force "lost control" during the riots, that the media were swept away in the frenzy and forgot their journalistic code of conduct, and that the judicial system, long afterward, also collapsed, unable to cope with the summit's "special conditions." The truth is, the system did not break down. On the contrary, it worked exactly as it was supposed to. That is why no matter how many times politicians, police, and journalists say, "Next time we'll do it better," it means that they'll do what they did then, only more effectively.

There has been a great deal of investigation concerning these riots. A political committee presented a report in which they accepted the claims of the activists— in summary, that all the riots were provoked by the police. Riots ensued on three occasions, the first when the police laid siege on the school where demonstrators slept. The committee concluded in its report that upon searching the school, no weapons were found and there was no evidence that preparations for riots had occurred. No charges were ever made against any of the 350 demonstrators detained. The second time rioting took place was on the Avenue, a shopping street in the center of the city. The disturbance occurred after police had attacked a peaceful demonstration. Many people were sitting down when the police rode on horseback into them to separate the "serious demonstrators from those that were not." Still, these riots lasted only about thirty minutes. The third time rioting arose was at Vasaplatsen, where the RTS party was held. The police—letting none walk away and beating those who tried—surrounded the park where partygoers had gathered. At that time, no one was armed, no faces were disguised, and the music had been playing for only twenty minutes. The report, written by a committee led by former Prime Minister Ingvar Carlsson, concludes that all riots were a reaction to police atrocities, and not the other way around. Even the police investigation states that at all three venues, the atmosphere was calm. It was only after the police attacked protesters that riots transpired. Still, not a single police officer has been convicted.

How can it be that the civil rights we take for granted can be so blatantly ignored? That the same pattern is repeating itself around the globe? That demonstrators can be shot at without any defendable reason? Politicians were handing out roses to the police for what our prime minister called a "job well done," while protests were still going on and I was lying in the hospital almost dead. How could this be "a job well done"? Riots on three out of four occasions, over ten bullets shot—the first time in seventy years that demonstrators have been fired at, a teenager possibly dying, hundreds of people wounded, over thirteen hundred arrested. To this day, only 70 demonstrators have been prosecuted and only 150 suspected of a crime, which means that over a thousand were denied their fundamental right to a peaceful protest. Demonstrators were locked in cages made specifically to hold large groups of people, to pack them in tightly and keep them for several days. Buses from all over Europe were stopped at the border, restricted from entering the country before the protests, much less the riots, had even begun.

The protesters who were brought to trial witnessed firsthand the hypocrisy of the legal system. Police witnesses changed the description of a suspect up to five times before being called to the stand. Movies from riots in other countries were shown in court. Evidence could be anything: literature the police had found in the home of the accused, or pictures of the suspect at other demonstrations. A great deal of effort was made to prove the suspect's previous involvement in political activism. Those proven to be politically active received twice as harsh a sentence.

Swedish law refers to "riot participation": it is illegal even to be at the scene of a riot whether you take part in it or not. Under this law, all the journalists who were present should have been convicted. They were not. This law also makes it diffi- cult to contradict police testimony, since to witness the riots would be to incrimi- nate oneself. After one young man was brutally attacked by the police, his mother pressed charges. The police then arrested her son. The investigation against the police was closed shortly after, and the man who had been attacked was sentenced to over a year in jail. Another activist was accused of ordering a crowd to charge at police. In crucial testimony, a police officer claimed that the suspect had spoken aggressively at an activist meeting a month earlier, stating that demonstrators were "going to give them hell." This meeting had been filmed, however, and it shows the suspect talking in a mild-mannered way about the importance of nonviolence. This officer had unquestionably committed perjury but was never prosecuted. The activist was sentenced to over two years in jail. This dedicated nonviolent pro- tester, from the YaBasta! or "white overalls" camp, is now serving time for waving his arms in the air. Did it matter that the crowd he was accused of ordering was moving in one direction, while he was waving in another? No. As this is being written, there remain completely innocent people serving time in Swedish jails.

I was one of the guilty ones, but I was not alone. There were many others just like me. We did not come to create riots, but we did not feel ashamed for throwing cobblestones and bottles at the police when they attacked us. I openly confessed these acts while in the hospital, but the prosecution still found it necessary to sub- mit fake evidence. In the videotape shown at my trial, several things had been altered. Pictures were out of order, scenes from other places and other times were spliced in, sound was added to make it seem as if there were protesters behind me, and portions of the original were deleted. Two journalists working for television secured the original tapes. At first, the police would not admit that they had sub- mitted false evidence, but they were forced to start an investigation and eventually acknowledged that the journalists' copy was the original footage. In one of the most media-exposed trials in Sweden, the police confessed to having tampered with evidence, but no charges were filed, since the tape "captured the atmosphere" of the incident. Nothing has been done to correct these atrocities. The police can admit criminal acts without fear of retribution.

There is a reason for this, of course. At the time of my shooting, I was completely alone, standing in front of over sixty police officers. I did throw three stones, none of them traveling even half the distance between me and the closest policeman. As the last rock left my hand, a shot was fired, aimed straight at my chest. Those in power typically don't like dealing with a story like mine, and luckily for them, almost no one in the press investigated it further. To do so, they would have to admit their own culpability. For example, one popular story picked up by newspapers a week before the summit reported that police had found a grenade launcher, when the object was actually a small slingshot. At press conferences, the police freely fabricated information, and the media printed it uncritically.

Power has another principle: too much of it will lead to a crisis, if not a complete breakdown. Have we reached that point? Capitalism runs rampant all over the globe, forcing everything in its way into subordination. We are told that this victorious progress enriches our lives, which roughly translates to the luxury of buying a McDonald's hamburger anywhere in Thailand. Here in my home town, politicians have been bulldozing anything that has been around for more than twenty years. Beautiful neighborhoods have been torn down, and those left standing are becoming increasingly expensive, bought up by rich people searching for something *real* and *picturesque*. The street where I lived ten years ago has been virtually transformed in about half that time. When I was younger, the street was lined with small businesses, but now there are three 7–11s and a number of other American chains. There has been a literal onslaught of corporate American culture. Of course, it is not American capitalism but the system itself that's at fault. It looks quite ridiculous, especially knowing that only one of the McDonald's and one of the convenience stores actually makes a profit. Out of the hundreds of magazines offered by 7–11s, most are owned and published by the same company. They have articles on the same Hollywood movie made by the very same media conglomerate. They contain ads for Coca-Cola and McDonald's. So I go to get my drugged-up beef, choose between Coke and Sprite, and what do I see? Ads for the same Hollywood movie! This is a snake eating its tail. How much of the world will be destroyed before capitalism eats itself?

Not much, possibly. In order to raise cows for the fast food industry, rain forests are destroyed. The potatoes for my fries are genetically modified without any regard for nature. Meanwhile, companies like Monsanto seek to patent basmati rice. They already have the majority of patents on the seed market. They modify the seeds to make them sterile so farmers have to buy new seeds every season. In the process, they have fundamentally changed the most important part of our planet's delicate ecosystem: the ability of nature to spread freely and transform itself. What our insurance companies will make of our gene banks, I try not to imagine. Health care and medicine only for those who can pay for them? It's not that far-fetched an idea. For a large portion of the world, it's already a fact. People starve as they watch farmland made into perfect rows of modified cash crops. As always, those combating these ills, with a pen or a rock, are called violent. It is tempting for me to call on George Orwell and his "newspeak" as yet another war is brought upon us to secure peace.

And what of justice? Every position in a hierarchy is the result of force. I hear some say that a just and peaceful world is impossible, that chaos and mayhem would ensue without rulers, that we would all kill ourselves if there were no police to keep us in line. But the world today is already in chaos: war, famine, and ecological destruction are the symptoms. It is a chaos that a few people benefit from, while the majority suffer. A world with no rulers, however, is the most developed form of civilization, requiring all to become involved in the decision-making ruling process. Besides, I cannot think of any system that could possibly be more violent than the one we have today. All alternatives have to be tried, and none should scare us more than the possibility that this might be as good as it gets, which in reality is the acceptance of endless slaughter and starvation.

The situation cannot be blamed on anything but the laws of competition themselves. No company could survive in this dog-eat-dog world if its executives suddenly started to *care*. Our rulers—and most of them are not politicians—are so possessed by greed—truly poisoned by it—that they can hardly be held accountable. I am not against progress or against *real* globalization, but the way the world is evolving isn't part of evolution. It looks more like the end of it.

The IMF counts the number of television sets in a Third World country and concludes that the quality of life is improving. But even Bill Gates recognizes that Africa needs drinkable water, not laptops. And Africans are not likely to improve their quality of life if the very foundations of life keep disappearing. Economic development is the magic wand that's supposed to cure all problems. But this is simply not true even in the very few instances where the money actually reaches the population. Life is never so hard as in places where ghettos are next door to luxury. Commercials create violence and even wealth seems devoid of meaning. As Donald Trump once said, "To be rich today is merely to own the largest amount of meaningless objects—that is, to possess the greatest amount of poverty."

The standardization of every aspect of our society creates a common battle-ground. Those who suffer directly at the mercy of land or factory owners are now being joined by the discontent in the middle class—middle class in the global sense, meaning most of us in the industrialized world. For many of us, it is not necessarily a political struggle for survival. It is more of a reaction to the sterile and pointless rat race this ultramaterialistic neoliberalism has cultivated. This is the strength of the New Left—one that is not constrained by dogmatic ideology and doesn't hold any doctrine more important than the people it is meant to serve. It is a movement that points out the difference between surviving and living. You cannot have a bit of freedom. You are either free or you're not.

Assembly line culture will have a hard time surviving the twenty-first century. The younger generation has grown up with ads tailored for them. They are sensitive to manipulation. It will be hard for politicians of the future to disguise their real motives with humanistic rhetoric. It seems that greed has finally put us at the forefront of a complete wasteland of values. What is left for us other than to reinvent ourselves and the society we live in? And as more people do just that, they see the tremendous difficulties that lay in front of any even slightly progressive idea. The state exposes itself, and this is not what democracy looks like. It is so much less than we deserve.

I did a lot of traveling when I was lying in my hospital bed. People had been praying for me all over the world, and I went to each of those places in my morphine-induced dreams, vacillating between life and death. I journeyed to London where I was shot while working as a waiter in a fashionable nightclub. The clientele was composed of the rich. They ate the delicacies of the world, puked under the tables, and then ate more. Drinking heavily, they climbed on the chairs, pushed aside the grapes and goose liver, and had sex with prostitutes. I was carried out on a stretcher, which had to be hidden so as to not offend the customers. After this, I went to India and saw the parade of a man claiming to be an enlightened god. I lost all my money and was forced to work as a slave laborer to buy my ticket home, surviving on peas and dirty water. After that I remember going to Denmark, only to be shot by Nazis. Now these memories make me laugh, reminding me how powerful the imagination can be. In its essence, it is free from boundaries and can find inspiration even in the grotesque inequalities of this world. I thank those who thought of me that month. I honestly believe it made a big difference. There is more magic in life than bullets. More powerful things too.

People are realizing more and more that those in power do not possess it absolutely. Liberate yourself, and the earth below you is conquered territory, someone once said. Since the riots, Gothenburg has had an upswing of culture. There is more music, and more people are politically involved, trying to make the world work for *us*. Hope and creativity will always be on our side. One day there will be enough conquered territory that we can turn our backs on those still clinging to the illusion of power. They will perish because of our lack of faith in them. Changes in nature can be violent and changes in human nature even more so. When we take our first breath of fresh air, it will all have been worth it.

Global Reorganization: Conference Proceedings, Santo Domingo, 1991

Frederick Buell

Storms of data blow across
oceans now, more than mere weather does.
Squatting guest workers, crunching hats,
fatalistic, mass, depart
far slower than executives who pass
from metropole to metropole, first class.
A whirlwind tries to strip Tobago bare.
A dustdark simoom rakes Ethiopia,
a sandstorm that thickens to converge
on the capital: the artificial structures,
like twisting water towers groan and snap,
and national boundaries, made up
by departing colonists flay thin with winds
sent hurtling over the desert. Eritreans'
cash condenses steadily into arms: they
shake the structure; stress points give way.

Change howls against the grain; disorder's common.
Here are white table cloths, and air conditioning.
Southeast of the Keys, a delegate has just
spoken of New Zealand in distress;
the welfare state toppled months ago,
and salaries kissed the bottom. And now
people have no pensions, schools, no savings,
no public health; a sudden alteration
from when the parent state subvented these for all.
Worldwide finance slashed those shelters off,
like tempests peeling districts of tin roofs.

Outside the room, beyond the swimming pool,
past the soaring palms, immediately the rubble
of half-undone infrastructure shows itself;
the same storm winds that ranged through Auckland
raising crime three-fold have torn things here:
100% inflation just last year,
doctors striking against public health,

which argued that their $400 per month
was more than the twisting island frame could stand.
From Venezuela, they predict the cholera:
in the west suburbs, where there are
six sewer outlets and three chemical
plant drainage fields, and some 40,000
inhabitants: for it ripe breeding ground.
Meanwhile, the teachers and the power co.'s shut down:
all who can have private generators
and schools; while thousands of small debtors
swarm the streets with desperate ingenuity,
scrounging their wits in micro-industries.

So the island battens down for a long gale.
It sets its infrastructure up for sale
and title deeds howl off toward the East—
on the Pacific Rim, most come, at last, to earth;
the rumors of an American free trade zone
have the Japanese and others quickly buying
all they can in the poorer South,
so that when trade gates open, they move North
where stuff is still for grabs. Under
west and eastern skies, though, the same storm,
centerless, unstable, tears up ground—
quite unpredictable, as when, say, water's forced
through a pipe, it shatters into turbulence;
and everywhere, weather switches, tricky winds pick up.
It's the macro version of the newest theory:
a sulphur fans its dusty wings in Beijing;
then a fortnight hence, gale winds wrack Manhattan.

We nail no futures, we descry no forms;
the only analogy that we can count on's,
apparently, the roughnesses that wail
round every structure, do so on all scales:
thus papers that race these streets, palmetto trash

that skids with the stirring of a larger gale,
mime fabrics torn with erratic micro-rents
from nasty conflicts, from twisted data nets.

Flotillas of the hard-working and the hungry drift
from back barrios past the cluster of hotels
then return in swirling patterns; a driven search
for make-do, finances, children, inheritance
of substance, stories, status, kin; inside,
the same afflatus strikes the conferees,
anxious about their footholds, small margins of ease,
connections, futures. All the time that they
seek impact in the talks they wrote to say
they feel also, at icewatered lamplit podium
the turbulence of that self-same ocean,
gnawing away the pilings they have built on.
The data storms are pitched at full blast here:
tracking them? It's an ok career
for a precariously invested service class;
their luxury's to speak of what might still
hurl them also in the common well,
or to anticipate it, and so let the crash
fall on others to the side. Served by white-clad waiters, they
construct, from their generalized anxiety,
pictures, precepts, models, theories that
solve little, but, in speaking, ease the heart.

Still further off, sequestered, the well-off
keep villas, bodyguards, Mercedes, clothes
and barred-off courtyards—perhaps the sort
of ride-the-maelstrom style you can pick out,
their children in North America, or Biarritz,
decontextualized cosmopolites. And this
like the red spot on Jupiter, is stable form
that moves on unpredictable chaos, chaos borne
by the middle classes, whose flailings wound

the hand-to-mouth strata below them—
though individuals alter, though some crime
leaves particular ones macheted, weltering
in common blood, the structure seems to stay,
though it drifts and shimmies, unpredictably.
Strange time it is, that, through the inane, hurls
so odd a species, so sensitive, so uncertain,
rolled by rolling ground, revolving worlds:
prolifically ingenious, like a palm in a hurricane,
lashing about, its split ends desperate, streaming,
individuals and branches longing to prevail,
all bound, by a wave-raked beach, to the same bole.
Frantic, it roots in to endure, spasmodically, heroically,
depths it cries out of, immemorially.

Fetishes and Rarities

Alphonso Lingis

As the human voice resounds over the perceived environment, it does not only hear its own echo, reverberating over the things and landscapes. Things talk back. They speak to us. They invoke us, call to us, respond to us. They are lures; they emanate rays of power. They direct us, mesmerize us, jinx us.

Animism recognizes a spirit *in* material things. There is a voice in things. But the voice is not their voice, the voice of matter; material things are animated by a spirit or by spirits. This spirit or soul is separate from them. Things are the relays of the voice of the spirit. On the forms, uses, and trajectories of things in social space, there are meanings put on them by humans.

Fetishism recognizes a spirit *of* material things. The voice is the voice of the things. Things act, emit directives on their own. The voice is the voice of their material bodies.

Contemporary philosophy is animist. An interpretative intention animates sounds or visual marks such that they function as words and phrases. A perceiving intention animates stimuli such that they function as sensations of sound, color, savor, odor. Internal relations, the meanings of things to other things, to the context in which they are found or the class to which they belong, the utility and value of things for other things or for the observer, are effects on the things of the identifying, classifying, relating activity of a mind. Things have no meanings apart from those that human attributions, motivations, and transactions endow them with.

Contemporary social sciences, however, are fetishist. They study the layout and movement of things—of resources, of energy, of equipment, of products—and find in them an explanation for the responses and intentions of humans. Economists seek in technological evolution the explanation for changes in production and in the laws of the market the explanation for changes in distribution. Art historians seek in the power of certain materials—stucco, plaster, plastic, acrylic, laser beams—explanations for the changes in artistic technique, intentions, and taste. Anthropologists seek in a study of the geographical and meteorological conditions of a region, its resources, and the available technology, an understanding of the political, cosmological, and religious ideology of a people.

Fetishes

In our biological space, things acquire the significance of nutrients. In our workplaces, they function as implements and equipment. The products of work have use value. In the global market, all things that circulate in the social field are commodities; they are subject to the calculation of equivalence, they have exchange value. Two sorts of things stand apart from the exchange of commodities: fetishes and rarities.

In the seventeenth century, Portuguese and Dutch merchants descended the African coast to trade—a first vanguard of what was to become global trade. There were objects—skulls, animal bones, fossil stones, crystals—that Africans were reluctant to offer in trade or would barter only for great quantities of the commodities brought by the merchants. In the eyes of the Portuguese and Dutch merchants, these objects were being assigned value far in excess of what any rational calculation of utility and exchange value would justify. Since the West Africans were taken to treasure "trifles," they could be duped; what the Europeans considered valueless—beads, for instance—could be exchanged for valuable goods. For the merchants, valuable goods were not goods of use value for themselves, but instead commodities—goods of exchange value: spices, silks, precious stones. The supremely valuable commodities were gold and silver.

These objects the Africans were unwilling to trade for what the European merchants took to be their real exchange value were objects that singularized themselves, were not perceived as equivalent to and interchangeable with others. They disrupted the circulation of goods and services; they stood out as singular and unexchangeable.

The merchants could only understand these objects as sacred to the Africans; they dubbed them *fetissos*, "fetishes." The fetish is a singular object, a unique or anomalous object. It stands apart from everyday use and exchange.

Unlike foodstuffs and unlike souvenirs, being absorbed into the person or history of someone does not singularize the fetish. Its singularity is not due to an outside spirit—that of a person for which it has unique sentimental value because of its association with some particular event in the biography of that person. Its singularity is likewise not due to its historical significance for a people because of its association with some cardinal event in their history. But the fetish is not simply an object that resists the significance and worth human dealings and transactions give to goods; it confronts humans and can move them.

The fetishes elicit passions. They are coveted, sought after, objects of greed. They are also objects to which the possessor is in thrall. They generate what are taken by the Europeans to be fanciful elaborations. The one who possesses them is possessed by them.

These "fetishes" were distinguished from idols, for example, from the Greco-Roman figures the Europeans were acquainted with, which visibly represented spiritual beings. In contrast with their Christianity, idolaters worshiped material representations of false spirits. Idols are free-standing; fetishes were especially things worn on the body—leather pouches worn around the neck containing fossils, stones, animal tusks, or fangs. They were not signifiers or allegories of a concept or an ideal. The Dutch merchants saw them as mere material things, which for the Africans possessed extraordinary power, capable of healing humans or infecting them with diseases or striking them dead.

African religion then did not distinguish the spiritual from the material, but instead feared and worshiped certain material things. African religion was materialistic. In fact Africa could not properly be said to have religion; it only had belief in magic.

Immanuel Kant wrote:

> The Negroes of Africa have by nature no feeling that rises above the
> trifling. . . . The religion of fetishes so widespread among them is perhaps a
> sort of idolatry that sinks as deeply into the trifling as appears to be possible
> to human nature. A bird feather, a cow's horn, a conch shell, or any other
> common object, as soon as it becomes consecrated by a few words, is an
> object of veneration and of invocation in swearing oaths.[1]

The concept of "fetish" invoked the *feiticos,* the appurtenances associated in Europe with witchcraft. They were taken to subject the human body to the influence of certain material things that, although alien to the body, function as its controlling organs. Applied to the things the West Africans kept out of the market, to which they had an apparently arbitrary attachment, the term *fetish* demonized these things.

The European discourse on fetishism in reality is animist. It says that the West Africans attributed to material things a voice and a power they do not have. They projected their own concupiscences and fears into them.

Sigmund Freud borrowed the concept of fetish, as understood by Dutch mercantile reports of West African practices, to designate things that European individuals prize obsessively, things that control their movements or repugnancies, without those individuals being able to explicate the properties in them that elicit such compulsive passions. For Freud the fetishes often worn on the body and taken to control the body are substitutes for a missing body part. This missing body part is originally the phallus, seen lacking in the mother. Thus, Freud attributed the power of the fetish on the fetishist to the ideas and memories of his unconscious mind.

> I announce that the fetish is a substitute for the penis. . . . It is not a substitute for any chance penis, but for a particular and quite special penis that had been extremely important in early childhood but had later been lost. . . . The fetish is a substitute for the woman's (the mother's) penis that the little boy once believed in and . . . does not want to give up.
>
> What happened, therefore, was that the boy refused to take cognizance of the fact of his having perceived that a woman does not possess a penis. No, that could not be true: for if a woman had been castrated, then his own possession of a penis was in danger . . .
>
> [A fetish] saves the fetishist from becoming a homosexual, by endowing women with the characteristic which makes them tolerable as sexual objects.[2]

Rarities

If the fetish was kept outside commerce in West Africa, the curiosity cabinets, which became popular in the same seventeenth century, exhibited things—curiosities or rarities—that were taken out of commerce in Europe.

The great monasteries and cathedrals of medieval Europe had displayed collections of relics. Relics differ from representations such as icons and statues; these represent the saint, while relics are parts of saints—bones or pieces of their clothing. The saint's power is really present in them, as is demonstrated by miracles performed by contact with relics—being touched with a relic or wearing it on one's body.

The *cabinets de curiosités* or *Wunderkammern* kept by the rich, cosmopolitan European intelligentsia interested in travel exhibited things that stood out as rare and fantastic. Such were relics of saints, but also giants' teeth and bones, unicorns' horns, and eggs, fruit, or burls shaped like human torsos or animal bodies. They exhibited freaks of nature such as two-headed ducks. They included ingenious mechanical contraptions and works of artistic virtuosity. They included antiquities—Egyptian or Greek statues and pottery. They contained exotic flora, fauna, and artifacts, first brought by Columbus and his successors to the cabinets of the Medicis and other southern noblemen, and later by Dutch and English traders to those of northern collectors.[3]

Rarities were collected in the space opened further and further by global trade. They had been acquired cheaply or expensively, but now, withdrawn from the market, whatever price could be put on them would be arbitrary.

Rarities have to be distinguished from keepsakes, things that are touched and loved and worn in that history, memory, and desire are attached to them.

Rarities were singular objects—things that defied classification—that broke the rules of the normal and the predictable. They confound the understanding. These extraordinary, exotic, or radically different things had power—the power to arouse a sense of wonder and marvel.

The curiosity cabinet displayed a collection of things taken from their place of origin and stripped of their context. It was not a pedagogical exhibit but a theater.

The curiosity cabinets are the theater of aesthetics of wonder that breaks with the narrative aesthetics of the religious and epic court art of earlier times. It removes an object from its natural, social, and cultural context to make it stand on its own. French philosopher Jean Brun identifies this aesthetics as a mercantile aesthetics, presenting things in the homogeneous and empty space of global exchange.

This mercantile aesthetics was to come into disrepute. It prized whatever provokes wonder—the fantastic and the grotesque. The high aesthetics of the courts and of the artists promoted taste, judgment, and style. The collections that merely indulged wonder came to be denigrated as mere objects of fancy, bric-a-brac, kitsch.

Natural scientists expressed their continued hostility to religion by denouncing the sense of wonder and fancy that led to the acceptance of miracles. The Enlightenment replaced wonder with doubt.

Yet the *cabinets de curiosités* functioned epistemologically to separate fact from theory, interpretation, and explanation. The shock of repeated contact with the unexpected and unpredictable functioned to isolate facts from the accounts of natural history, however coherent, consistent, and complete.

With the rise of universities and laboratories, the curiosity cabinets of collectors and intellectuals came to be enlisted for pedagogical purposes. The collections were sorted out and rearranged. They were reorganized according to the eighteenth-century taxonomies of Linnaeus, Buffon, and Lamarck. From being collections of the anomalous and bizarre, they became collections of series and sequences. The butterflies preserved were pinned to show their genus, species, and sex. University faculties set out to display complete collections of butterflies, tree leaves and fruit, seashells, and mineral samples.

Whereas the curiosity cabinet had presented a theater of heteroclite things shown out of context, to provoke wonder before the unclassifiable, monstrous, and awesome, now the scientist showed exhibits that first exhibited principles of identification and classification, a taxonomy, a commanding rational system. Rock samples, tree leaves, seashells, or butterflies were arranged in a rational system to illustrate the order of nature. The exhibits now solicit comprehensive understanding and make prediction possible.

Medical schools acquired exhibits of anatomy, of deformities and diseases. Science faculties and laboratories acquired mineralogical and biological exhibits and exhibits of technological devices. Universities and cities acquired natural history and science museums.

When the overthrow of monarchs and aristocrats led to the confiscation of private art collections, the principles that had transformed the curiosity cabinets into natural science exhibits and museums were applied to art collections now in the hands of the state and opened to the public. Artworks were identified and classified by geographical and cultural provenance and chronology. History and then evolutionary biology stimulated concern with cultural evolution. The art collections were arranged to show how the Buddha image, which first appeared in Afghanistan in the wake of the Hellenistic culture spread by Alexander the Great, spread into India, China, and Japan. They were arranged to show a chronological and causal relationship between the Italian and the Flemish Renaissance.

Such collections desacralized the altarpieces taken from old churches of Europe, the statues of gods and goddesses from ancient Greece and Rome, the idols of Asia, and the fetishes of Africa and America. Graves and tombs were desecrated; Egyptian mummies and the bodies of native North Americans were put on exhibit in museums. Religions themselves were museumified, according to rational identifications and classifications, and their rituals and artifacts exhibited according to rational principles of evolution—wherein fetishism, the religion of material things, figured as the most primitive religious expression of humankind.

The natural history, science, anthropology, and art museums played a fundamental role in the construction of the concept of objectivity. Wonder and curiosity give way to understanding. Rarities are disenchanted; they are exhibited as objects, variables of rational taxonomies and classifications.

True fetishes are objects that constitute subjects. Whereas animism envisions things as anthropomorphized objects, fetishism sees humans objectified by the spirit of the material things they encounter.[4] The fetish elicits passions in humans, concupiscence and fancy, the passion to possess and the passion for one's mind and one's body to be possessed. These passions constitute humans as sensuous and as suffering.

To disenchant fetishes is to understand them as objects, to explain the powers to elicit attachment and obsessive wonder in them to be the rebound effects of the concepts the fetishist has about them—the false concepts he has about them. It is to recast them in the perspective of animism.

It is to replace the covetous and possessed, the sensuous and suffering fetishist with the rational observer—identifier, classifier, interpreter. The rational observer confronts nature as a well-appointed judge, demanding that it answer with yes or no the question he himself formulates. The rational observer is an autonomously determined subject.

Commodity Fetishism

What Marx declares to be fetishized in capitalism are commodities. Commodities are goods and services viewed as having exchange value. The exchange value of a thing can well diverge from its use value. Things of the greatest use value, such as air and water, may have no exchange value, due to their immediate availability and abundance. The exchange value of a thing may diverge completely from its use value. Such is the case with money, which is not acquired for its use value as a material thing, as gold or paper, but exclusively for its exchange value. Scarcity as well as the quantity of human labor that went into its manufacture or availability, and not the material properties of things, determines the value of commodities.

Its scarcity, and the quantity of human labor that it absorbed, are invisible properties of the thing. The scarcity of a commodity on the market, as well as the quantity of human labor that went into it, are themselves determined by the network of relations between owners, producers, and distributors. This network of human relations is also an invisible determinant of the value of a commodity.

Marx then reverses the ascription of fetishism. Material commodities, inasmuch as they are exchangeable for money, for gold, control the passions of capitalists. Commodities are fetishized inasmuch as they are valued; they excite passions of greed and fancy for their exchange value. Money and commodities taken as fetishes in capitalism are not material things in their visible, material properties but valued for their invisible goods. And while for West Africans, to take something as a fetish is to hold it outside commerce, in capitalism it is precisely inasmuch as a thing is wholly cast into commerce, inasmuch as it figures as a commodity, that Marx says it is fetishized.

What connects the two concepts of fetish is the notion of a power of the things on us. As effects of the power of the fetish, the humans are objects, sensuous and suffering substances, thrown into movement by things. For fetishes elicit passions in humans, the passion to possess or to be possessed, greed or fancy.

These powers of the fetish in commodity fetishism Marx wishes to reduce. They are, in his view, magical powers. And false powers. Marx reinstates animism: the voices that speak in things are but echoes of human voices. Things have no other meaning or value than that which humans have projected into them—the scarcity and quantity of labor that the institutionalized network of human relations has put in them.

We are now in the midst of the third industrial revolution—the information revolution. Miniaturization reduces the raw material costs of information technology; robotization reduces the labor costs. Information is the principal raw material and the principal product of high-tech industry. Information is wealth. Prosperity is the acquisition, accumulation, and production of information.

The new information technology makes available to us, as never before, the languages and the symbolic systems in which all cultures, but also all natural landscapes and species—everything that we have perceived or can perceive—have been identified, recorded, classified, compared, interpreted. Before viewing any products of industry, we can download from the Net site photographs of them, along with their specifications, uses, and availability. Before buying a book, we can download an abstract of its contents and the reviews published of it. Before going to an exhibition of an architect or painter, we can download films of his or her complete work and read the studies written of the work. Before going on a trip to West Africa, we can download all the information about its geography, climate, economy, political system, architecture, language, religion, cuisine. Before going to view the baobab trees of the Sudan, we can download a description of the species, their modes of propagation, the diseases that may attack them, the uses to which they can be put.

Thus, we would no longer have any naive, firsthand experience of manufactured products, cultures, other species, or natural places. We perceive what has already been identified, described, classified, compared. Our perceptions and encounters are culture specific—media culture specific.

The identifications and descriptions we download are in conceptual language or in symbols and graphs, that is, in generic and general forms. The photographs are of standardized or typical items or individuals. A photograph of a work by Robert Mapplethorpe makes his photograph for us one of a class of reproductions, as a photograph of the Great Pyramid of Cheops makes our vision of that pyramid an exemplification of what we have already seen. All our perceptions follow conceptual identifications. We see what has been conceptualized in advance. We see tokens of types, instances, examples, or representatives of categories.

But to become cultured is not simply to have only educated perceptions and experiences. The information with which we come to encounter products, cultures, other species, and natural places is also filed, indexed, and retrieved according to the specific capabilities of the media technology. Two-dimension low-definition television and digital information storage process information in technology-specific ways, for the way information directs and shapes our perceptions varies with the quantity, speed, and format in which we receive that information.

Information is marketed for distribution. On television, news is marketed as infotainment. It is edited, framed, spliced, dramatized so as to attract and hold the attention of viewers. Information is intended to be retrieved by specific target groups of viewers. Information about consumer goods and services, about museums and concerts, or about places that seek to attract tourists or legislative protection are edited, narrated, cut, lit, dramatized differently for different target groups of information-consumers. Nature programs are filmed and narrated as detective stories, tragedies, comedies, farces, fundraisers. Information about peoples and cultures will be edited according to specific agendas.

Henceforth, whenever we encounter things, artwork, cultures, species, and places, we perceive them as examples or representatives of categories, models, prototypes, narratives classified, conceptualized, edited, dramatized, filmed, and narrated in the information banks.

Today the information economy induces an information culture. The cultured person is not simply one who has access to the information highways; he or she has his or her personal collection of sites and files. By classifying, editing, framing, splicing, dramatizing them in their own way, individuals define their own identity, establish their status, measure their worth. They communicate with networks of other media users at chat sites.

Does the cultured person then encounter things, artwork, cultures, species, landscapes—or information about things, artwork, cultures, species, landscapes? Editing, framing, splicing, classifying, dramatizing information that has already been programmed, edited, framed, spliced, classified, dramatized?

Is the encounter with things themselves still possible today? Is it still possible to know the power of things, the directives in things, the voice of things? In our culture of commodity fetishism, is a culture of true fetishism possible? In our societies regulated by the ethics of economics, our economic ethics, is the primordial ethos of luck still possible?

The Sublime

How much is given on the planet, the things that are sublime! How much is not just the best on a continuous scale but is on a level utterly above all the others, a level too where things are incomparable with one another. The sequoias are not just taller than other trees, more exalted. You can't just say, "Well, I saw the virgin pine forests of the Canadian Rockies, so I got close to what the sequoias are. All I have to do is imagine trees taller still, more uplifting." When one day you get to the sequoias, you see the unimaginable. And then, incomparable with the sequoias, the baobabs await you in Africa, the banyans in India!

Among the sacred places one immediately locates on this transcendent level are Rheims cathedral in France, the Hagia Sophia in Istanbul, the temples of Khajuraho in India, Teotihuacán in Mexico, and Borobudur in Java. And also the Colca Canyon in Peru, Mount Machpuhare in Nepal, Lake Atitlán in Guatemala, the sandscapes of the Sahara, and the icescapes of Antarctica.

Anyone who has done it knows that it makes sense, if it is all you can manage, to save up for years in order to take off at least a few days from work and responsibility and fly to France just to see the *Mona Lisa,* fly to Japan just to spend a morning in the Ryongi Zen sand garden in Kyoto, fly to Peru just to spend, if that were all that was possible, a day in Machu Picchu.

There are transcendent encounters with living nature: the day you came upon a leopard, free, in the jungle in Sri Lanka, sprawled over the limb of a tree not ten feet above the ground, the leopard opening one eye when your feet rustled the leaves and then, with lordly disdain, closing it again; the night when, seated in a small whaler over shallow waters with pure white sand thirty feet below illuminated by the moon, you watched the sharks pirouette in the transparent waters under you; the day when, in the mountains of Nicaragua, you came upon the nest of a hummingbird in a cactus plant, woven of spider webs and containing one minuscule egg and one newly hatched hummingbird chick.

These givens in Nature, givens of Nature, are gifts. They are there by grace and by good fortune. They are rarities that we come upon by luck.

Their forms and trajectories speak to us. They bespeak their importance and their sublimity.

They are directives. They affect the sensuality and direct the movements of our bodies. They take possession of us. We are there to serve them.

The encounter with these things is happiness—a happiness not pursued, earned, paid for, but happiness as fortune and good luck. A happiness known not in appropriation but in exposure. Wonder and awe are the opening of the inner diaphragm toward what is without any proportion to human measure. A happiness that is felt in exhilaration, in expropriative ecstasy.

Notes

1. Immanuel Kant, *Observations on the Feeling of the Beautiful and Sublime,* trans. John Goldthwait (Berkeley: University of California Press, 1960), 111.

2. Sigmund Freud, "Fetishism," trans. James Strachey, in *The Standard Edition of the Complete Psychological Works of Sigmund Freud* (London: Hogarth Press, 1961), 21:152–155.

3. Peter Pels, "The Spirit of Matter: On Fetish, Rarity, Fact, and Fancy," in Patricia Spyer, ed. *Border Fetishisms: Material Objects in Unstable Spaces,* 105. (New York: Routledge, 1988).

4. Ibid., 101.

Honey, Sugar, and Rose

Lorrinda Khan

Beginnings

It would be easy to tell how my life ends. I see the end so clearly, but isn't it the same with any journey? Doesn't the traveler forget the dream by the end of the trail? The real challenge is to tell where and when my life began. Not birth—that would be too easy. I mean life. When did I start to see?

I first left the United States early in my thirties. I could tell you that I left it to find my life or something like that. The truth is that I left for the stories. I love them, and like any good junkie, I knew that I had to find them no matter what the outcome or the cost. So one day I loaded everything I owned into a U-Haul and dropped it off at the safest and most reliable storage I could find, and my life began. I do love stories—fat ones, thin ones, stories that are the beginning, and even sometimes those that are the end of a life, a career, or a mission. In truth it doesn't matter. I love stories bigger than life, filled with Hollywood charisma, or those that are understated, profound truths. Don't you see? My life bored me. Running to work day in and day out, I realized I needed a story of my own and here, wherever here is, I don't hear the voices of the other storytellers. There are sounds here, on the street men call out, but I don't hear them. Something strange happens when you spend time with people you cannot understand. I hear the music of the vendor's voice as the echo hits the hot blacktop, but this is not my language. Not my mind's language. It is only the tool I use to buy their goods. The sounds have no effect on my voice—here my voice is everywhere.

My voice is like the birds' songs. When I first came to this dream, I thought there were no birds here. Now I realize they were only hiding. The morning is theirs, long before the noise and dirt rise—before the streets fill with people. Only then can you hear the birds call to you. Uncanny creatures, they will not remain long enough to hear you stir. We have an agreement: I do not venture too close to my open window or door and they sing for me. And as they do, their music blends with my voice.

Love in Two Tongues

I never belonged to anyone before. Nor was I ever understood. Not by those who spoke my mother tongue. To them I was 'tard—short for *retard*. Awais never noticed that I don't belong here. To my husband I am American. On Sunday he left. Two huge suitcases filled with wedding gifts. Each hand-picked by me. I watched his plane depart, trusting that Allah's will be done—A.K.A. you have no control over this—wanting to go with him. Knowing without Urdu or Punjabi, I couldn't pass there either.

In Miami, shop girls seeing his dark hair and eyes jabber at me in Spanish. I answer with a confident *si,* hoping my accent doesn't give me away. Older women leer at my light skin and green eyes, angry I would take one of their boys. How can I tell them that he doesn't speak Spanish; it is one of my languages. They are furious when they try to speak to him and I answer. All I can think is, *No preocupan, mi esposo no es Latino.* But then I remember the Dominican expression, *No tienes una case; no tienes una matrimonio*—without a house, there can be no marriage. I wonder if he felt the same sting in Ohio—corn-fed boys staring at their lost prize.

When I married, my Victorian lit. professor warned me that if I ever traveled with my husband, his family would lock me in a closet—like a poor blonde Hollywood starlet that he once knew. I imagined her golden locks, leather pants, and stiletto heels all covered with black hajab. My instructor's warning made me wonder more about his bias and intolerance than any fictive cruelty that my husband's family might inflict on me. As his sister's wedding nears, I imagine our own wedding day and the sincerity of his commitment to me. In truth, I know a soul as compassionate as his could not develop in a household that was not filled with a loving and nurturing family.

Now his sister marries. I imagine her adorned in gold. I imagine their prized daughter, unpacking suitcases filled with box after box of American kitchen gizmos for her house. The first question asked when a couple is engaged is whether the family is Urdu or Punjabi speaking. It is a funny question; all speak Urdu. Is it the mother tongue? Better if they share the same language inside the house.

Honey, Sugar, and Rose

When your mother gives me *mathai* to eat at breakfast while at her home in Wah Cantt, I am reminded of a time when you had returned from Pakistan. I had waited alone for you in our large apartment in America, packing boxes scavenged from the Winn-Dixie supermarket. Empty **Bounty** paper towel and canned tuna boxes made our habitation look more like a warehouse than a home. When you returned, our apartment was nearly empty; we were moving and had no food to eat, so we sat on the floor and ate the sticky *galaibi* sent by your mother. We drank too dark, bitter tea with cream. The scent of honey, sugar, and rose filled my nostrils, luring me to imagine your excursion without me.

While you were gone, I had ventured to the local library, where I wondered at romantic images from *National Geographic* of Pakistani village women dressed in dusty red and blue embroidered *shalwars*, herding water buffalo. Pictures of dump trucks painted with murals of rockets and missiles and a veiled woman's eyes. I did not know then what sort of sound those trucks would make: thousands of cowbells announcing the trucks' presence in the lane next to your father's white Toyota Corolla as we make our way to the Islamabad airport to send you away. Nor did I know the women were simple nomads who had escaped Afghani soil. It is an inadequate image to represent a whole population, when in reality so very many other women live in Pakistan too.

As I look at my breakfast plate, I wonder why I eat mathai now; mathai is for weddings, births, or celebrations. Your parents give it to me for I am their guest, and I know it would be rude not to eat the sweets that represent their joy that I am staying with them. Your father has counseled me on the Quran, which teaches us that whenever we feel unhappy about life, we should look not to those above us but to those below and *Thank God* that we are not in their place. Your mother asks me daily why I do not wear my *tops,* earrings in Urdu, and I tell her that it is because you have left us, and jewelry is for celebrations. In her heart, your mother knows the truth—that I long for you—and shakes her head and says "No Awais. Plain. Plain"—all the while, wishing I would wear the more ornate dresses and jewelry. A year ago, this would have made me think she was stifling me, but now I know that it is because she wants to set her American daughter apart from the nar-row images of Pakistani women that fill library magazines—women crushed by heat and exploited by clever American cameramen. Still, I do not put them on. Perhaps it is because I could never be confused for one who had suffered so much.

Face Value

On Sony TV, Technicolor girls in red and gold *shalwar kamez* perform traditional dances around hay wagons. Their true loves (always in Levi's and a Polo shirt) give the real clues as to when the film was made. In Urdu drama, true love prevails over trials of family, love misplaced, villains, and tyrants. Love is at the heart of every song and every dance. A woman's exaggerated facial expressions encourage her admirer. Her head sways left, then right, then left again to show pleasure. The woman's eyes quickly catch the eyes of her beloved, enticing him to sing for her. The instant his attention is caught, she modestly looks away, continuing her dance while layers of golden organza rise and fall as she spins. The slight variations in embroidery and cut of each woman's dress suggest to the viewer which region she is from. Face value is placed on the demeanor and dress of the women. Loyalty is shown to her beloved, culture, and society in the red and gold of her organza.

   This same idea is at work in Ramadan prayers; for the holiday, I wear a brightly colored shalwar kamez. On the moist Florida earth, I sit on plastic sheeting among other women. Each woman is wearing the dress of her native country. The early morning dew makes the ground soft and fragrant. All the women are sharing prayer rugs or blankets to protect themselves from the clammy sensation of the plastic. Those of us who were born in the United States leave our blue jeans and T-shirts for the more ornate costume of our husband's native land. From my dress, the other women know my husband is from Pakistan. My outward appearance shows a cultural connection, which is rarely evident to the outside world. Dressed in shalwar kamez, I am reminded of the first time I heard the Pakistani love songs; of my husband singing to me in full voice, eyebrows raised, smiling and laughing in my kitchen. During the prayer, all the women press their shoulders against one another. I feel the warmth of the women next to me. During the prayer, I am aware of the rise and fall of their chests. The heat of their bodies reassures me that I am accepted here. The women know me completely by my dress and the emotion in my facial expressions. The mixing of Pakistani and American culture that comes from my experiences is unmistakable in the subtle changes in my movement.

Cooking Lessons

I call my friend Layinah to ask how to cook the couscous I bought at the Arab market. I think it should be boiled. But how can I be sure? *Fabrique au Maroc*—ten minutes to prepare—the French instructions definitely say ten minutes. This I guess from my Spanish, never having taken French. The Arabic is inscrutable— at least I can pronounce some of the words. Koranic Arabic leaves little room for cooking vocabulary. Still only ten minutes. I recognize the Arabic number ten. At first, Layinah cannot understand what I am asking her despite her fluency in English. I try several variant pronunciations of couscous. Five minutes into our discussion, she says, "Ahhh couscous," in her mixed French-Arabic accent. I am accustomed to being misunderstood by friends from other countries. I have learned to speak slowly on the phone, changing my vocabulary slightly, opting for more European-English words and phrases. Quickly she tells me she has never made the grain dish in question. "My mother, um, makes it on Fridays after mosque." She has watched. There is hope. She asks if I have a Moroccan pot. I am worried again. No one told me Moroccan pots were different. What if I can't find this pot? She thinks I should talk to Fouzia. If I am lucky, "She'll know how to make this dish." Maybe she has a pot. Fouzia calls me about ten minutes later. She says, "Ahhh couscous," more quickly than Layinah had. I imagine the conference they had in French before she called me. Fouzia also has never cooked couscous. She tells me it is very hard. Tomorrow she will bring me the special pot also fabrique au Maroc.

When I met my husband, I told him I didn't know how to cook, thinking Pakistani girls knew something more than I did about cooking. I worried how I would feed him. In truth, I did cook then; I had completed course work in a program for chefs. I knew I shouldn't emphasize this. Eight years later, I have learned how to combine cumin, curry powder, and garam masala with garlic and ginger to make foods taste right. This takes time and experimentation, knowing how the spices typically taste in traditional foods, so that when you adapt them, you don't violate what a native palate would consider the correct balance. There is no easy way to understand this balance. One must simply know the flavors. Not only understand but enjoy. He isn't keen on the taste of American meat and potatoes. All half-cooked to him.

I try new foods to satisfy his needs. Fouzia's pot is sort of a double boiler. As she explains to me, I simply put the couscous in the top of the pot and put water in the bottom and boil for ten minutes. "Then do this with my hands." She makes a rolling motion with her fingers to signify the separation of the grains. While I look at the pot, I realize the holes for the steam are too large and the couscous is too small to stay in the top. I conclude that I will not be able to make the couscous without her mother's guidance. She is in Morocco, and it is too late. I can't return the pot without trying. I should have bought the American adaptation in a box, a much simpler instant solution. At home the couscous doesn't cook. I place cheese-cloth in the top of the pot to keep the couscous from slipping through the holes. I try to steam it for an hour, but it's still hard. I roll my fingers as she showed me, separating the clumps of grain. The couscous is partially soft and slightly sticky in places, and the grain burns my fingers. The next day they will ask me if I was successful. Layinah tells me that her brother teases her with a French expression, "A girl cannot marry or be a good wife until she can make this couscous." I am glad my husband doesn't speak French. I am glad he doesn't know this.

What Miracle Is This?

As our Range Rover inches over boulders covered with mud and parts of trees, it repeatedly slips close to the cliff's edge in order to make its way through the passage between the Karakoram mountains—past the glacier, along the river where villagers have planted rice and poppies to the formation of this cavernous mouth—an opening to the north. As each tire vanquishes the large rocks, my husband's sister and I are bounced high into the air giggling, half-heartedly thinking one good slip and we might meet our deaths in the icy river thousands of feet below.

Before we left, a Pakistani army soldier inspected the tires of our car and told us to proceed despite the trees, rocks, and mud that filled the road we were now on. He promised that *the road to Kashmir was a good one.* Improvements under the new government included dynamiting the mountain range to expand the old road. But the engineers had not planned well, and with the rains came dangerous landslides that destroyed the only path to a land where people built walls to get rid of rocks. A land where Pakistani and Indian soldiers fought for the line of control and where I heard a voice that repeats itself to this day: *Climb into this place. Rest. Eat. Here you are my guest.*

Opportunity came with the landslides. The mud covered the road and slowed our car to a crawl, so that children from the mountains above could run to greet us as we passed. Good and bad alike. Dozens of mischievous little boys in muddy *kamezes* without any pants chased us yelling, "One rupee." And there we met a young girl and her sisters. We gave them Danish butter cookies. She had been so timid as she held her small hand out for the offered gifts.

I have learned that crossing over is not so difficult dressed in shalwar kamez. To the people of this place, it is no longer apparent in my face, in my eyes, that I do not belong.

In this land of mud houses, glaciers, and children who collect berries for dinner, I have learned not to look too long at the muddy silt in my teacup.

Reparation

I could not look at the old man with his right arm dangling. It was little more than five pounds of shredded flesh with skin stretched tight across bone and an indentation where muscle should have been. Even with years of preparation: watching hundreds of car crashes and gunshot wounds, action films full of stabbings and explosions, Americans can swallow. Even then I could not look.

The Afghani man held up the price of my guilt: one crooked stained finger for one rupee. As if as little as a penny could buy back the sorrow, the guilt of American bombs and wars. Still I could not look, so my mother paid twenty rupees for us both. Here there are children by the hundreds, left lame by a war they were not alive to see. They make their way on crutches between cars in the scorching Pakistani sun selling newspapers and sliced coconut.

Where the freeways meet in Islamabad, the injured have gathered to ask the well-fed drivers, before they turn their cars from the city, to pay the cost in rupees of walking on the mine fields left by Russian and American military. The men, women, and children, stained by Pakistani dirt, are left without enough food and water to survive. Their forms are evident from miles away, for they are covered with the dust of exile, the dust of sorrow.

Sleeper

You grow in my belly, a little terrorista or would they call you a sleeper, one of millions—suspects of the unthinkable. Your cells inhabit my form. I did not know when I planned for you it would be like this. I did not know they would hate so. I am sorry for that which you will face. You overtake my body, and for you my darling, I have become a ravager of oranges—a lover of vanilla when all I ever wanted was chocolate. You, my sweet daughter, drive me to drink gallons of orange juice, rejecting any drink not rich in vitamin C.

In my dreams, things are better for you. In my dreams, people continue to progress and learn to hate a little less. In my dreams, you have the ability to learn and grow free from distrust and racism. But in reality, the pendulum swings back the opposite direction. They undo all the compassion that was learned. Don't worry, my sweet love. I know that you are like your father, a sleeper waiting to show your full potential.

I feel you—they will see you as foreign, but you are really half of me—as you roll and kick my insides. My stomach hums with your heartbeat. Your blood mixes with mine, until I am as foreign as you are. This they cannot see. You are like the water that vibrates my kitchen faucet—nothing can slow your mounting pressure. In time, my darling. For now, you must grow and sleep until it is your turn to face the unthinkable.

Early Grief

These dreams are proof of my loneliness. Before, when your presence was deep inside for me, you were closer to me than any other. A rush of fluids swirled from me to you. We were united by umbilical cord and placenta—that which failed us both. Not enough oxygen to support the passage from womb to light. I did not expect you then. Not so early. I was not permitted to keep you anchored deep within, protected by blood and flesh, safe from the outside world.

Perhaps it was natural that thoughts of my first years taxed my mind as I was prepared for surgery. The color of the operating room was identical to the walls of my childhood home. The rhythmic sound of Spanish bounced off the sea-foam green cement floor. Fear prohibited any comprehension of the nurse's directions as the doctor performed the epidural. Unsure what to do, I tried not to breathe, forcing them to pull my body into position. Pressure first, then pain. Unable to hold my breath any longer, I cried, "I do not understand you," until I realized there was no one who could say "almost done" in my mother tongue. I wanted to walk away—to touch the floor with my bare feet—but the anesthesiologist had bound my arms, leaving me spread across the operating table like a crucified scarecrow. Before I could make my escape, I felt the first cut, a curve, a smile to pull you through—then like a farmer positioning straw stuffing, he searched for your rump—pushing and pulling you into position. One good push and you were gone—separated from me with speed and skill. The suction formed by his swiftness left a vacuum where you were. I could only hold my breath as I waited for the signs of your respiration: one short squall, then you were whisked from the theater. Your father, wanting to protect you from the very beginning, followed closely to inspect your progress as you were treated by the pediatricians. For the first time in seven months, I was alone. Promptly the surgeon sealed your exit layer by layer—uterus, muscle, fat, and skin—stitch by stitch. I imagined you tunneling out of me, like an escaping refugee, deprived by my body of food and air. Seeing that the epidural had worn off so that I could feel your escape, I am given more drugs, sealing our fate. For three days, I cannot wake to hold you.

Now in wakeful moments, I am aware of not your hum but rather the angry burn of the arc from which you came and the formation of scars over the space it has left behind. Cheated of our last months together, of a safe and secure habitation for you, my love, I can only say, Know this my daughter; no one has ever inhabited my dreams so.

Devotion

It is said in the Quran that when a baby is born, all of the mother's sins are forgiven. You are my pardon: the source of newness—certain salvation. As I look at your small form, I am more virtuous, kinder, more prudent. All passion falls away except that I feel for you, my love. It is said that we never truly own anything in this world. I think that is wrong, for I belong to you. Nothing is truer than that. When a child is born, Arab women change their name to *Ummo*, meaning "mother of." Now I am Ummo Mahrukh; all else has been erased.

Pillow Talk

My darling daughter, you will hear that Americans are too worried about the danger in everything. They worry about airbags and seatbelts and X-rays and microwaves and sun exposure and second-hand smoke. Americans worry about body fat and fiber in their diets. Americans worry about taking medicine during pregnancy. Americans worry that their babies will sleep on too soft beds and turn blue in the night or pull too many covers over their heads and sink into oblivion. American grandmothers buy bumpers for their grandbabies' cribs so their soft heads do not slip through the rails.

And you will also hear that Pakistani mothers do not think that babies are injured by too much comfort. Pakistani mothers do not know about the safety of car seats or firm mattresses. Pakistani mothers have never had to worry about what medicines they take. Pakistani mothers see the softness of the baby's head and worry that they would be uncomfortable in an unyielding American-style bed. For this reason, Pakistani children's cots are filled with plush mattresses and soft pillows to protect them from the unforgiving world. Pakistani grandmothers have never heard of bumpers or of babies' heads falling though rails; instead they worry about the shape of their grandchild's head, telling their daughters always to use the pillows and turn the baby's head to prevent lumps—the surest sign of a neglectful mother.

Somewhere between the debate of too much and not enough exists your cot. Each pillow has been the subject of thoughtful consideration and deep discussion. While you softly sleep, Achi Bahati, Didi, and I have long phone conversations in a mix of broken Urdu and English about your head and your heart and our love for you. You, my darling, with an American mother and Pakistani grandmother, are to be protected from both too much danger and not enough comfort.

In the Village

Jan Clausen

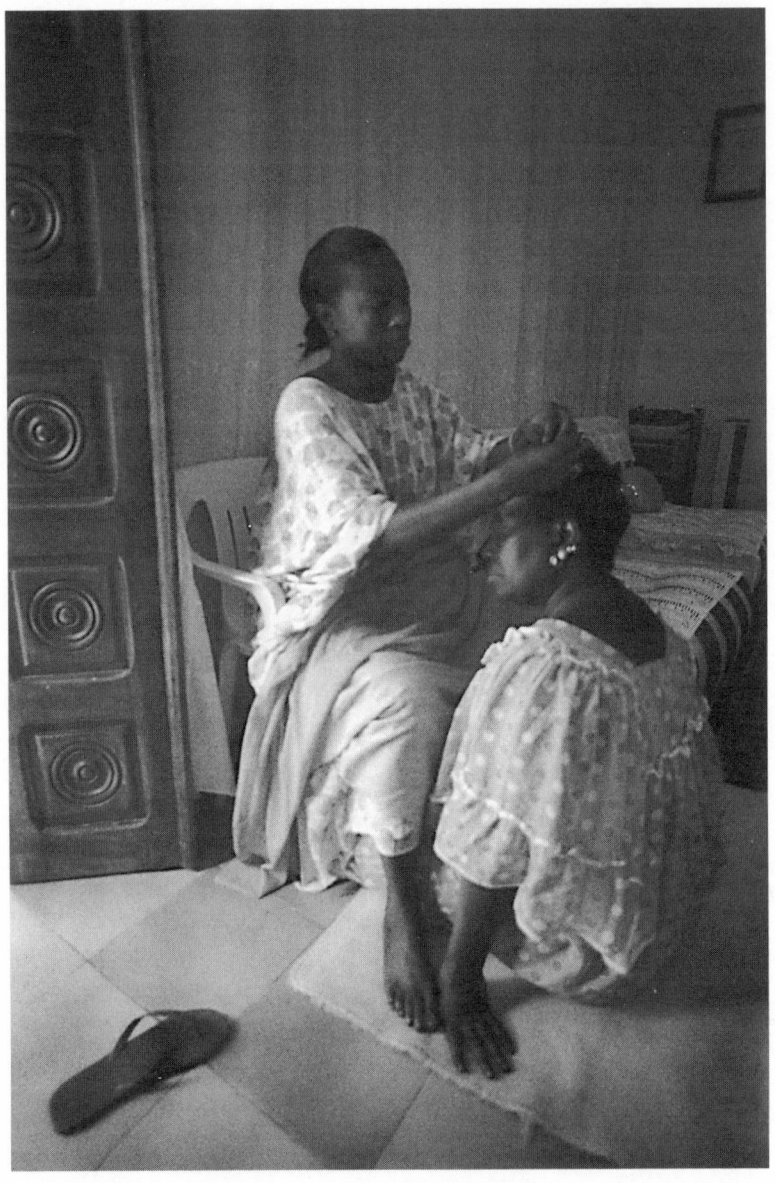

Kerry Stuart Coppin, *Untitled: Woman Braiding Hair / African Home / Dakar, Senegal*

A lilting lift
of clean banana leaf,
dry mutter of windmill palm—
the voice of sea air
walking in her garden.
The voice of goat.
The voice of dove.
Old woman grating coconut.
The young dasheen.
The little rain.
(The 30 years in England.)

The stone feast,
bull killed to flatter death.
Paired butterflies yellow
in the withered corn.
The rum shop tune.
The moneygram.
Jack Iron on the ground.
(The teacher daughter up in Edmonton.)

The lizard wall,
the tambran shade,
the neighbor's rooster
on the step.
Tall children trudge
the ruined road,
ears stopped
with a city rhythm.
(The tourist visa overstayed.
That gray world, East Flatbush.)

Old man abed,
old maker, unmade—
who worked,

got sons and daughters
on three islands.
Paid women keep him clean,
sing hymns in his kitchen
with the radio.

Lace curtains.
House full of flies.
(Bel Air, Beau Lieu,
old cruelty of sugar.)

The stroke of broom,
the harp of heat.
The long-eared sheep
that scale the crumbling graves
above a perfect blue
unrescued reef.
(Old laws
against beating drum,
blowing shell,
lifting cutlass
in the road.)

> *When my father*
> *came from Aruba*
> *—I was 6—*
> *I remember*
> *he lifted me*
> *up.*

(A struggle
in the distance
of history.)

Kuku.
Okro.
Bluggoe.

Husks
in the heat.

Ash
on the edge
of wind.

Ibra Ibrahimovic, *Untitled*

The Snow in Ghana

Ryszard Kapuściński

translated by William Brand

The fire stood between us and linked us together. A boy added wood and the flames rose higher, illuminating our faces.

"What is the name of your country?"

"Poland."

Poland was far away, beyond the Sahara, beyond the sea, to the north and the east. The *Nana* repeated the name aloud. "Is that how it is pronounced?" he asked.

"That's the way," I answered. "That's correct."

"They have snow there," Kwesi said. Kwesi worked in town. Once, at the cinema, there was a movie with snow. The children applauded and cried merrily "*Anko! Anko!*" asking to see the snow again. The white puffs fell and fell. Those are lucky countries, Kwesi said. They do not need to grow cotton; the cotton falls from the sky. They call it snow and walk on it and even throw it into the river.

We were stuck here by this fire by chance—three of us, my friend Kofi from Accra, a driver and I. Night had already fallen when the tire blew—the third tire, rotten luck. It happened on a side road, in the bush, near the village of Mpango in Ghana. Too dark to fix it. You have no idea how dark the night can be. You can stick out your hand and not see it. They have nights like that. We walked into the village.

The Nana received us. There is a Nana in every village, because Nana means boss, head man, a sort of mayor but with more authority. If you want to get married back home in your village, the mayor cannot stop you, but the Nana can. He has a Council of Elders, who meet and govern and ponder disputes. Once upon a time the Nana was a god. But now there is the independent government in Accra. The government passes laws and the Nana has to execute them. A Nana who does not carry them out is acting like a feudal lord and must be gotten rid of. The government is trying to make all Nanas join the party.

The Nana from Mpango was skinny and bald, with thin Sudanese lips. My friend Kofi introduced us. He explained where I was from and that they were to treat me as a friend.

"I know him," my friend Kofi said. "He's an African."

That is the highest compliment that can be paid a European. It opens every door for him.

The Nana smiled and we shook hands. You always greet a Nana by pressing his right hand between both of your own palms. This shows respect. He sat us down by the fire, where the elders had just been holding a meeting. The bonfire was in the middle of the village, and to the left and right, along the road, there were other fires. As many fires as huts. Perhaps twenty. We could see the fires and the figures of the women and the men and the silhouettes of the clay huts—they were all visible against a night so dark and deep that it felt heavy like a weight.

The bush had disappeared, even though the bush was everywhere. It began a hundred meters away, immobile, massive, a tightly packed, coarse thicket surrounding the village and us and the fire. The bush screamed and cried and crackled; it was alive; it smelled of wilted green; it was terrifying and tempting; you knew that you could touch it and be wounded and die, but tonight, this night, you couldn't even see it.

Poland.

They did not know of any such country.

The elders looked at me with uncertainty, possibly suspicion. I wanted to break their mistrust somehow. I did not know how and I was tired.

"Where are your colonies?" the Nana asked.

My eyes were drooping, but I became alert. People often asked that question. Kofi had asked it first, long ago, and my answer was a revelation to him. From then on he was always ready for the question with a little speech prepared, illustrating its absurdity.

Kofi answered: "They don't have colonies, Nana. Not all white countries have colonies. Not all whites are colonialists. You have to understand that whites often colonize whites."

The elders shuddered and smacked their lips. They were surprised. Once I would have been surprised that they were surprised. But not any more. I can't bear that language—that language of white, black and yellow. The language of race is disgusting.

Kofi explained: "For a hundred years they taught us that the white is somebody greater, super, extra. They had their clubs, their swimming pools, their neighborhoods. Their whores, their cars, and their burbling language. We knew that England was the only country in the world, that God was English, that only the English traveled around the globe. We knew exactly as much as they wanted us to know. Now it's hard to change."

Kofi and I stuck up for each other; we no longer spoke about the subject of skin, but here, among new faces, the subject had to come up.

One of the elders asked, "Are all the women in your country white?"

"All of them."

"Are they beautiful?"

"They're very beautiful," I answered.

"Do you know what he told me, Nana?" Kofi interjected. "That during their summer, the women take off their clothes and lie in the sun to get black skin. The ones that become dark are proud of it, and others admire them for being as tanned as blacks."

Very good, Kofi, you got them. The elders' eyes lit up at the thought of those bodies darkening in the sun, because, you know how it is, boys are the same all over the world: they like that sort of thing. The elders rubbed their hands together, smiled; women's bodies in the sun; they snuggled up inside their loose *kente* robes that looked like Roman togas.

"My country has no colonies," I said after a time, "and there was a time when my country was a colony. I respect what you've suffered, but, we too have suffered horrible things: there were streetcars, restaurants, districts *nur für Deutsch*. There were camps, war, executions. You don't know camps, war and executions. That was what we called fascism. It's the worst colonialism."

They listened, frowning, and closed their eyes. Strange things had been said, which they needed time to take in.

"Tell me, what does a streetcar look like?"

The concrete is important. Perhaps there was not enough room. No, it had nothing to do with room; it was contempt. One person stepping on another. Not only Africa is a cursed land. Every land can be like it—Europe, America, any place. The world depends on people, needs to step on them.

"But Nana, we were free afterwards. We built cities and ran lights into the villages. Those who couldn't read were taught how to read."

The Nana stood up and grasped my hand. The rest of the elders did the same. We had become friends, *przyjaciele, amigos.*

I wanted to eat.

I could smell meat in the air. I could smell a smell that was not of the jungle or of palm or of coconuts; it was the smell of a kielbasa, the kind you could get for 11.60 zlotys at that inn in the Mazury. And a large beer.

Instead we ate goat.

Poland . . . snow falling, women in the sun, no colonies. There had been a war; there were homes to build; somebody teaching somebody to read.

I had told them something, I rationalized. It was too late to go into details. I wanted to go to sleep. We were leaving at dawn; a lecture was impossible. Anyway, they had worries of their own.

Suddenly I felt shame, a sense of having missed the mark. It was not my country I had described. Snow and the lack of colonies—that's accurate enough, but it is not what we know or what we carry around within ourselves: nothing of our pride, of our life, nothing of what we breathe.

Snow—that's the truth, Nana. Snow is marvelous. And it's terrible. Snow, because in January, January 1945, the January offensive, there were ashes, ashes everywhere: Warsaw, Wroclaw, and Szczecin. And bricks, freezing hands, vodka and people laying bricks—this is where the bed will go and the wardrobe right here—people filing back into the center of the city, and ice on the window panes, and no water, and those nights, the meetings till dawn, and angry discussions and later the fires of Silesia, and the blast furnaces, and the temperature—160 degrees centigrade—in August in front of the blast furnaces, our tropics, our Africa, black and hot. Oh, what a load of shit—What do you mean?—Oh, what a lovely little war—Shut up about the war! We want to live, to be happy, we want an apartment, a TV, no, first a motor scooter. A Pole can drink and a Pole can fight, why can't we work? What if we never learn how? Our ships are on every sea, success in exports, success in boxing, youngsters in gloves, wet gloves pulling a tractor out of the mud, Nowa Huta, build, build, build, Tychy and Wizów, bright apartments, upward mobility, a cowherd yesterday and an engineer today—Do you call that an engineer? and the whole streetcar bursts out laughing. Tell me: what does a street-car look like? It's very simple: four wheels, an electrical pick-up, *enough, enough,* it's all a code, nothing but signs in the bush, in Mpango, and the key to the code is in my pocket.

We always carry it to foreign countries, all over the world, our pride and our powerlessness. We know its configuration, but there is no way to make it accessible to others. It will never be right. Something, the most important thing, the most significant thing, something remains unsaid.

Relate one year of my country—it does not matter which one: let us say, 1957. And one month of that year—say, July. And just one day—let us say, the sixth.

No.

Yet that day, that month, that year exist in us, somehow, because we were there, walking that street, or digging coal, or cutting the forest, and if we were walking along that street how can we then describe it (it could be Cracow) so that you can see its movement, its climate, its persistence and changeability, its smell and its hum?

They cannot see it. You cannot see it, anything—the night, Mpango, the thick bush, Ghana, the fire dying out, the elders going off to sleep, the Nana dozing, and snow falling somewhere, and women like blacks, *thoughts,* "They are learning to read, he said something like that," *thoughts,* "They had a war, ach, a war, he said, yes, no colonies," that country, Poland, white and they have no colonies," *thoughts,* the bush screams, this strange world.

Two Women, Two Worlds

Audrey McCollum

The equatorial sun is burning through the mists that swirl out of the surrounding forest. A shaft of light from the doorway of our thatch-roofed lodging dances across the Papua New Guinea highlander's curved lips as she speaks; it reflects off the dome of her forehead and the dark flesh cushioning her cheekbones. She leans forward, her voice low and intense.

"People ask, 'Why do this white woman and white man come to see you so many times? Why do they contribute to your center for women?' They say, 'Maybe they are your own father and mother come back from the dead.'" She studies my face, her ebony eyes glistening.

"I wish," she says, "I wish that you really *are* my mother."

Words elude me. I'm shaken by the cruelties my friend, Pirip, has described. Now, in November of 1996, and after 13 years of striving, I understand her mission as well as my own.

In March of 1983, our Twin Otter aircraft threaded its way through jungle-cloaked mountains, tossed by swirling updrafts. Bob, my husband, and I stared uneasily at the precipitous limestone ridges that almost grazed our wings.

Finally we approached the mile-high Wahgi Valley. Bracketed by tall ranges, it followed the Wahgi River for over sixty miles. This was the cradle of highland agriculture over 9,000 years ago.

The first Caucasians didn't glide down from the sky; they stumbled in on foot. When Papua New Guinea became an Australian protectorate after World War I, it was forbidding. Swamps or densely forested lowlands rose toward a volcanic spine that was thought to be too wild to support human life.

It astonished gold prospectors to discover populated valleys in the mountains in 1930. It astonished dark-skinned highlanders to confront men so pale that they seemed like spirits of the dead.

Yet pale men established an enduring presence here as explorers, missionaries, and Australian patrol officers, and it continued after Papua New Guinea became independent in 1975. Peter van Fleet, a former patrol officer keenly interested in anthropology, ran a small lodge that became the base for our first explorations.

As afternoons advanced in the Wahgi Valley, women trudged along the meandering roads, returning home from forests, gardens, or markets. Suspended from the crowns of their heads, coarse fiber netbags, *bilums,* bulged with enormous loads. One, extending the length of a woman's spine, might be stretched taut with produce. Another on top might cradle a baby, and a bundle of firewood might crown the woman's head.

The women's movements were restricted by their burdens, sometimes heavier than 100 pounds. They turned their heads slowly and stiffly as though their necks had rusted in the afternoon rains.

In times past, highland men didn't carry domestic loads—they strode ahead of women and children, carrying spears, bows and arrows, prepared for attack. But now?

"Men have stronger bodies," I said to Benjamin, an indigenous guide who worked with Peter. "Why do women carry heavy loads?"

"It is right that they should," he quipped. "A bride is so expensive."

"It must hurt their necks," I said.

"They are used to it," he said calmly. Girls as young as three were given a tiny bilum and encouraged to carry one *kaukau*—a sweet potato—home from the gardens where their mothers tended the crops. By seven or eight years, they might carry 30 pounds.

The bilum, made by forming intricate loops from one continuous strand of fiber, was considered a symbol of the womb, yet to my eyes it was an emblem of a burdened life. I wanted to hear women speak for themselves and Peter offered to help. "I know a teacher who speaks English well, and she's interested in women's affairs," he said.

Telephone and telex were available in towns, but most communication took place on foot. Peter sent a messenger to the school where Betty Kaman taught. Betty sent out messengers to find Pirip Kuru, an advocate for local women.

We gathered in the lodge at dusk. Pirip was about five feet tall, full-figured, and clothed in a puff-sleeved loose smock and a wrapped skirt. Her wiry black hair was cropped short, and a furrow ran across the crown as though it had been dented by years of bearing bilums.

Pirip seemed dignified but shy, reserved but alert. She didn't trust her own English but seemed to understand mine. And she shared with Betty a fluency in pidgin, a melange of Melanesian, German, and English.

Elegant and formal, Betty was the interpreter of our three-way conversation. She was an experienced schoolteacher whose family cared for her four children while she taught.

"I sent to Australia for nursing bottles so I could continue teaching while they were babies," she explained with a touch of hauteur, "and my husband is a graduate of the University of Papua New Guinea. He is a successful coffee grower—coffee is the most important export crop in the highlands."

"Have you been married long?" I asked.

"Yes, 12 years. When I married, my family was presented with many pigs, bird of paradise plumes, and 6,000 *kina*. That was my bride price," she said proudly.

"The kina, was that cash?" I asked. The shell of the gold-lipped pearl oyster, the kina was now also a minted currency.

"No, pearl shells." It took her husband's family years to gather the fortune, Betty added. "At times I would like to be free and independent, and that might be possible. As a professional woman, I could earn a salary; if I returned to my parents they would accept me back because they own land and coffee, and they would be able to pay back my bride price. It would be different for Pirip. Her parents would have distributed her bride price. They would probably beat her and force her to go back to her husband."

"*Beat* her!" Pirip's face was inscrutable. She had been silent, sitting forward in her chair, hands on her outspread knees, continuously watching Betty and me.

"You have beautiful dresses," I said, wanting to draw her into the conversation. Pirip's outfit was made from a vivid cotton print. She smiled, exposing two rows of startlingly perfect teeth, and spoke to Betty in pidgin, still strange to my ears.

"She sewed her dress herself," Betty explained. Pirip was a churchwoman; her pastor encouraged her to become skillful on a sewing machine. Then Pirip began to dream that Wahgi Valley women could learn to make better clothes than the second-hand garments imported from Australia since missionaries and government officials began insisting that people cover their bodies.

"What did you wear before?" I asked Pirip who answered with sparkling eyes as Betty translated her words.

"We wore tapa cloth from special tree bark. For celebrations, my parents dressed me with feathers and furs that they collected from animals; they painted my face and decorated me in a beautiful traditional style—I was dressed half naked." Pirip erupted into laughter that shook her sturdy shoulders.

"Pirip sees her new skill in sewing as a symbol of moving into modern times. She thinks women can produce clothing to sell in the markets so they can earn some personal funds," said Betty, explaining that Pirip walked from woman to woman, and 200 responded. The South Wahgi Valley Women's Association was formed, and Pirip was named President.

"You are an important woman," I said to Pirip, and her smile curved like a quarter moon.

Each woman earned two kina by selling her surplus crops in the market and contributed the money to the association which then bought sewing machines and fabrics.

Now Pirip spoke in an urgent tone.

"She longs for textiles from America, and wonders if you could send her some," Betty told me.

I tried to explain how difficult that would be, but I floundered. Pirip had no way to appreciate the 10,000 miles from New Hampshire to New Guinea, the cost of shipping, or the probable import taxes. Yet Pirip's hope was easy to understand. When Australians first entered the highlands, they encountered people who had not even developed the wheel. The highlanders' first sightings of that revolving device occurred when gold prospectors flew planes in. It's said that tribesmen crawled under those strange big birds to learn whether they were female or male—that they could understand.

Those planes, and others during World War II, were laden with products of Western technology. For a people with no experience of industrial manufacturing, this influx of goods seemed magical. If so much came unbidden, why not more in response to ritual and desire? Why shouldn't Pirip imagine that I could supply endless bolts of cloth?

But I couldn't, and when Pirip realized that, her upper body sagged.

"Tell me more about what you hope to do," I urged her.

"Pirip wants to help women modernize their domestic skills," Betty explained. Welfare workers, based in the towns, were ignoring rural women's needs. Infant and maternal mortality were high, and female anemia was widespread. Visiting the Minj Health Center required a long walk or fare for the PMV—a public motor vehicle, typically an open truck filled with standing passengers.

"So how is the women's association progressing?"

"Pirip says that among the original 200 women, many were beaten or threatened with beatings by their husbands who fear that an association may bring unwelcome change into their lives," Betty said soberly. "Maybe 100 remain in the association."

"But in the last election, Pirip became a candidate from her district for the provincial government—we have both a national parliament and a government for each province—and she did well. There were 18 candidates, 17 of them men, and she ranked sixth in the count of votes. She will try again."

Pirip dreamed of building a center for the association, Betty explained. When a parcel of land for lease was advertised by the government, Pirip applied and it was awarded to her along with a grant of 27,000 kina (about $34,000) for the center. But the funds were embezzled and never reached the women.

Watching me closely, Pirip spoke rapidly.

"Pirip asks, 'Is it possible that any help could come from America?'" She doesn't miss a beat, I thought, amused and admiring. I was captured by the thought that women in the Upper Valley where Bob and I now lived—a region in New Hampshire and Vermont that straddles the Connecticut River—might reach across the world to women of the Wahgi Valley. So I promised to take back Pirip's story and see if any funds could be raised. Pirip moved very close; gazing directly into my eyes, she began crooning and caressing my knee. Then she spoke.

"Pirip says she never dreamed that a woman from America might come to Minj and talk to her," Betty told me.

Pirip studied my face intently. What did she see?

After 30 years in Connecticut, where Bob and I met, married, raised our offspring, and developed professional careers, he was urged to become dean of the Dartmouth Medical school in New Hampshire. It was an irresistible invitation.

The wrench of our move took me by surprise. I left my intimate friends, supportive colleagues, and trusting clients. Now I was needing to be needed again.

I was eager to learn more about the culture of Pirip's people, the Kuma, so one evening Peter nosed his Land Rover cautiously along narrow lanes to a traditional house. Windowless, with a thatched roof, walls of woven strips of *pandanus* (screw pine), an earthen floor, it was lighted by a kerosene lantern rather than the usual central fire and jammed with people. A courting party was underway.

"The ceremonies are called *turnim head* and *carry leg*; you'll see why," Peter said. To the throb of an hourglass-shaped *kundu* drum, five couples filed in and sat back on their heels side by side, garbed in what Pirip had termed "beautiful traditional style." Skirts composed of multiple strands of twined fiber fell gracefully between the girls' thighs, and amber *cuscus* (tree kangaroo) pelts hung between their high, taut breasts. They wore necklaces of animal teeth and earrings of fluffy white feathers.

The males sported intricately woven bark belts with narrow fiber aprons called *laplaps* hanging in front, and bunches of strap-like cordyline leaves termed *as gras* suspended behind. Youths of both sexes had painted red ochre masks around their gleaming eyes, and black cassowary feathers soared above their headbands of *cuscus* fur. Some male watchers had adorned their foreheads with circular bailer shells, and kina shell crescents gleamed on their chests. Boars' tusks hung at their throats, and a few older men had thrust semicircles of bone through their nasal septums.

Men secretly practiced love magic before courting parties, since they gained prestige if girls swayed toward them and invited them to carry leg. They lost face if that didn't happen. Sexual initiative belonged to the girls during this interval in their lives.

The kneeling young people began swaying toward each other and then away, toward and away, in response to the insistent drumbeat. Oiled brown bodies gleamed in the lantern's glow as each couple's heads turned in unison so that their noses met and parted. Then each girl extended her legs across her partner's right thigh, and they started turnim head once more. Again and again, the teasing motions spurred giggles and rising excitement. Many shoulders were swaying, mine included, and erotic energy pulsed through the crowd until, pair by pair, the aroused couples slipped away to enjoy a night of passion.

Marriage ended sexual freedom for women. Since the aim of marriage was to enlarge the clan, adultery had to be prevented. A wife was forbidden to talk with a man except in her husband's presence.

Too, a girl's close ties to her birth family were ruptured when she was led or forcibly carried to her husband. If his homestead was several days' walk away, she rarely visited her kin again.

That image stirred a dormant ache inside of me.

Polygamy was still common here, Peter told us. It enhanced male prestige, showing that a man could amass much bride wealth, and it secured ties with other clans, and since it was *tambu* for a man to be intimate with his wife during the years she nursed her babies, it offered sexual outlets.

Benjamin, Peter's guide, had two wives. "Do your wives get on well together?" I asked one morning as we jounced along a roller-coaster road.

"My wives get on well enough," Benjamin said.

"I've heard that some wives are jealous of each other," I persisted.

"That can happen," Benjamin admitted. But his wives lived a long steep trudge from each other. Benjamin pointed out the separate ridges on which he had built a thatched hut for each wife—she shared it with her children and pigs.

"With *pigs?*" Bob erupted.

"Yes. Each pig has a separate stall for the night; they are house-trained so the stall stays clean. A man without a pig is a nobody," explained Benjamin. Women were responsible for their care.

"I will show you how my people make a garden," he said as we approached a sloping plot of land. Men had cleared it by slashing and burning off the vegetation, and they'd dug interconnecting drainage ditches so that the hillside looked like a tilted checkerboard.

"Sometimes the women tie themselves to a tree or a rock so they will not fall. They dig pits in the ground and place their babies there inside their netbags," said Benjamin as we toiled up.

Banana trees and sugar cane were growing at the edge of the garden; men planted and tended those crops. Crops low to the ground were planted, weeded, and harvested by women. Some women were planting kaukau with simple wooden digging sticks. They were bending straight-legged from their hips or crouching down on all fours, still managing to chat and smile.

"The men are just standing around," I said to Benjamin.

"You see, when there was a great deal of clan warfare, the men would stand guard while the women worked," he explained.

Later, Benjamin drove us to a household where a *mumu* (a baked feast) was being prepared. Sticks had been shaved into a pile of tinder, then the leader (Big Man) of the group looped a strip of bamboo around a bundle of twigs. Grasping the bundle firmly with his toes, he pulled the strip back and forth until sparks flashed out and the tinder began to smolder. Soon a fire was blazing, heating large stones.

A traditional Papuan woman suckles a piglet. Pigs are considered to be valuables among many highland people, and women are entrusted with their care. A puny or ailing piglet might receive this special treatment. Photo by Robert McCollum.

When the stones were glowing, women arranged them in a pit, using tongs made from sticks split at one end. They layered the stones with moist banana leaves, folding in corn, pumpkin, peanuts, kaukau, *pitpit* (a wild cane that tasted like asparagus) and various greens. The meal was served on banana leaves and was delectable.

The diet was supplemented by birds, fish, marsupials, and snakes that men hunted with bows and arrows. Men also built dwellings and some worked for cash in the foreign-owned coffee or tea plantations that spread across the fertile valley after World War II. A few had small plantations of their own, but many men were seen idle along the roadside, some crouched around a deck of cards throwing bets. Everywhere there were stories about *rascols,* men without meaningful work who preyed on others, assaulting and stealing.

"Highland women seem to work much harder than men," I said.

"That is true," Benjamin conceded, "and it is only right. It costs so much to buy a woman."

Another afternoon, we lurched up a rutted mountain road to the homestead where Benjamin's parents lived. After welcoming us with smiles and pats on our arms, his tiny withered mother fetched a key. The woven pandanus men's house was secured with a modern padlock.

Inside, the posts and roof gleamed with black resins from the ever-glowing fires. Pigs' jaws, bronzed by the smoke, hung from the crossbeam as a record of ceremonial exchange. There were three crude wooden beds and space for woven mats. This was where Benjamin's father and male kin spent daytime hours socializing, and nights in sleep.

"Closer to town," Benjamin explained, "some men now sleep in family houses— the missionaries say they should. But many preserve the traditional way." He turned to Bob. "To sleep with a woman," he said solemnly, "can cause a man to become weak."

Kuma people believed that females were intensely sexual; their sexuality was desirable but dangerous too. Intercourse could cause a man's taut and shining skin—the hallmark of vitality—to crumple into flaccid folds. Childbirth fluids were considered toxic and menstruating women were secluded to certain areas to protect men from their soiled aprons. They had to avoid walking through newly planted gardens because a drop of menstrual blood could sicken men. Kuma women had powers that men couldn't control.

Perhaps, I conjectured, Kuma men had drawn the line against those powers by excluding women from their own flamboyant roles as ceremonial and political transactors. Like western women, Pirip was trying to enter the male domain.

After we returned to New Hampshire, Pirip's aim infused me with fresh purpose and led to new connections with Dartmouth faculty, students, and regional women's groups. I delved into anthropological literature and rethought assumptions about our own culture, enhancing my growing therapy practice. In our labored correspondence (Pirip asked kin and friends to serve as scribes) I encouraged her aim of building a women's center, and garnered small contributions amounting to $500 (now 600 kina).

I proposed a March, 1984, meeting in Madang, a northeastern seaport, since Bob and I planned to explore Papua New Guinea's small islands by ship. I had no response from Pirip, so I was stunned when she met us, having borrowed a government vehicle and driven for 19 hours non-stop with her husband, their male friend, Jonah and two of her five children.

As she showed me a bankbook containing her association accounts, Jonah explained that the women had earned 700 kina cleaning the jail and other Minj properties. Pirip had been assured that with my contribution, the provincial government would provide matching funds.

"But I don't have the money with me," I said, dismayed, explaining that it seemed safest to have the funds transferred to her bank after we made contact again. Pirip looked despairing and I was appalled—hope had fueled her exhausting drive.

"With the help of men in her family, Pirip has built a bush house center near her family house, and women have begun gathering there to produce artifacts for sale," said Jonah. "When she has accumulated the several thousand kina she needs, she will build a permanent center on her leased land next to the police station and develop the programs the women want."

"Pirip, you're a *strongpela meri tru* (very strong woman)," I said. Cheered, she told me about her childhood in the mountains above Minj, living much as Benjamin had shown us. The daughter of her father's third wife, she had eight brothers or half-brothers but no sisters. She hardly mentioned her mother but said, "Father treated me as a valuable wealth in the family; sometimes he cut ripe sugar cane or banana and asked me to come in the *haus man* and sit down and eat with him—he loved me very much."

After hours of talk, Pirip needed to start home and our ship would soon leave port. When we said goodbye, I felt growing affection for this woman from another world—a bond that would spur six more trips to her country.

But I had let her down; for me, that's the stuff of nightmares.

My father was cursed by inherited wealth. Fashion in clothes, parties and travels defined my parents' leisured lives: the "season" in Biarritz or St. Moritz where the international "smart set" gathered—children were watched by dutiful nannies; fox hunting in Virginia; glittering balls in Newport mansions.

When his fortune shrank in the 1929 stock market crash, Father couldn't handle a transition from playboy to salaried worker. One night I saw him teeter on the windowsill, bellowing in a whiskey-rasped voice, "Look out below, here I come," while Mother clutched his ankle and yanked him back inside. Then he left our home and came back, left and came back, then left again—I never knew when it would happen or why. Like many children of turmoil, I sometimes imagined that it was all my fault and it was up to me to fix it, whatever "it" might be.

Most of my memories elude chronology. But I vividly recall that my younger sister, Jackie, woke up sick when she was ten. When I told Mother about Jackie's fiery, spotted skin, she began phoning for a doctor. We had no regular doctor and, in fact, no regular phone. In her slow slide into madness after Father left for the final time, Mother reclined all day on the living room sofa garbed in a negligee—lost in a reverie that gradually became demonic. She feared opening her mail, so the bills piled up unpaid. Utilities in our apartment were often cut off.

Jackie had German measles, said the doctor, explaining that it would have to run its course. "She shouldn't read much," he cautioned. Her eyes were inflamed.

"But my homework!" she moaned.

"Don't worry," I said. "I'll bring your assignments home, I'll read to you."

But I usually lingered at school, and there was supper to fix—mother hadn't been reared to cook. The night before she went back to school, Jackie impaled me with her clear blue gaze.

"You promised to help me with homework every night. You didn't do it."

That was only one of the many times I disappointed her. When she died an early alcohol-induced death, I wondered if my neglect had played a part.

Now, years later, did Jackie's shadow lie across my relationship with Pirip? Had I failed Pirip as grievously as it seemed? I was unsure, but the day after Bob and I got home, I transferred the $500 contributed by Upper Valley women to Pirip's bank in Mt. Hagen. It was received, but a second donation that I gathered never reached her. It was apparently stolen.

We drove eastward out of the tumult of Mt. Hagen, the provincial capital where our plane landed in March of 1989. There was a hubbub of traffic now—cars, PMVs, and grinding trucks that belched black diesel vapors into the morning freshness.

Roadside businesses had sprouted at the outskirts: tires and batteries for sale, and shops for automotive repair. And in the bustling market the few elderly men who sported as gras wore it protruding below a western-style jacket.

Finally we sped along the two-lane Highland Highway and turned south near Minj market. We moved slowly down a side road searching, and there she was. When I called her name, her mouth gaped in disbelief, and then she began to cry. As I leaned toward her, she hugged me tightly, her shoulders heaving with sobs. Her tears trickled down my neck, flowed inside my tank top, and oozed into my bra—an intimate communion. I hugged her back and produced a pidgin greeting.

"*Mi anamas tru long lookim yu gen*" (I'm very glad to see you again). Pirip stared in open-mouthed surprise, and then wailed and sobbed more intensely, clinging to my arm.

"This is our customary way to show when we are happy to meet," Agua, our current guide, explained as Pirip led us into her family compound. In a clearing beyond the sleeping and cooking houses, we saw a new *Haus win* (rest house). This was the women's center, a handsome heptagonal structure. Glass windows had been set into two of the seven walls which were made of pandanus woven in an intricate pattern. The steep thatched roof rose to a phallic peak—a style I had seen on men's houses.

Kuru, Pirip's husband, bounded forward laughing and shouting and hugged me, holding my cheek against his until my face was wet from his tears. Then we gathered inside the haus win—Kuru, his brother Gabriel, Pirip's son-in-law Chris, Bob, and over 20 women. Gabriel was the spokesman.

"You see, there is a Provincial Council of Women; the president is Betty Takip," he said. "The Provincial Council has been allocated 20,000 kina to be divided among the districts, but Pirip's group has not received any funds. This group must make an application, which costs 50 kina, and Betty decides on the applications. Unfortunately, funds allocated for women by the national government, and distributed by the provincial government, often do not reach rural women.

Wearing traditional garb, Kuma women plant *kau-kau* (sweet potato), the staple food, in a new garden. Photo by Robert McCollum.

"In the time of Pirip's mother, men were preoccupied with warfare as well as hunting. Women had autonomy in their own domain. Since warfare has been abolished, men are more involved with family affairs and they keep women subordinate. They boss women around and control family resources. Women have access to medical services and education, but only if the man of the family decides it should happen because it involves an expenditure of money. Women are very much burdened."

"Does bride-price continue?" I asked.

"Yes," said Gabriel, "but that has changed too. It is often presented as cash, and men now view it as the purchase of a woman that entitles the husband to treat her as property.

"Pirip began her women's work around the time of independence in 1975," Gabriel went on. "She has faced many obstacles—women's allegiances to their own clan groups, male opposition to change, and her own illiteracy."

"What's your own work?" Bob asked as Gabriel paused.

"I am an educator. I have offered to teach the women to read and write."

"Wonderful," I said. "But I'd like to hear what changes the women would like to see." After the men ambled out, a young woman named Elizabeth Tuan explained the women's silence: "It is our custom that women do not speak until the men have finished speaking. Now Pirip would like to make you one of the registered members of her group—there are 30 women and six men who assist with construction."

"That would be an honor," I said.

"Pirip says this bush house with seven sides was her idea. Many of Pirip's ideas were taken by Betty, and she wonders if Betty might have taken the missing money too. I am working with these women to get a grant of 200 kina."

"I'd like to contribute 200 kina that I've saved from my work at home," I said, dismayed about the lost funds. I handed the bills to Pirip, who stuffed them inside her smock. Then the other women pushed me outside where they put coronas of blossoms on my head and around my neck. To my amazement I was lifted up by seven women, all smaller than I, and carried completely around the building.

When my feet were back on the ground, Elizabeth drew me behind the Haus Win. "I am a coordinator—there are two in each province," she said in a voice just above a whisper. "I try to help women become modern—for example, to build separate pig houses for their health, and to learn how to use cooking and eating utensils. And I am encouraging them to start on a small project, maybe raising chickens."

But we were interrupted as a group of smiling women surrounded us, touching my arms, my cheeks—I felt cradled in their warm embrace. They led Bob and me to where a mumu had been served on banana leaves, and we all sat on the ground, shaded by arching bamboo, and happily munched kaukau and roasted corn.

Pirip's kin had built a large sleeping house which would become a guest house for tourists, but it wasn't ready for us, so as the light waned Agua urged us to leave since the highway was unsafe after dark.

Our vehicle had been transformed: the bumpers, mirror, door handles, roof rack, and front fender were festooned with blossoms. Bob had been garlanded too, and the group closed in to say good-bye. When Pirip hugged me tightly again, it was hard to pull away. Tears stung my eyes as every passing car or truck honked a salute.

"We decorate the car for important people," Agua explained.

Being important was a heavy responsibility. I had doubts about Elizabeth Tuan's aims: Would forks really improve women's lives, or only the lives of fork salesmen? And raising chickens could be fruitless since feed was costly and the expense might never be recovered. I'd hoped to hear about the women's own goals and judge whether I was touching their lives in a constructive way.

I didn't see Pirip again for three years. Bob and I joined the widespread protests against President Bush's inexorable momentum toward war in Iraq. Then, in January of '91, I attended a national meeting of mental health professionals concerning violence. Operation Desert Storm was bearing witness to the central theme of the conference: the United States had developed a "culture of destruction."

There were 25,000 murders every year, half-erupting out of domestic violence. Around four million women were beaten by male partners each year, and 800,000 were raped.

A suicide occurred every twenty minutes. Thirty-five thousand were confirmed each year but it was believed that up to 100,000 actually took place.

We were pounded by ugly realities about our country, which the U.S. Senate Judiciary Committee later declared the most violent in the developed world.

I wanted to go back to Papua New Guinea. I wanted to find Pirip and say, "Dear sister, please slow down."

But she had failed to answer several letters, and when Bob and I arrived at her homestead in '92, she was away. Her daughter, Ruth, explained that Pirip had misunderstood the dates, and told me sadly that husbands had opposed the women's association and some women became contentious. Then, in a payback raid, many local homes were burned. Men went away and their women followed.

"Mama Pirip hasn't given up," Ruth, declared as we left to explore other parts of her country.

"Damn, damn, damn," I muttered under my breath as we drove away, frustrated at the frenetic pace of our lives, shaped by dates and schedules. Pirip would be disappointed again.

Bob and I traveled among riverine people where we saw close-knit family groups meeting their needs through barter; women were highly esteemed for their fishing skills. Young men, wanting to reconfirm their clan identities, were reviving initiation rites suppressed by missionaries.

The meaning of "progress" eluded me as Agua drove us to Minj on another journey in '93.

"Do you have a family now, Agua?" Bob asked.

"Yes, I have two children. They live with their mother among my people in the mountains. I have a van, and I stay with them on weekends."

"Has your job changed your life?" inquired Bob and Agua grinned.

"If I did not work for wages, we would not have things like a car, better clothes, better education." Agua had four years of schooling.

"Is cash bringing any problems?" Bob asked, and Agua looked grim.

"In Hagen, there is much gambling, drinking beer, even raping women. Some men are making homemade guns from pipes and not long ago, the post office caught guns coming through the mail. They traced them to a missionary; he was importing guns."

"To sell?" I asked in horror. Agua shrugged.

At Pirip's homestead, she introduced her second oldest son, Mike.

"Are you in school?" Bob asked—this was Tuesday morning.

"I've finished eighth grade, and I have two more years in secondary school, but I'm taking a year out to help with mama Pirip's work. Most younger men are no good," Mike declared. "They don't have any work, they do nothing. They just play around—they play darts, drink beer."

Four buildings stood in the compound, two still under construction—the intended guest house and another "for teaching and projects," Pirip explained. Her speech flowed between Pidgin and English now.

"The association does not have money to complete the buildings," she said when we gathered inside. "Could you help us get money from the American government? I know it gives money to people in other countries."

"I don't know how to do that," I said regretfully, explaining that aid went first to countries in which people were dying of starvation and disease.

"But it is very important to have buildings so people can see what has been done. I have worked for women for so long," Pirip said in a faltering voice.

"And you should feel proud. But what are the good things in women's lives, what would you all *not* want to change?" After a thoughtful silence, several women began to talk.

"We have freedom to work or not to work."

"The family takes care of each other."

"We always have food."

"We would not change keeping pigs. Pigs are very important, like money, for celebrations, for bride-price. Women are responsible for pigs."

I wished I could write those words on an enormous poster and mount it on the roof! Knowing little about life in other lands, these women didn't grasp the importance of what they said.

Just then, others carried in aluminum pots full of food. Today, attesting to women's growing prosperity, instead of the "heart-healthy" mumus we previously enjoyed, every morsel was unctuous with pig fat. Grease slimed my mouth and oozed down my chin as I ate a kaukau, washing it down with canned soda from a trade store.

When we stood up after eating, Pirip clutched her knee.

"Do you have a problem with your knee?" I asked.

"She has a problem with her weight," said a woman, laughing. I couldn't smile—on their customary diet, the active highlanders were lean.

My wish to understand what had shaped Pirip's feminism drew us back in '95 and '96, and her personal story emerged—haltingly, painfully, with Mike as sporadic interpreter. Here I report only the essence.

Kuru, whom Pirip had happily married, took four more wives. Apparently infertile and jealous of Pirip, the fifth wife had stabbed her and murdered her firstborn while Kuru, unfathomably, restrained Pirip.

Entrapped by a coalescence of Kuma tradition that would have blamed and shamed her had she left him, and new Christian teachings of submission and forgiveness, Pirip remained a dutiful wife and bore five more children. But she became a dauntless feminist, declaring that "The most important aim is for women to make choices, not be ruled by men."

With her permission, I published her story in a book, and took copies to her in '99. The awe, wonder, and delight she and her family expressed were profoundly moving. Her subsequent letters conveyed that her struggles gained spreading recognition through the book, and she achieved status comparable to that of a male highland leader—a "Big Man." She was elated.

Yet Pirip also wrote of her bewilderment at the turmoil in her country. Striking deals with politicians and abetting widespread corruption, multi-national corporations plundered the nation's gold, copper, and timber, poisoning streams and destroying forest cultures. Asian bank crises led to rampant inflation, increasing the cost of materials needed for the center.

A grant from New Zealand funded a small loan-low interest scheme for women, and Pirip gained status as a project advisor. But because of inexperience with cash management as well as inflation, many women were unable to repay their loans. Pirip was often blamed.

Furthermore, with rivalries among women continuing, Pirip's struggle to attain official recognition of the South Wahgi Women's Association was prolonged. When it was accomplished and the buildings were completed, a gala opening was planned. Unbelievably, though, the first Wahgi Valley twister in Pirip's lifetime destroyed the buildings. She vowed to continue her efforts, but a long silence ensued.

On September 8, '03, news streaked across the globe. By e-mail!

"From Pirip Kuru: we wish to inform that we have lost our father and husband, Mr. Kuru, on the 8th August, 2003. After our ceremonial activities, we are now looking forward to staying together as a family unit to looking after ourselves. We hope everything at your end is ok. Good luck and may the good Lord bless you all." Signed by her eldest son, Collin.

I had long believed that Kuru's support of Pirip's feminist efforts expressed contrition about his earlier cruelty, and I e-mailed my sadness. The response came soon:

"Dear Audrey Mccollum,

Hello and thank you very much for the e-mail. The e-mail that you used is in the new building of the Provincial Council of Women in Western Highlands Province and Mama Pirip is the executive member of the province and she is the President of the Minj District Council of Women so on behalf of her, you can use the office e-mail."

"Mama and the Provincial Council of Women's President Mrs. Paula Mek recently started Literacy school at their center in Mt Hagen. And we will also conduct another Literacy school here in our district when the building is completed.

"We see that you have done a lot to make the book known to every race on the globe. Thank you . . . and it was very kind of you to send us the photo of your two grandsons, their life is full of good prosperity to come, tell them that we are sending our Love and best wishes to them and families.

"Sad days, we are all very sorry to hear that you and Mr. Bob will not make it to Papua New Guinea once again due to Mr. Bob's health but it doesn't matter we'll always communicate until your family and ours will one day meet.

That's all and may the lord bless your family."

Mrs. Pirip Kuru and son Mr. Mike Nomb Keyessan

At Eden's Edge

Ellen Dissanayake

On the pavement, slim-hipped, tight trousered touts
Smile conspiratorially
And offer in three languages
To help me buy gems, find a hotel.
Like the shopkeepers, they turn away when it is revealed
That my misleading aspect has a local habitation and a name,
Is not therefore likely to dispense fiscal or carnal largesse.

On the path homeward, a bell rings—
My white face—and reflexively
Children who used to hid behind *akka's* skirts
Call out in English "Where are you going?"
"Give money!" "Toffee!" "Two rupees!"
Their elder brothers, hitching at their sarongs,
Snigger, boldly say "Hel-lo," "Tch-ch,"
Even though my European eyes survey the ground
More modestly than any monk or Kandyan maid's.

Resembling in size and shade the enterprising men
Who once gauged and packaged the bounty of this favored land
And arranged for its lucrative transfer elsewhere,
I can hardly complain of being treated as an object for exploitation.
Turn-about, as they say, is not unfair.

One must appreciate the irony:
It is I, the Westerner, who now seek moderation and repose,
While Lanka hastens to discard her measured ways
And fall, derelict, at the feet of a bloated, outmoded image,
Grinning Mammon.

Yet Irony is not all. There is Pathos as well.
For when Lanka regrets what has been lost
(Nay, headlong thrown unheedingly away),
It will be too late.

This was the last paradise.
There will be no more Edens
(As I, by chance or fortune, fleetingly found)—
Not even short-term ones—
To flee to.

Jenny Matthews, *Beach Camp, Gaza, October 25, 2000*

Fences of Enclosure, Windows of Possibility

Naomi Klein

A few months ago, while riffling through my column clippings searching for a lost statistic, I noticed a couple of recurring themes and images. The first was the fence. The image came up again and again: barriers separating people from previously public resources, locking them away from much needed land and water, restricting their ability to move across borders, to express political dissent, to demonstrate on public streets, even keeping politicians from enacting policies that make sense for the people who elected them.

Some of these fences are hard to see, but they exist all the same. A virtual fence goes up around schools in Zambia when an education "user fee" is introduced on the advice of the World Bank, putting classes out of the reach of millions of people. A fence goes up around the family farm in Canada when government policies turn small-scale agriculture into a luxury item, unaffordable in a landscape of tumbling commodity prices and factory farms. There is a real if invisible fence that goes up around clean water in Soweto when prices skyrocket owing to privatization, and residents are forced to turn to contaminated sources. And there is a fence that goes up around the very idea of democracy when Argentina is told it won't get an International Monetary Fund loan unless it further reduces social spending, privatizes more resources and eliminates supports to local industries, all in the midst of an economic crisis deepened by those very policies. These fences, of course, are as old as colonialism. "Such usurious operations put bars around free nations," Eduardo Galeano wrote in *Open Veins of Latin America*. He was referring to the terms of a British loan to Argentina in 1824.

Fences have always been a part of capitalism, the only way to protect property from would-be bandits, but the double standards propping up these fences have, of late, become, increasingly blatant. Expropriation of corporate holdings may be the greatest sin any socialist government can commit in the eyes of the international financial markets (just ask Venezuela's Hugo Chavez or Cuba's Fidel Castro). But the asset protection guaranteed to companies under free trade deals did not extend to the Argentine citizens who deposited their life savings in Citibank, Scotiabank and HSBC accounts and now find that most of their money has simply disappeared. Neither did the market's reverence for private wealth embrace the U.S. employees of Enron, who found that they had been "locked out" of their privatized retirement portfolios, unable to sell even as Enron executives were frantically cashing in their own stocks.

Meanwhile, some very necessary fences are under attack: in the rush to privatization, the barriers that once existed between many public and private spaces—keeping advertisements out of schools, for instance, profit-making interests out of health care, or news outlets from acting purely as promotional vehicles for their owners' other holdings—have nearly all been leveled. Every protected public space has been cracked open, only to be re-enclosed by the market.

Another public-interest barrier under serious threat is the one separating genetically modified crops from crops that have not yet been altered. The seed giants have done such a remarkably poor job of preventing their tampered seeds from blowing into neighboring fields, taking root, and cross-pollinating, that in many parts of the world, eating GMO-free is no longer even an option—the entire food supply has been contaminated. The fences that protect the public interest seem to be fast disappearing, while the ones that restrict our liberties keep multiplying.

When I first noticed that the image of the fence kept coming up in discussion, debates and in my own writing, it seemed significant to me. After all, the past decade of economic integration has been fuelled by promises of barriers coming down, of increased mobility and greater freedom. And yet twelve years after the celebrated collapse of the Berlin Wall, we are surrounded by fences yet again, cut off—from one another, from the earth and from our own ability to imagine that change is possible. The economic process that goes by the benign euphemism "globalization" now reaches into every aspect of life, transforming every activity and natural resource into a measured and owned commodity. As the Hong Kong—based labor researcher Gerard Greenfield points out, the current stage of capitalism is not simply about trade in the traditional sense of selling more products across borders. It is also about feeding the market's insatiable need for growth by redefining as "products" entire sectors that were previously considered part of "the commons" and not for sale. The invading of the public by the private has reached into categories such as health and education, of course, but also ideas, genes, seeds, now purchased, patented and fenced off, as well as traditional aboriginal remedies, plants, water and even human stem cells. With copyright now the U.S.'s single largest export (more than manufactured goods or arms), international trade law must be understood not only as taking down selective barriers to trade but more accurately as a process that systematically puts up new barriers—around knowledge, technology and newly privatized resources. These Trade Related Intellectual Property Rights are what prevent farmers from replanting their Monsanto patented seeds and make it illegal for poor countries to manufacture cheaper generic drugs to get to their needy populations.

Globalization is now on trial because the other side of all these virtual fences are real people, shut out of schools, hospitals, workplaces, their own farms, homes and communities. Mass privatization and deregulation have bred armies of locked-out people, whose services are no longer needed, whose lifestyles are written off as "backward," whose basic needs go unmet. These fences of social exclusion can discard an entire industry, and they can also write off an entire country, as has happened to Argentina. In the case of Africa, essentially an entire continent can find itself exiled to the global shadow world, off the map and off the news, appearing only during wartime when its citizens are looked on with suspicion as potential militia members, would-be terrorists or anti-American fanatics.

In fact, remarkably few of globalization's fenced-out people turn to violence. Most simply move: from countryside to city, from country to country. And that's when they come face to face with distinctly unvirtual fences, the ones made of chain link and razor wire, reinforced with concrete and guarded with machine guns. Whenever I hear the phrase "free trade," I can't help picturing the caged factories I visited in the Philippines and Indonesia that are all surrounded by gates, watchtowers and soldiers—to keep the highly subsidized products from leaking out and the union organizers from getting in. I think, too, about a recent trip to the South Australian desert where I visited the infamous Woomera detention center. Located five hundred kilometers from the nearest city, Woomera is a former military base that has been converted into a privatized refugee holding pen, owned by a subsidiary of the U.S. security firm Wackenhut. At Woomera, hundreds of Afghan and Iraqi refugees, fleeing oppression and dictatorship in their own countries, are so desperate for the world to see what is going on behind the fence that they stage hunger strikes, jump off the roofs of their barracks, drink shampoo, and sew their mouths shut.

These days, newspapers are filled with gruesome accounts of asylum seekers attempting to make it across national borders by hiding themselves among the products that enjoy so much more mobility than they do. In December 2001, the bodies of eight Romanian refugees, including two children, were discovered in a cargo container filled with office furniture; they had asphyxiated during the long journey at sea. The same year, the dead bodies of two more refugees were discovered in Eau Claire, Wisconsin, in a shipment of bathroom fixtures. The year before, fifty-four Chinese refugees from Fujian province suffocated in the back of a delivery truck in Dover, England.

All these fences are connects: the real ones, made of steel and razor wire, are needed to enforce the virtual ones, the ones that put resources and wealth out of the hands of so many. It simply isn't possible to lock away this much of our collective wealth without an accompanying strategy to control popular unrest and mobility. Security firms do their biggest business in the cities where the gap between rich and poor is greatest—Johannesburg, São Paulo, New Delhi—selling iron gates, armored cars, elaborate alarm systems and renting out armies of private guards. Brazilians, for instance, spend US$4.5 billion a year on private security, and the country's 400,000 armed rent-a-cops outnumber actual police officers by almost four to one. In deeply divided South Africa, annual spending on private security has reached US$1.6 billion, more than three times what the government spends each year on affordable housing. It now seems that these gated compounds protecting the haves from the have-nots are microcosms of what is fast becoming a global security state—not a global village intent on lowering walls and barriers, as we were promised, but a network of fortresses connected by highly militarized trade corridors.

If this picture seems extreme, it may only be because most of us in the West rarely see the fences and the artillery. The gated factories and refugee detention centers remain tucked away in remote places, less able to pose a direct challenge to the seductive rhetoric of the borderless world. But over the past few years, some fences have intruded into full view—often, fittingly, during the summits where this brutal model of globalization is advanced. It is now taken for granted that if world leaders want to get together to discuss a new trade deal, they will need to build a modern-day fortress to protect themselves from public rage, complete with armored tanks, tear gas, water cannons and attack dogs. When Quebec City hosted the Summit of the Americas in April 2001, the Canadian government took the unprecedented step of building a cage around, not just the conference center, but the downtown core, forcing residents to show official documentation to get to their homes and workplaces. Another popular strategy is to hold the summits in inaccessible locations: the 2002 G8 meeting was held deep in the Canadian Rocky Mountains, and the 2001 WTO meeting took place in the repressive Gulf State of Qatar, where the emir bans political protests. The "war on terrorism" has become yet another fence to hide behind, used by summit organizers to explain why public shows of dissent just won't be possible this time around or, worse, to draw threatening parallels between legitimate protesters and terrorists bent on destruction.

But what are reported as menacing confrontations are often joyous events, as much experiments in alternative ways of organizing societies as criticisms of existing models. The first time I participated in one of these counter-summits, I remember having the distinct feeling that some sort of political portal was opening up—a gateway, a window, "a crack in history," to use Subcomandante Marcos's beautiful phrase. This opening had little to do with the broken window at the local McDonald's, the image so favored by television cameras; it was something else: a sense of possibility, a blast of fresh air, oxygen rushing to the brain. These protests—which are actually week-long marathons of intense education on global politics, late-night strategy sessions in six-way simultaneous translation, festivals of music and street theatre—are like stepping into a parallel universe. Overnight, the site is transformed into a kind of alternative global city where urgency replaces resignation, corporate logos need armed guards, people usurp cars, art is everywhere, strangers talk to each other, and the prospect of a radical change in political course does not seem like an odd and anachronistic idea but the most logical thought in the world.

Even the heavy-handed security measures have been co-opted by activists into part of the message: the fences that surround the summits become metaphors for an economic model that exiles billions to poverty and exclusion. Confrontations are staged at the fence—but not only the ones involving sticks and bricks: tear-gas canisters have been flicked back with hockey sticks, water cannons have been irreverently challenged with toy water pistols and buzzing helicopters mocked with swarms of paper airplanes. During the Summit of the Americas in Quebec City, a group of activists built a medieval-style wooden catapult, wheeled it up to the three-meter-high fence that enclosed the downtown and lofted teddy bears over the top. In Prague, during a meeting of the World Bank and the International

Monetary Fund, the Italian direct-action group Tute Bianche decided not to confront the black-clad riot police dressed in similarly threatening ski masks and bandannas; instead, they marched to the police line in white jumpsuits stuffed with rubber tires and Styrofoam padding. In a standoff between Darth Vader and an army of Michelin Men, the police couldn't win. Meanwhile, in another part of the city, the steep hillside leading up to the conference center was scaled by a band of "pink fairies" dressed in burlesque wigs, silver-and-pink evening wear and platform shoes. These activists are quite serious in their desire to disrupt the current economic order, but their tactics reflect a dogged refusal to engage in classic power struggles: their goal is not to take power for themselves but to challenge power centralization on principle.

Other kinds of windows are opening as well, quiet conspiracies to reclaim privatized spaces and assets for public use. Maybe it's students kicking ads out of their classrooms, or swapping music on-line, or setting up independent media centers with free software. Maybe it's Thai peasants planting organic vegetables on over-irrigated golf courses, or landless farmers in Brazil cutting down fences around unused lands and turning them into farming co-operatives. Maybe it's Bolivian workers reversing the privatization of their water supply, or South African township residents reconnecting their neighbors' electricity under the slogan Power to the People. And once reclaimed, these spaces are also being remade. In neighborhood assemblies, at city councils, in independent media centers, in community-run forests and farms, a new culture of vibrant direct democracy is emerging, one that is fuelled and strengthened by direct participation, not dampened and discouraged by passive spectatorship.

Despite all the attempts at privatization, it turns out that there are some things that don't want to be owned. Music, water, seeds, electricity, ideas—they keep bursting out of the confines erected around them. They have a natural resistance to enclosure, a tendency to escape, to cross-pollinate, to flow through fences, and flee out open windows.

As I write this, it's not clear what will emerge from these liberated spaces, or if what emerges will be hardy enough to withstand the mounting attacks from the police and military, as the line between terrorist and activist is deliberately blurred. The question of what comes next preoccupies me, as it does everyone else who has been part of building this international movement. The question punctuates a very old and recurring story, the one about people pushing up against the barriers that try to contain them, opening up windows, breathing deeply, tasting freedom.

Kerry Stuart Coppin, *Untitled: Gathering of Women / Courtyard / Dakar, Senegal*

Waltzing Matilda

Najem Wali

translated by Marilyn Booth

All I have left from this story is a white Caribbean suit, a Panama hat, and a cassette tape that I've carried persistently in my left shirt pocket. And a pair of white shoes which, if I hadn't lost them in the course of my journey, would complement the suit, which I'm wearing now.

It must have been in the autumn. October, to be more exact. Spring doesn't tend to go on for very long in Basra, and one could wear clothes such as these only in a moderate season. It almost had to be October twentieth, in fact, since I recall now that I heard a particular sentence coming from Mathilda's mouth, words that ring in my ears even now.

"Thirty years, as of today—you've gotten that far. Time to leave this graveyard, and you've got to do it."

Our unit had come to Basra twenty-seven days before. Unlike other units, we weren't sent directly to the front. Ours was of a different makeup and mission: we were a collection of airborne storm troopers, one of those new squads that had emerged with the war. And since chemical weapons hadn't yet been used (in all probability), they had kept us in the city, waiting for an appropriate time to deploy us.

At that time Basra was packed solid with military units, so much so that they couldn't find any place to lodge us; neither the naval base nor the Abu'l-Qasim camp had any space at all. They did not want to send us as far away as the air base in Ash Shuayba or Az Zubayr; clearly, they thought it important to keep us near the Shatt al-Arab, the broad waterway formed by the Tigris and Euphrates, and the borders. So they bivouacked us in al-Watani Street, in a dormitory belonging to the University of Basra that had housed Arab students from outside the country, most of whom had disappeared after the breakout of war. Any remnants of this throng were sent to the new residential buildings erected for the students near Karmat Ali City.

That's why we were only a ferry ride away from the other side of Basra. Every quarter hour, as long as there was no bombing, the ferry crossed the wide expanse of river. In that direction—toward Tannumah—the border was no more than twenty kilometers away.

But that was the prewar geography. Once the battles had started, the front began right at the Shatt, down from the corniche, and with this scenario we were separated from the war front by only a trench filled with dirty water, which one could cross swimming if things came to that.

That was the time when visiting Mathilda became part of my routine. I had known her since my university days. Mulhem, my friend from Baghdad, and I used to go to her late in the afternoon, after classes were over for the day. Or we would walk down directly from the residential quarters. But this time I couldn't visit her unless the battalion had gone on exercises and scouting duties. I was placed with six other soldiers. They called us the "hall watch" because the battalion adjutant, after studying our files which had come from the security authorities in our cities and towns, believed that we—assuredly—comprised a danger to the Iraqi army as long as we held on to our weapons. He didn't know what to do with us, until he came up with the idea of handing that duty to us. We—the "magnificent seven," as we called ourselves—stayed behind to mount guard over the two large halls where the soldiers slept as well as a smaller chamber allotted to the officers. When my duties were done, I would leave without anyone taking notice.

Mathilda was, in some sort of way, my own special secret. Even at night we soldiers couldn't be there because of the officers' presence, for they were there to drink away every evening. I slipped away to her every day between noon and two P.M. I would rap on the windowpane twice, hard, then once lightly, followed by three more quick taps. At that, she would push aside the red curtain and, when she had satisfied herself that it was I, she would open the door for me. I would come in to the tavern which wasn't normally open by day.

Mathilda was in her early sixties as far as I know, and I was just turning thirty. As I said, it must have been October, precisely the twentieth, because as I remember, she was the one who, a week before, had decided on celebrating my birthday.

"Don't you remember," she asked me, "it was your friend Mulhem who gave me the task, one time, of procuring a bottle of champagne."

She laughed and went on. "He told me it was for the sake of celebrating the birthday of our stubborn, heedless friend."

I'd be the first to admit that Mulhem had taken me by surprise on countless matters. My impending birthday wouldn't have passed through my mind if it hadn't been for his repeated reminders. I had remembered it only once—and that was in his presence. Joking, Mathilda had proposed that we consider the first of July an Iraqi national holiday, since it was entered as everyone's birthdate on all Iraqi IDs.[1]

"Wednesday, the twentieth of October, at 10:33," I said almost automatically. My mind was wholly taken up by the image of my grandfather, inspector of date production in the Basra environs, who in his entire life had committed but one good deed, which was to record the day, month, year, and indeed the very hour in which I was born in his own private register, which he carried in his vest pocket as long as he lived.

At the time, as I recall it, Mathilda (to whose joking we were accustomed) had a ready response. "So was your grandfather sitting between your mama's thighs, with a stopwatch in his hand?"

Mathilda spoke formal Arabic with us. It was that sort of Arabic, she claimed, that she had learned effortlessly. But whenever the alcohol rose in her head she would start reminiscing in the Basran dialect. Had it been up to her, that's the only Arabic she would have spoken. But as she would say, she spoke formal Arabic "automatically," ever since first hearing the interminable commentaries of high officials in the presence of her husband, back in the fifties, as they warned him against his partiality to Basra. Her husband had been the minister of date production in the forties. He had brought her with him to Basra after one of his trips to Greece, during World War Two.

Though she was perfectly aware that countless stories swirled about her person and had since her arrival in Iraq, she did not tell us the whole story in one sitting. She related it in installments to pique our interest, luring us into a state where we sometimes believed we were living in a world of the imagination.

Thus had the people of Basra woven their many stories about her. Indeed, my grandmother even insisted that Mathilda, and no one else, was a peasant's daughter who'd been snatched away by an Englishman, and now she had returned married to a government minister! But my grandfather made fun of that story, even as he retold her story to me on different occasions. As usual, he remembered the very day and hour, the month and the year, for he had remained faithful to his profession as an accountant even in matters that had nothing to do with numbers and sums.

So it was that before he embarked on his story, he would pull his little notebook from his vest pocket and read the date. On the eighteenth of April in the year 1945, at 9:17, the three inspectors of dates, who were in the midst of counting and inspecting trays of premier-quality dates stuffed with almonds and walnuts and destined for China and Great Britain, had to leave work, leave the storeroom of the International Railroad Station where the trays were stacked, and go to the district authority building to supervise the array of dates and milk under preparation for presentation to visitors, and to be present among the delegation collected there to welcome the minister and his madame.

On that spring day—my grandfather would say—we saw a young woman in her twenties, of medium height, thin but elegantly so, her eyes large and black, arm in arm with the minister, who was dressed in a white suit, panama hat, and white shoes. The young woman was carrying a white parasol that hid her dark blonde hair, which he described as having a lighter streak, worn in a short cut. Resembling the hair of Greta Garbo, would add my father, devoted filmgoer, who was dogged about adding his beloved phrase every time he heard my grandfather telling the story. And that would draw my grandfather to comment. "Hero from Gabo land . . . may your future be promising . . . discoverer of penicillin."

In any case, my grandfather did not stint in describing her beauty, swearing that her eyes were full of a magic he had seen only once in his life, in the eyes of a sea nymph who appeared to them in the Gulf as they prayed the dusk prayer on deck, en route to Mecca. Otherwise—he would say in response when I expressed my doubts about what he had said—what could have made the second bowl of milk, which she requested from him because she loved the milk and dates given as a gift to the delegation, drop from his hand when he looked into her eyes as he passed the bowl to her?

On that day it had been exactly two years since their wedding, and for the occasion the district put together an anniversary celebration. That evening they drank and danced to exhaustion—the tango and the salsa. At that time only a few knew the source of those dances; or her origins would have been guessed from the start.

She seemed insistent on keeping her origins a mystery. In front of us she was adamant about calling herself a citizen of the world. She said she had left her village of Macondo, surrounded by sites where the dolphin played, long before. But the world citizen settled upon her future that evening, and allowed herself to choose, this time. She chose Basra as the place she would remain in forever, and because she was so tired of departures, as she admitted to us one time.

And in the middle of the night, said my grandfather—for Mathilda had no desire at all to relate these events—the customers at the Shtura Hotel, where the minister and his wife stayed, woke up to Mathilda's screams. Those who rushed to the room found the minister dead. The doctor who performed the autopsy reported that he had eaten a great number of dates that evening, and because of his high cholesterol level his body (he was a man in his fifties) could not handle it. There was no logic to this official cause, since dates contain no cholesterol.

In the course of the next two days, the minister was buried in the Cemetery of Hasan al-Basri in Zubayr. Mathilda stayed on for a week, sleeping at his grave, only to surprise everyone with her decision to stay in Basra. With the money she inherited, she bought the tavern opposite Mary's Bar and in front of the national playgrounds. Mathilda wouldn't comment on the story when I told it to her. The only thing she said came in response to my question: "Why did you decide to stay in Basra?"

"I fell in love with Basra, love at first sight, *habuubi*."

When I didn't leave the subject easily she gave me another answer. "I'm a citizen of the world, and Basra is the Macondo of the East."

I would insist. "I don't think Macondo exists except in the mind of García Marquez."

She would laugh at that. "Macondo is what created García Marquez, not the other way around." She stared into the distance and added, "Isn't Basra a reality?"

So I ask her again. "Is that why you're so fond of its people?"

And at the time a sort of wonder glints in her eyes. "Basrans have something of the Caribbean soul in them. Departures, traveling—that's destined for them. If not on the high seas, they're sailors roving across the land." After a short silence, she adds, "The city lacks only dolphins to be a Caribbean city."

It seemed to me that the story of the dolphins might be the most legendary of the stories, as opposed to what Mulhem thought. He insisted on the truth of the whole story. And before Mathilda launched her story, she brought out a small chest to show us a lovely group of pictures she had collected.

"Pictures are your traveling case," I told her.

"No, they're the essence of my life," she said.

In more than one of them we saw the image of a man in a white Caribbean-style outfit, wearing a Panama hat and white shoes.

"Pablo." She was pointing to the man. "That's how we rested after dancing to 'Guantanamera.'"

She was stretched out next to him, in the same costume I've seen on that woman in some painting or other, but I can't remember which one. (Could it be a Gauguin?) Dark skin, tall, dark blonde hair with a yellow flower to one side. In the photo, they're lying close together, laughing, a clear blue sky stretching above them, its far reaches touching an endless sea, small waves showing here and there. And the swaying palms on the shore cast their branches to both sides, brown sands yielding beneath their bodies and white sea flowers above.

"What's 'Guantanamera'?"

"Originally a Cuban song, in which a man's speaking to his Caribbean love."

Mathilda showed us more than thirty photos of herself with Pablo. She looked happy in all of them, and Pablo's face was positively alight.

"Pablo came from Spain after the collapse of the republic."

So she was the Caribbean love and Pablo was the fine Spaniard who had come to Macondo, encumbered with his country's collapse.

Silent, she noticed our wonder. "Actually, he came to the island, as he told me later, to join up with the armed peasants."

She put the photos back into the little chest, and we could see a wistfully tender look on her face.

"Once the soldiers chased him for an entire night. They followed him from Cartagena de las Indias until they surrounded him in the outskirts of Macondo, where the dolphin sites are. In that area and precisely on nights when the moon is full, the female dolphin came onto the shore searching for handsome males."

She laughed, and then her voice became more serious.

"That evening I was in the Macondo suburbs. The sea was still clinging to my skin when I saw him, wearing a Caribbean suit, Panama hat, and white shoes."

She turned her back on us, as if she was fully occupied in putting the little chest back on the table next to the wall. But to tell the truth that sea smell had never stopped emanating from Mathilda.

And so that is how Mathilda would take us with her to worlds of which we had absolutely no knowledge. And why not? For when we first came to her, my friend Mulhem and I, it was another era. There was no war going on. Mulhem wasn't a prisoner. I wasn't a soldier in the airborne storm troopers division. Basra was at its most splendid, its evenings resplendent and alive. Mulhem was studying English literature, his mind occupied with Byron and Yeats and Coleridge. And I was studying Spanish literature, all caught up in Lorca, Machado, and Alberti. Mathilda's tavern was crammed with sailors coming from everywhere. In a word, I'd say that her bar was the center of the world as far as we were concerned, and before time bound us with its storm and tossed every one of us into a different corner.

I wasn't the only one having these thoughts. She was thinking the same. When she talked of those days everything came to life all at once, as if things had happened yesterday rather than ten years or more ago, as if she was determined not to get old.

"We age only in relation to others."

I would tell her that she hadn't changed much. She would shake her head and laugh, and say to me, "Thanks for your flattery. But then, you were always different from the others."

I hadn't said it to flatter. She really hadn't changed very much, especially in her personality. When she opened the door, she still would say to me, "Come on in, lo-o-o-ve! Habuubi!"

She pronounced that sentence the same way every time, knowing that I loved her Basran habuubi. I would find her in a kitchen apron, her hair every which way, as if she'd just gotten up from sleep. She'd have a kitchen knife in one hand, and at the bar there would be a large plate of peeled cucumber, sliced tomatoes, peeled yams. She was in the midst of chopping onions on a wooden cutting board. To be fair, I should mention that she always stopped working for a few minutes, when I arrived. She would pull out a bottle of something she had made herself. Anything but *araq*.

"Araq is the Iraqi suicide drink." That's what she would say, jokingly, alluding to a comment I had made to Mulhem in front of her the very first time we had come to her tavern. Ever since that night, she'd remembered that I don't drink araq. I might not have been so persistent about visiting her throughout those years had I not known of her distinctive liquor supply, varieties that her friends among the sailors brought her from all over or that she made herself from grapes or dates.

"We'll put it on the bill?"

Again, jokingly, reminding me of the never-ending period when I was always broke. She would put a small glass on the table for me, and another for her, and pour into both, but she didn't drink while I was drinking. She just clinked her glass against mine saying sahha! To your health! In all languages. *Yamas. Saluta. Salud. Cheers. L'chaim.*

L'chaim always came last. "I know you are a good fellow, different from the rest," she would say to me.

And then I could take my first sip, while she continued to slice yams and tomatoes. She would take a drink only when she heard the distant voices of the battalion chanting, "Oh, you cub of Zayn al-Qaws, greet the Al-Qastal, tell him we've come, we've come and not gone."[2]

She knew it was time for me to leave. She put on the cassette tape that Mulhem had given to her at the beginning of the war. She raised her glass to knock it against mine, and we drank in silence and quickly. A secret, shared gloom enfolded us, Mulhem's absence mingled with the coming of the battalion.

"I've gotten tired of those wretched songs," she would say. So I teased her a little. "Your sentence is an appeal for destruction, like that l'chaim. Annihilation." After a sigh, she would answer. "Is there an annihilation greater than the punishment of hearing these songs?" Mathilda sounded sad; she truly seemed to want to leave everything behind, this time.

"I'm tired. Everything has changed. My tavern is no longer what it was, and Basra is no longer Macondo."

That was the refrain with which she ended her conversation every time, and so ran the course of our days. Nothing except repeating the stories of the past. Did we have anything else left to us? She was the one who talked, more than I did. She complained about the situation in two or three sentences, no more, but she showed no real desire to leave, and appeared stalwart in front of events, or as if she was struggling to hold on—stubbornly—to whatever determination she possessed. At least, that's how it looked to me. Until the day came when she let me know that she simply could not bear it any longer.

"I'll leave. I can't stand the officers in my tavern any more, or the sounds of the streets being hit, the big guns strafing, airplanes circling up there."

Sensing that my dejection was getting the better of me, a grief she could easily make out on my face, she would say as she accompanied me to the door, "Maybe you need to go away, too. Tomorrow you'll be thirty, habuubi."

I would just shake my head, confused, and at that she patted me on the shoulder. As if she knew exactly what was going through my head, she asked, "Are you thinking about Mulhem?" Seeing that I didn't know where to turn, she gave me a kiss on the cheek and added, "You're a good fellow, you're different from the other young men, like him, the two of you are made of different clay but with one spirit. He also wanted to leave."

Then, as if a crazy idea had occurred to her, she added, "I've got some special champagne for you here. Tomorrow we'll celebrate your birthday." As I went out, the words of the song accompanied me, all the way to the hall, where soon enough the anthems of the squadron would assail me.

> Wasted and wounded . . .
> I'm an innocent victim of a blinded alley
> And tired of all these soldiers here
> No one speaks English and everything's broken . . .
> Old Bushmill's I staggered, you buried the dagger . . .
> To go waltzing Matilda, waltzing Matilda
> You'll go a waltzing Matilda with me . . .

Mulhem arrived in Basra before I did. He was attached to the missile battery. Actually, their unit had bivouacked in Al Faw. One day he claimed to have an illness that could only be treated in the military hospital in Basra. Luckily for him the physician who examined him was a young fellow, a recent graduate. The doctor found out his pretense and said right out, laughing, "Tell me the reason you're here. A girl?"

Mulhem laughed too, and told him candidly that he longed to visit Mathilda and to give her "this cassette," taking it out of his pocket.

Mathilda was so happy to see him. "Do you know that the two of you are completely unlike the rest of the students and soldiers, I don't know why!" she said to me when she had me listen to the tune for the first time. I answered her teasingly, "Maybe because Mulhem's aunt is a poet, like our famous Nazik al-Mala'ika. And me, well, maybe because my grandfather told me about you."

She laughed. "Even though you are different, there's something the two of you share, a sort of mysterious transparency." Then we'd start in nostalgically on the old days. Or rather, she did most of the talking. She always translated the lyrics to the song because she knew that my English was too rudimentary to help me understand what the song was talking about. When she joked with me, saying, "Mulhem knows English better than you do," I would counter with, "My Spanish is better than his." And then she would recall her mother tongue, to which she hadn't alluded at all. But I was sure I knew it.

"*Hala.*"

"No one says this 'Hala,'" I would tell her, "unless they've known it since child-hood."

With a seriousness tinged with sarcasm and traces of pain, she asked, "How would *you* know?"

"Mathilda, you know that I was in the Spanish department at the university, and you know that Mulhem's degree is in English."

"Listen to me," she said with a sigh. "Concentrate on what I'm saying. And tell me if what you were saying is true." So I listened, as she seized my arm as if to pre-pare me for the next scene.

> I'm an innocent victim of a blinded alley . . .
> Now the dogs are barking and the taxi cab's parking
> A lot they can do for me . . .
> Your silhouette window light
> To go waltzing Matilda, waltzing Matilda
> You'll go a waltzing Matilda with me.

And when the song filled me with melancholy, even if I didn't know exactly what the words were saying, I knew that what I had said was bunk.

So then I confess to her, and she says, "Forget it." Then she begins talking about the song and its history, and about Tom Waits. "Did you know that originally it was a song sung by the first Australians? Before the English came in, the native Australian would leave home with a bag on his shoulder, and when he stopped to rest on the road he would set a fire and start singing to Matilda, who was really his traveling bag."

I ask her if these were the same words we were hearing now.

"No." She began to sing the original lyrics.

"So, what is the difference between that and the new song?"

She told me that Tom Waits, a white singer of the blues, had revised it to say something, this time around, about the soldiers coming home from the Vietnam War.

I told her I felt the song was talking about all soldiers.

"That's why Mulhem gave it to me."

We're quiet. She tells me a secret, shyly.

"Do you know, the last time he was here, before leaving for his last trip and dis-appearing . . ." She was quiet for a little. "He asked me to waltz with him. He told me he couldn't take it and was going to turn himself in."

I drained my glass, and asked her if we could rewind the tape and dance together. She opened her arms and leaned toward me across the table, gave me a kiss on the cheek, and said, "I have another song here that's for you, and that's what we'll dance to."

That happened on the last day I saw her. Her cheeks went rosy when she said it, and there was a shine in her eyes, a flash like you see in the eyes of teenagers. Then she was as before, sitting across the table from me. She turned up the sound, and at the same time, with her other hand, she adjusted the yellow flower fixed to the left, among her blonde curls.

"Do you like this dress? I put it on specially for your birthday."

She was wearing a blue ensemble, embroidered with birds and waves and white sea flowers. I nodded. She pushed over the glass of champagne, perhaps the last one, from the first bottle on the table.

"We'll kill the second bottle!" she said, pulling another bottle from the refrigerator. "We'll drink everything we have, today. The bar is reserved for us, and only for us, today."

I laughed and remembered the little sign that she had hung on the door: Bar closed temporarily due to illness. As I drank the new glass rapidly, I said to her, "Yes, we'll drink everything today, even araq."

My voice must have sounded sad, because she put down the glass that was already between her lips and looked at me. I looked down. "Don't tell me, as he did, that it's your last day here!"

Mathilda, of the intuition that never gets it wrong, knew that we were on the point of leaving. She had noticed how I came to her that noontime, not my usual self. I nodded, while my fingers stroked the glass that both palms gripped. She poured me a new glass.

"We got orders to move. We're leaving."

She gave me a gentle look and said something in Spanish. "*Tienes el carino de Pablo.*" You have Pablo's gentleness. I didn't say anything, because I knew that it was she who would talk this time. For a moment we remained silent, though, drinking and listening to Tom Waits, until I saw her moving suddenly behind the bar, in the direction of her room. She disappeared but was back in moments, in her hand a travel bag made of treebark. She set it down on the table. She gazed at me, and then opened the bag to take out a white Caribbean suit, a Panama hat, and a pair of white shoes.

"Pablo's suit. I still have it. A birthday present for you." She pushed it across to me. "Take it. Wear it tonight. It brings luck."

I took it.

"Pablo didn't want to wear it, that night when we were in the harbor at Piraeus."

I didn't understand her meaning. I figured it was a hallucination brought on by the stuff we were drinking. Until I remembered the story she had told us about the two of them.

Pablo had fled after the revolt of the fishermen and smugglers in Macondo and Cartagena de las Indias had fizzled. He'd gone to Greece. And she carried his small treebark case and crossed the ocean with him. Fifteen months he fought at the side of the partisans against the royalist forces supported by the English army. She moved with him all over Greece. No matter; she herself didn't go into battle, except that Pablo's comrades insisted she accompany them, because she brought luck with her wherever they went, "like the female dolphin," as they said over and over in her presence.

One day Pablo came to her saying that his comrades had decided to send him to Italy to fight with the partisans in San Remo. She didn't understand these things but he told her that his Spanish origins would help him to move freely in the areas under the control of the Italian government, since Spain and Italy were allies during the war. In any case she wanted to follow him again, and she would follow him to the ends of the world. For, "this is the destiny of the dolphin female when she loves."

The port was in an unbelievable state of chaos that evening, as a result of the bombing by the Allies. The two of them had to get to a foreign-registered freighter that would be going via Italy. But that voyage did not happen. They lost each other in the crowds.

Mathilda did not despair. It seems, though, that she ended up in a different ship, one that carried dates. When the bombing ended, she was standing with the little traveling case in one hand, and an elegant man whose features had a touch of Caribbean was standing in front of her. At first she thought he was from somewhere in South America; later on she learned that he was the Iraqi Minister of Date Production. He asked her in English, which she had a difficult time understanding, what she was doing there. She told him the story. The man smiled and told her that it was too late to change the course of things now. The ship had already begun to move. She couldn't find anything to say; she asked him where the ship was headed.

"Basra."

He asked her politely to accompany him, and so it was that she moved from the spot she had occupied, the little bag still in her hand, the case that contained the little chest carrying pictures, the white Caribbean suit, the Panama hat, and the white shoes—that bag she had carried with her on every journey.

And when she told the story, Mathilda always insisted, over and over, that because Pablo wasn't wearing those clothes, they'd had bad luck that evening.

"But the minister was wearing that very same suit when he died," I said to her lightly.

"Ah, your grandfather's story," she exclaimed, as she always did. And sighed heavily. "Forget about it, and take the suit."

I was prepared to do everything. I knew one thing only, which was that I would not walk into the university residential quarters where the army slept ever again.

As if Mathilda knew my thoughts, she said, "In war, nothing has meaning except escape or imprisonment."

I spoke with a childish stubbornness or perhaps because of the alcohol in my veins. "So did Mulhem take the other suit?"

"He was right when he called you the pigheaded one."

Her fingers stroked my temple. "Don't think of anything now except leaving. You have to get out of this cemetery." She smiled. "Tonight, Pablo's coming. One of the Argentinian sailors. An old friend, whose ship arrived a few days ago. They loaded it with dates today, and they're leaving at dawn."

To all appearances I was listening carefully, but I guess I had drunk enough to make my head spin, and certainly she noticed it. She led me to her room in back. I didn't see the round table on which sat a platter of pineapple, coconut, and other Caribbean fruits. I didn't see the old iron bed over which pictures of the saints and the white dolphins hung above the silk pillow. I didn't see the photos of the ports hung there: Bombay, Barcelona, Lattakia, Tripoli, Limasol, Agadir, Marseilles, Liverpool, Hamburg, Sao Paolo, Porto Alegra, Cartagena, Rotterdam; nor her photos with Pablo in the Caribbean suit, the Panama hat, and the white shoes. And I didn't see the two large posters of Macondo. I didn't even sense Mathilda getting me to lie down, or hear her saying, "I'll wake you up when Pablo arrives, so you can leave." I was in a stupor, from Mathilda's drinks, from the fragrance of coconut, the scent of the Caribbean that lay over the place, and the sounds coming from the record player that sat near the bed, which she turned on before she went out.

"Guantanamera . . . guajira . . . Guantanamera . . . Guantanamera . . ." As if the song was coming from very far away, while through a tiny window above my head, I saw clearly a small island swimming in the light, dolphins playing near the shores, and the palm fronds swaying, heavy with fruit. A female dolphin swam near to where I lay, by my side a mulatta woman reclining close to me, in the depths of a ship carrying dates, where I lay, in the white Caribbean suit, Panama hat, and white shoes.

Notes

1. By order of King Faisal II, whose birthday was July 1, all Iraqis born before 1958 had this date as their official birthdays.

2. Zayn al-Qaws was a border town belonging to Iran until September 22, 1980, when Saddam Hussein raised the Iraqi flag there. Al-Qaztal was an Arab military commander in the battle of Al-Qadisiya in the time of the caliph Umar bin al qatab against the Persian Imperium. The soldiers are saying that they have come to liberate this place and will not leave it.

Black Tea

Kathleen L. Housley

My black tea
　　bought in Arizona
　　brewed in New York
　　by a family
　　of Italian descent
　　from leaves picked
　　on Indian plantations
　　by women workers
　　whose wages have been cut
tastes of spring rain.

An Alternative to Progress

Bill McKibben

The eastern end of the village of Gorasin, on the edge of the Louhajang River in the district of Tangail, in the nation of Bangladesh, has no store that we would recognize, no car, no electric lines, no television. No telephone. There are just small fields, a cow, some chickens, barefoot children, banana palms swaying in the breeze. The call to prayer from a nearby muezzin drifts over the croplands. It is about as far from the center of the world as you can possibly get. And that may be the point.

Hovering over all the issues about the World Bank and the World Trade Organization and the spread of genetically modified crops, hovering over everything that's happened since the 1999 Battle of Seattle is a big question: Is there really any alternative to the General Course of things? Is there some imaginable future that does not lead through the eternal Westernization, the endless economic expansion, that is the gospel of our time? Is there some alternative to Progress?

Gorasin is one of those places that suggests there might be. "Suggests" is about as strong as I'd like to get. Alternatives get quickly overwhelmed in the modern world, co-opted or submerged beneath the staggering flow of business as usual. But, at least right now, life in Gorasin is worth a look.

If we think about Bangladesh at all, it is as a basket case. A hundred and thirty million people crowded into an area the size of Wisconsin. Constant flooding, with the regular scattering of killer cyclones. A 10-letter word for woe.

If you ask the World Bank what needs to happen in Bangladesh, their answer—detailed in a report called "Bangladesh 2020"—is to turn it into another Thailand or, better yet, another Singapore: to ramp up its growth rate, produce crops like cut flowers for export, "manage" a "transition" to urbanization, and exploit its huge supply of cheap labor to allow a leap up the development ladder. "There is no alternative to accelerated growth." If you ask Monsanto, the key is high-yielding varieties of rice, including new genetically engineered strains: "golden rice," say, designed to eliminate vitamin A deficiency. If you ask international donor agencies, the secret is more microcredit, like the pioneering Grameen Bank projects that have captured worldwide attention in recent years. "If you want to work on misery, Bangladesh is the ultimate misery you can have," says Atiq Rahman, of the Bangladesh Center for Advanced Studies, a local NGO.

Those are the standard views: that Bangladesh lives in a state of backwardness that can be "fixed" through an application of technology, capital, exposure to the discipline of the markets. To quote from the World Bank report, "Backwardness in the form of cheap labor gives Bangladesh a strong competitive potential edge." In other words, an inexhaustible supply of poor people willing to work at low wages is its greatest asset. In the words of Rahman, who co-authored the Bank report, Bangladeshis are now at a "survival" stage and need to make a "quantum leap" to some higher level of development, a leap that inevitably leads to urbanization, an export-oriented economy, more fertilizer, big electric power plants. And when you look at the country's sad statistics for nutrition, for life expectancy, for literacy, then it's easy to defend the conventional wisdom: The average person dies at 60, and the infant mortality rate is 10 times that of the United States.

But there is another way of looking at things, a Gorasin way, one developed closer to home, less despairing and less grandiose at the same time. "People say that it's a miracle Bangladesh can survive its food and energy crises, that it somehow perseveres," Sajed Kamal, a solar energy educator, told me as we walked the town's fields. "The real miracle, though, is that you could contrive a way to have a food crisis. If you stick something in the ground here, it grows." So Bangladesh, it's worth noting, is able to feed itself.

Our guides that day were the people who lived in Gorasin, who lived in small huts, smaller than trailer homes. They were showing us sesame seed plants, loofah sponge gourds, eggplants, sugarcane, bamboo. Onions, pulses, all manner of local leafy greens. All grown without pesticides, without fertilizer, and without seed imported from the laboratories of the West. Gorasin sits in a large self-declared pesticide-free zone, one of several organic oases established around the country by adherents of the Nayakrishi, or "New Agriculture" movement. The movement arose in response to numerous environmental hazards that the villagers believe were traceable to pesticides.

"When we women went to collect water, we would be affected," one villager was saying. She was twenty-something, beautiful, gregarious. "Our skin would absorb the poisons. We would get itchiness, get gastric trouble. Now we've adopted our own solution. The water is pure again."

"The cows used to eat the grass and drop dead," one man added. "And then the villagers would fight each other."

"We grew up with a saying: 'We Bengalis are made of rice and fish,'" said another man. "Then the fish started catching diseases. We are not scientists, but we made the connection between pesticide and fish death. Since we've started organic farming, the fish are now healthier and more plentiful."

"A fertilized plant jumps up fast and falls right over," said a third. "Our plants are strong and healthy. Theirs, you eat it and you get sick. The minute you say 'Nayakrishi' in the market, though, people will pay more, because they know they're saving on health care."

A few miles away, at the Nayakrishi training school for the Tangail district, 25 varieties of papaya are growing. A hundred and twelve varieties of jackfruit, all cataloged by the farmers by taste, size, color, season, habitat. Wicker baskets and clay pots in a darkened shed contain 300 varieties of local rice, 20 kinds of bitter gourd, 84 varieties of local beans.

"Do you know how much it costs to build a gene bank like the ones where botanists store plant varieties?" asks Farhad Mazhar, a founder of the Center for Development Alternatives, known by its Bengali acronym, UBINIG, the Dhaka-based NGO that helped launch the Nayakrishi movement. "No scientist can afford to catalog hundreds of varieties of rice. But farmers are doing it as part of household activity. Our little seed station has more vegetables than the national gene bank, which spends millions. But we can do it for free."

For free, and in the process, they insist, they can rejuvenate village life. Farida Akhter, Mazhar's partner running UBINIG, is one of Bangladesh's leading feminists. She set up the nation's only women's bookstore and led a long fight against contraceptive abuses by international agencies. But if you ask her what single step would do the most to improve the lot of Bengali women, she does not hesitate: "I'd want rural women to have control over seeds again. That's women's power, or was before the multinationals started selling their new varieties in the last few decades. Traditionally, the woman is the one who knows what a good seed is, what will germinate, how to store it. Maybe they like the sound of the seed when they flick it, the weight of it on the winnowers, how it looks. They'll cut a seed with their teeth and listen to the sound it makes. They know how to dry it, how many times to put it under the sun, and whether to use the morning sun or the afternoon sun. Men used to discuss with their wives what kind of crop to raise for next year. But now they listen to the seed seller. The woman has become redundant, a burden."

Farhad Mazhar was in Seattle for the WTO protests. "I strongly believe in globalization," he says. "I'm not a national chauvinist. We need more interaction at the international level. We need cultural exchanges, all that sort of thing. But that's not happening here in Bangladesh, and it's not happening in all the other countries like us. We're just a source of raw materials." Certainly not a source of ideas. Ideas flow the other way.

Bangladesh became a country in 1971, following a brief civil war. "Civil war" is actually a misnomer: Pakistan, backed rhetorically by the United States, carried out what may have been the most efficient genocide of the 20th century, killing as many as 3 million Bengalis in nine months before a resistance army aided by Indian troops drove them out. That carnage was followed in short order by famine and cyclones. Then a military coup shut off the new nation's political life. Since then, Bangladesh has made the world news only sporadically, usually when the waters of the Ganges and the Brahmaputra overflow their banks. (Two or three thousand need to drown before it makes the back pages of American newspapers.) As a relatively calm Muslim country, without geopolitical significance and with a minuscule economy, it would be hard to imagine a less newsworthy place. But 1 human in 50 now lives there, and its grand history stretches back into the mists far enough to qualify it as a cradle of civilization. Still, for the rest of the planet, its only outstanding feature today is poverty.

"Poverty is the most salable commodity we have here," says Khushi Kabir, a longtime grassroots organizer. Experts jet in, stay at the Sheraton in Dhaka, issue reports, and leave. Local academics vie for "consultancies," making bids that sometimes require kickbacks to government officials. And the expert advice has often gone spectacularly wrong. A huge Flood Action Plan, for instance, called for ever-higher embankments to keep the rivers at bay. But Bangladesh is not Holland: The huge silt deposits kept raising riverbeds, and the floodwater that eventually topped the dikes had nowhere to drain. "One area in the southwest was under-water for 10 years," says Kabir.

Later, in an effort to curb diarrheal disease, UNICEF helped drill thousands of deep tube wells around the country and ran advertisements urging people to stop drinking surface water. But they neglected to sample the subsurface geology, and so tens of millions began drinking water contaminated with naturally occurring arsenic. The water has killed some already; others, disfigured by the melanoma lesions that arsenic causes, can no longer be given in marriage. UNICEF's new ads tell people not to drink from the tube wells.

Other international aid has worked better: The country's fertility rate has fallen quickly and the International Center for Diarrheal Disease Research has cut the incidence of cholera, which is endemic in the region. But local activists say the benefits aren't worth the costs: "Absolutely we would be better off if everyone try-ing to 'help' us just went home," says Mazhar. "If they did, then the people in the country would be able to come up with their own ideas." Those ideas would, nec-essarily, center on village life. Though Dhaka, a chaotic megacity with a population uncountably north of 10 million, dominates the political life of the nation, 80 per-cent of Bengalis still live in rural areas. Which is not to say that they live in Iowa, or the Punjab, or any of the other places that the word *rural* conjures in our minds. In the first place, Bangladesh is almost as much liquid as solid. There is water everywhere you look, and much of the year many villages are accessible mostly by canoe. Land holdings tend to be tiny, many under an acre. And the place feels, to a Westerner, almost unbelievably crowded. The population density dwarfs that of India or China; it approaches the density of Hong Kong. Even in rural farming dis-tricts, there is simply no such thing as a lonely road. Rickshaws, bicycles, buses, draft animals, and pedestrians jam every vista. One Bengali said the reason his country did not excel at most international sports was simple: "Where is the room for a soccer pitch?"

That picture of a standing-room-only floodplain sounds pretty desperate to our ears, as if the population of our Eastern seaboard were ordered to somehow make a living in Chesapeake Bay. But at least for the moment this huge population of Bengalis manages to feed itself. Partly that's a result of the "Green Revolution," the rice strains that, whatever their toll in pesticides and fertilizers, have boosted grain yields. But mostly that's a function of the simple biology of a hot delta. Floods regularly renew the soil, the sun shines most of the year, and so fruit trees grow in two years to a girth that would require five decades on a New England hillside. Plants jump from the ground. There's an almost obscene lushness everywhere. And the large population means that there are plenty of people to manage that lushness, to help make the most of it.

Here's what I mean. We were sitting one day on the front porch of a one-acre organic farm about an hour from Dhaka. It was a hobby farm, whose owner was mostly concerned with his rosebushes. Still, without getting up, we could see guava, lemon, pomegranate, coconut, betel nut, mango, jackfruit, apple, lichee, chestnut, date, fig, and bamboo trees, as well as squash, okra, eggplant, zucchini, blackberry, bay leaf, cardamom, cinnamon, and sugarcane plants, not to mention dozens of herbs, far more flowers, and a flock of ducklings. A chicken coop produced not just eggs and meat, but waste that fed a fishpond, which in turn produced thousands of pounds of protein annually, and a healthy crop of water hyacinths that were harvested to feed a small herd of cows, whose dung in turn fired a biogas cooking system. "Food is everywhere, and in 12 hours it will double," Kamal said.

So what do you do with that kind of fertility? The World Bank report recommends that you figure out ways to grow "higher-value" crops for export; they cite the Colombian cut-flower industry as an example. It could supply vegetables to other parts of Asia, "graduating from a minor supplier at present to a major player in the long term." That would probably generate the most money, cash that would be plowed into expanding the industries that could take advantage of the country's cheap labor pool. Or you could follow UBINIG's advice and focus on farms like those of Gorasin. "Any 'development' policy here must give agriculture priority," says Farhad Mazhar. "Don't destroy it any further, because you've got no way to take care of those people." The choice you make will depend on your sense of the future. The sheer growth in human numbers—Bangladesh's population may double again by 2020—could mean that you have no choice but to make a mad dash for modernization, figuring out every possible way to convert your country's resources to cash. But it will also depend on how you see the people living in Bengali villages. Are they desperately poor? Or is, in Mazhar's words, "the whole Western construction of poverty" suspect? "The real question," he insists, "is, What are the livelihood strategies of the bulk of people, and what kind of development enhances or destroys those strategies?"

That is, do you want a few lightbulbs run off rooftop solar generators, or do you want to run electric lines to the three-quarters of the country that currently lacks them? Do you want more people moving to the cities, or do you want to develop an organic agriculture that can absorb more labor? Those are questions, not answers. Rahman, the development expert, says that rooftop solar is only a beginning: "Once people have the 'little power,' they want 'big power' from electric lines," he says. Even though big power in a poor country can imply expense, pollution, dependence.

Here's another way of asking the same thing: How do you address the problem of vitamin A deficiency? Large numbers of poor people around South Asia suffer from a variety of micronutrient deficiencies—their diets lack sufficient iron or zinc or vitamin A, also known as beta-carotene. If you don't get enough, you can go blind. In 1999, European researchers announced they had managed to genetically modify rice so that it would express vitamin A to anyone who ate a bowlful, as surely as if they had popped a vitamin pill. Within a year the major biotech companies had announced agreements to license the technology free of charge to poor nations. As *Time* magazine put it last year, "The biotech industry sees golden rice as a powerful ally in its struggle to win public acceptance." An industry group ran a massive ad campaign touting the new technology with a rapid-fire montage of children and farms against a backdrop of swelling music.

But the advertisements look a little different from the organic farms of the Bengali floodplain, where farmers insist they have a different solution to the problem. The Nayakrishi movement held a small seminar for peasant farmers on the new technology at an open-air meeting hall in the Tangail district one day while I was there. A Filipino agriculture expert discussed the plans—that by 2003 the International Rice Research Institute would be producing genetically modified seeds for them to plant. The farmers—illiterate, most of them—kept interrupting with questions and sermonettes. They weren't concerned about frankenfoods. Instead, they instantly realized that the new rice would require fertilizer and pesticide. More to the point, they kept saying, they had no need of golden rice because the leafy vegetables they could grow in their organic fields provided all the nutrition they needed. "When we cook the green vegetables, we are aware not to throw out the water," said one woman. "Yes," said another. "And we don't like to eat rice only. It tastes better with green vegetables."

This is neither simplistic nor sentimental. In fact, there's plenty of evidence to show that as the Green Revolution spread in the last four decades, nutrient deficiency followed close behind. A plant like bathua, a leafy vegetable that provided beta-carotene to Indians for an eternity, becomes such a competitor of wheat once you start using chemical fertilizers that it requires herbicides to destroy it. A steady decline in the consumption per capita of vegetables, fruits, beans, and spices took place in Bangladesh even as the consumption of rice increased. Plants growing wild around the margins of Gorasin's fields provide massive quantities of vitamins A and C, or folic acid, iron, and calcium. But the spread of any high-yielding variety like golden rice tends to reduce that crop diversity. "There may or may not be issues of biosafety," said the Filipino expert. "The real question is, Do we really need this?"

Again, the answer depends on how you see the world. Maybe it's too late for Bangladesh to go back to a balanced diet, particularly in urban areas where bathua and amaranth are hard to come by. There's a kind of inevitability to the argument for a technological, capital-intensive future that comes from a scarcity of successful counter-examples. There aren't many places that have chosen an alternative path. Kerala, perhaps, the state of 30 million people in the south of India that has achieved Western levels of life expectancy, literacy, infant mortality, and fertility on an average income per capita of $300 per year. But the World Bank and Monsanto don't talk about Kerala; they talk about Thailand and Singapore.

"The Nayakrishi fields can be twice as productive as 'modern' agriculture," says Mazhar. "But I can't get anyone from the World Bank to come out and test my claims. We don't fit with the model." The Nayakrishi movement is small, with only tens of thousands of farmers in a nation with tens of millions. And although it is growing, it remains insubstantial against the sheer scale of Bangladesh. But Nayakrishi hints at other ways of addressing other issues, like energy: The Bangladesh Rural Advancement Committee has begun using microcredit programs to help peasants finance solar systems for their rooftops, and biogas generators for their cookstoves. The dung from three cows lets you cook all your meals for a day and frees you from crouching by the fireside to feed rice straw to the flame. That's a kind of progress that doesn't show up easily in anyone's statistics, but you can feel it in the strain on your back at the end of the day. It's a kind of progress that could conceivably mix with newer technologies. In his recent primer, *Food's Frontier: The Next Green Revolution,* Richard Manning notes that Western researchers are just beginning to focus more intensely on how people have grown food for generations.

There are few certainties when talking about the future of places like Bangladesh. Here's one, though: The most important Western export to Bangladesh in the next few decades will almost certainly be the higher sea level caused by global warming. When the Bay of Bengal rises a foot or two, the waters of the Ganges and the Brahmaputra will back up when they flood, unable to flow smoothly into the ocean. The Bay of Bengal rose a few inches higher than normal in 1998, and that year the floodwaters covered vast swaths of the country for as long as three months. Forget the fertility-promoting "normal" floods of the Bengali summer; this was 90 days of wading through thigh-deep water—more or less because Americans can't manage to stop driving Explorers. That near-geological force may be enough to end all these debates, to shut off the experimentation and innovation that offer curious and unexpected twists on what we've taken to calling development. Which would be the biggest shame of all.

The night we left Gorasin, we sat in the courtyard by everyone's small huts. The whole village of 35 or 40 people was on hand. Two babies were using a grapefruit as a ball, which every person in the village would roll back to them with great smiles. It takes a village to raise a child, indeed, and to raise a crop. And to raise a song, as well: One of the men, Akkas Ali, mentioned that he had written a hundred songs praising organic agriculture, tunes he and the other men had sung at local markets in an effort to convert other farmers. We ate fat bananas, and rosy grapefruit, and listened as the sun set. "Nayakrishi has corrected my mistakes," he sang in a reedy Bengali, as the rest of the village clapped rhythmically. "Food from Nayakrishi is so much better. No longer do I eat the poisons. Why should I eat that life-destroying stuff? Bangladesh will come to an end, unless you turn to Nayakrishi. If you use organic fertilizer, the Almighty will be behind you, And you'll be having no more gastric problems." As I say, the sun was setting over Gorasin. I have no idea if this represents a vision of the future, or a fragment of a fleeting past. It depends on how you look at it.

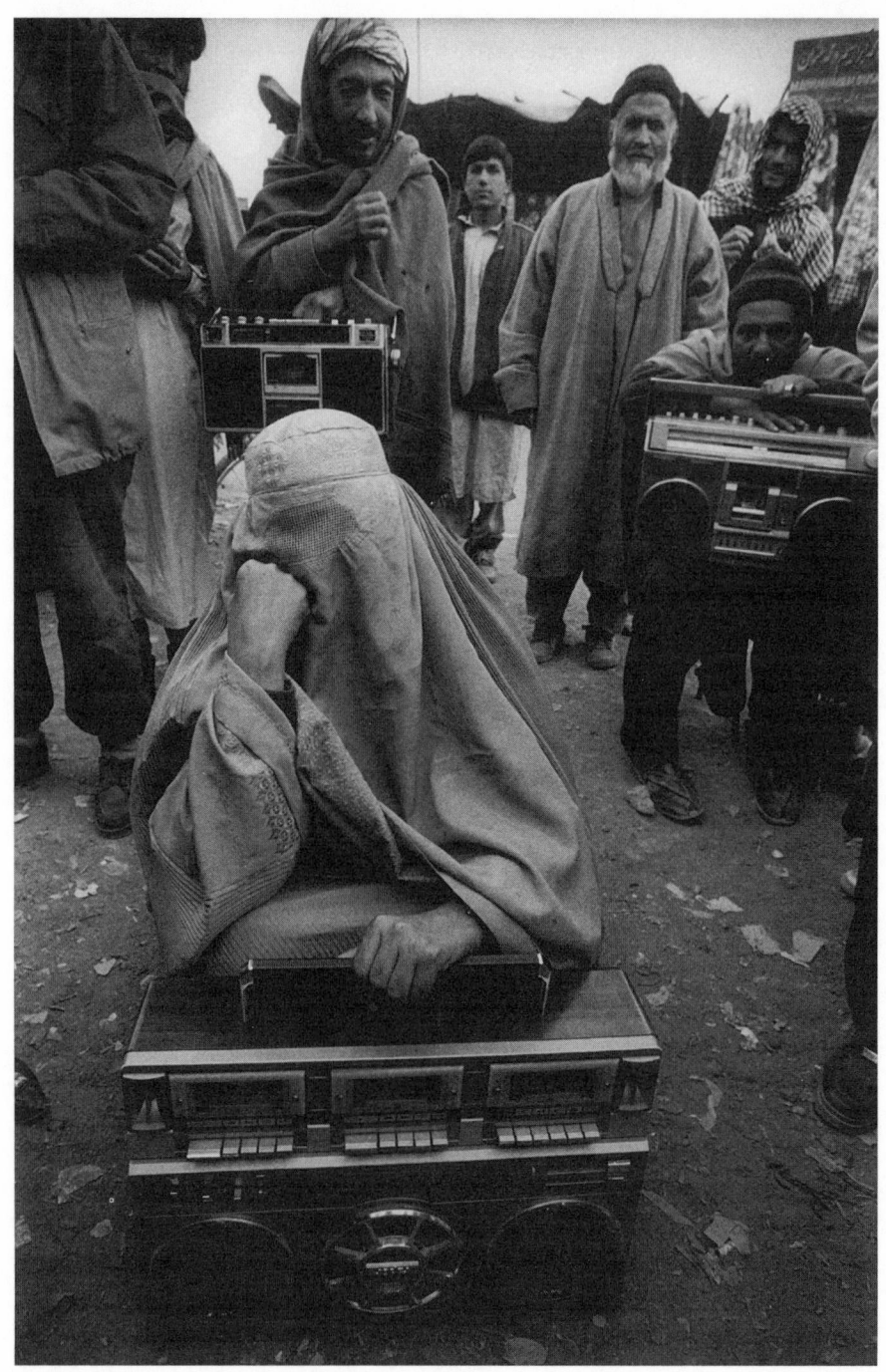

Jenny Matthews, *Kabul, Afghanistan, December 5, 2001*

The Globalization of Evil: Words from Baghdad and Belgrade

Nuha al Radi and Jasmina Tesanovic

Correspondence between Nuha al Radi and Jasmina Tesanovic started in January 2000, when Nuha read Jasmina's war diary in Granta, four years after she had published hers in the same magazine. The correspondence between these two women, one an Iraqi and a Muslim, the other Serbian and a Christian, began with Jasmina's words, "We were supposed to be enemies."

Sun, 5 Mar 2000 14:04:38
Dear Nuha,

I know when people write about their dogs, it means something else, especially when they are living in a dictatorship. But your diary says a lot. You always have this feeling you could have done better, that's why I don't read mine. I think it is the light tone that bothers you. It is the heavy tone that bothers me.

This weekend I was in Lugano, and spent a large portion of my time there locked in a toilet because I didn't have the coin to get out. Nobody bothered to help me. The lock works when you close the door, but in order to get out you have to have the right coin. What kind of fascism is that? Lately—since we have anarchy and killings and life has become cheap—I've started to appreciate the kind of order that keeps you locked in a bathroom above personal needs. It's not like America. The hypocrisy here is very European, much less political, more anti-political and cheap.

I wish you luck with your visa neurosis. I got my Italian visa too when I didn't care anymore.

Yours,

Jasmina

Mon, 06 Mar 2000 08:43:53

Dear Jasmina,

You are right about the light tone being difficult, but then people are always telling me I never take anything seriously. That's not true. Everyone has their way of dealing with life. My censorship was necessary because of the dictatorship I lived in, and because others were at risk. But I feel hypocritical when I have not said all that I should. I have not read my diary again except when it was being translated into Arabic. Then I had to. Anyway it is done now. The printed word does not go away.

I'm still trying for my visa, otherwise I'm just visiting friends, seeing movies and going to concerts. Tonight I'm going to see a Spanish classical guitarist.

Love,

Nuha

Tue, 7 Mar 2000 18:53:44 +0000

My Dear Nuha,

Our political/personal stories are identical—what criminal patterns the world repeats.

My film "Jasmina's Diary" had an audience of a million people and God knows how many festivals, but I didn't get any money. From the start, my crew and I got very little. We were forbidden from showing it in Serbia.

It is a German film and Serbia has cultural sanctions. The country's allowed to make money on our art and misery, but we are forbidden to survive. That's why, when I feel that a publisher or agent is honest, I don't care about money because they always pay you back. But when they are not honest big money turns into humiliation.

I keep quoting and mentioning your diary, telling people about the similarities between us. I made similar comparisons between Serbia and Iraq before knowing you, but our friendship has given me written proof. Your diary is good. Sometimes censorship works the other way round. All the best political and passionate poetry was written in Italy during fascism for the same reason: They had to find new ways to capture their experience. I envy you for your concerts and exhibitions. Here everything is dead. Once it was a world scene.

Yours,

Jasmina

Wed, 8 Mar 2000 15:57:39 +0000

Dear Nuha,

Sometime ago I erased all of your letters by mistake. I have only our notes from the last few days, but I'm the kind of person who erases things deliberately but says it was by mistake.

I keep talking about you all the time, the similarities, differences. I call our correspondence "The Globalization of Evil."

Yours,

Jasmina

Wed, 08 Mar 2000 09:01:59

Dear Jasmina,

You are a genius! What a wonderful idea, "Globilization of Evil." I have just come from meeting women parliamentarians, all ex-presidents' wives and ministers. At one point in the evening a girl of about twenty got up to speak. She had been jailed by the Israelis in the south, kept in a prison called Alkhiam, and tortured. She told us how the Israelis would torment their captives. If the prisoners refused to succumb, the Israelis would bring their sons or fathers, sisters, and torture and kill and burn *them*—just gruesome, horrific. She was twice incarcerated.

After she finished, I went and talked to her. She turned out to be a member of Hisbollah, an Iranian-backed Shia party made up primarily of Lebanese fighters. "Weren't you afraid of torture?" I asked, but she said, "If you believe, it is not a problem." This little girl was amazing. She's trained as a fighter, but she's not allowed to go south anymore. Now she does her work from Beirut.

The one thing I fear is torture. If I was to go back to Iraq, maybe no one would bother me, but one cannot be certain and I don't think I could take being tortured. Then again, one doesn't know how one would behave in such circumstances.

A Palestinian woman was the best speaker at the meeting. She lost her visa when she left Jerusalem and now she can't go back. An Algerian woman told us that much of the killing that goes on is done by the Algerians themselves. For us poor Iraqis we have it internally with an evil dictator and externally with an evil

America—they are the one keeping the sanctions. I guess Britain too, though I think they're America's skirts now. Somehow I have a weakness for the Brits, but no such feeling for the Americans.

I just got an email saying that there may still be a chance for Cyprus. I am still waiting for a visa to go there for my exhibition. Just when I had given up.
Love,
Nuha

Wed, 8 Mar 2000 20:27:17 +0000

"Globalization of Evil." Sometimes I like ideas based on opposing political correctness. This word, "globalization," is so in, and yet, what do we get out of it?

I failed to go to any meetings today. I visited my mother's grave with my father and watched him cry.

My father and her were never religious—unless communism can be considered a religion—so this was the right day for us to visit. She always celebrated collective feasts as her own, the International Women's Day was her true birthday. She even had me on March 7th, only one day before, as she used to claim, so that my birthday lasted two days.

She was a feminist in a communist old-fashioned way, which has often been proved more efficient and true.

Your description of the women's meeting reminds me so much of our meetings of Women in Black. We had one in Zagreb in '96, where an Arab woman explained how she was saving the Jews that were imprisoned in her country and vice versa. It was so moving and brave, exactly what the essence of Women in Black is—to fight the evil in one's own country, not to globalize it. There goes the title. It closes the circle and opens a new one.
Much love,
Jasmina

Thursday, March 9, 2000 09:00:57 PST
Dear Jasmina,

I can't understand this evil. How can some people be so vile and still have such a large following? Look at Pinochet. Why can't people see what he did during his reign? Or Castro. Are people afraid of him or are they just too poor to act? Maybe they are more concerned about earning a living? With Saddam I know people follow him out of fear and opportunism, but Pinochet has no power, so why do people pretend? Am I being very stupid?

I like to visit graveyards but not those that house people I know. I still haven't been to my father's grave. I like to think of people I know as traveling in another place. I can't relate to a mound of earth.

Yes, I realized when I was at the women's meeting that it was probably like your Women in Black. The world is much the same in such matters, maybe that's why globalization has grown so popular. Now it is an invasion into food and clothing, which will make life very boring. I am glad I saw a bit of the world before mass culture took over. Nowadays young people have such little to choose from.
Love,
Nuha

Friday, March 10, 2000 14:38:46 +0000
My dear Nuha,

Do you feel political censorship lurking everywhere? I am so angry with the West. I feel safer with my own country than with the so-called allies of democracy, which is a very unusual story for me, since I was brought up by the West.

I just learned that I cannot have a bank account abroad because of the new list of unwanted people (I am not on it) and the tightening of economic sanctions. All the money I earned from my book, on which I live, can only be transferred if my President doesn't fall to the Hague tribunal. It was a possibility a month ago, but now, no way. "Personally we would love to do it," the bank clerks say, "but orders are orders."

I feel like turning down all the business trips they are counting on, the discussion with the Hague tribunal judges, the publishing of my book for very little compensation, my travels via Budapest with sleepless nights so that I can be on time. But then, if I don't do it, I have nothing to do. I am one of the few who has the opportunity to travel, buy medicine for family and friends, fight back against economic sanctions and the world's misconception of Serbs, speak out and be published. So I will do it with the energy of true hate. They made me a Serb who hates the West. I am not a saint. I cannot live on thin air and be happy.

I think that this is how criminal leaders get followers, not only out of stupidity, fear or a need for money, but when there is no other place to go. Yes, I have participated in many discussions on how globalization is a loss of cultural identity, market pressure, etc. But I'm afraid that when applied to my own country it turns the other way. We love to have Benetton and McDonald's here. It makes us feel that we belong to the world and to one another.

For us it is a matter of luxury to be a member of the globalized world, instead of being identified as a bad Serb who eats *cevapcici,* our local shish kebab.

The good thing about the globalization of evil is that it binds us together, even if in pain. An old Bosnian woman raped in war will tell you a story identical to that of a teenage American raped on a U.S. campus.

Bad things and bad people get together easier than good ones. It's like how children immediately pick up their older siblings' negative habits. I've seen it happen too many times and yet I cannot find an answer.

I also visit graveyards to see other people's graves and their pictures, never my own. My own are never dead. I've been writing a lot lately—mostly of my mother. In my stories she is never alone. She is the history of this country.

Yours,

Jasmina

Friday, March 10, 2000 05:26:16

Dear J,

I've just had my e-mail full of ranting and raving wiped out by a power cut. It's difficult to rant with the same amount of feeling the second time around, but I'll try. I've programmed it to save automatically in case the same occurs again.

You make me laugh. Do you know that all Iraqi bank accounts are frozen in the U.K.? Nowhere else but there, I guess, because there are a half a million Iraqis living there. When you ask why, the clerks explain that it's the U.N. law. I say, how come no other country does it? When you tell them that, their faces go blank.

There used to be so many stories of similar things happening because poor unsuspecting Iraqi's would come from abroad and put all their money in the bank, only to be told that they were not allowed to take it out. Sometimes the bank clerks are not aware of this but, by the time the computer spits out the information, it is already too late. It's western democracy and humanitarianism—so they keep telling us. At least we are not hypocritical. We are known to be corrupt, undemocratic and inhumane, but at least it's not a double standard. I can rant and rave forever, but I might as well be hitting my head against a brick wall. The trouble is that I was educated in the West so my disillusionment is enormous. There is no trust left. Whatever they say, I know they are lying to suit their own political needs.

The Cypriots are not giving me a visa because it is nearly impossible for an Iraqi to get one unless you have an oil deal. They keep saying your file is lost, making excuses as the months go by. I was told the only way was to be washed ashore and the police would pick you up and put you in prison for three months. After that you could stay. How do you like that?

I am sorry I'm not able to pacify you but much the same has happened to us and for so many years now that we have grown blasé about mistreatment.
Love,
N

Friday, March 10, 2000 20:36:02
My dear Nuha,

The strange thing is that, with stories as bad as mine, you do pacify me. We are so different—you a Muslim and me an Orthodox and both of us fake Brits, disillusioned world citizens publishing in *Granta*. It means that the problem is not in us, but in those who make the rules and the rules are obviously made according to money and power. We cannot change our blood and breed, but we can change those rules.

I've had my own decent share of bank account problems. The worst was in 1993. I was on a Greek island with my small daughter and carried around our money for food and board. The Greeks were saying, don't leave your shoes on the beach, somebody will pick them up, so I went to a bank and asked to leave my money there, FOR A WEEK. "Yes, yes," they said.

A week after they refused to give it back to me: sanctions. You can put money in but not take it out. I was left with almost nothing, a small child, far from home, no consulate, no phone lines. The girl at the bank didn't blink. She loved being "civilized," being part of the European community.

It was tremendously hot, but I took my little girl and we hitchhiked to Thessaloniki, where the central bank was located. We slept in the park. It was 40 degrees centigrade. The director of the bank didn't blink either. He said, "Not possible," in bad English, then went away. I was penniless and desperate. I started crying and my little girl, only eight years old, tried to console me. Then a woman came up to me and said: I will give you my money, you take a local bus, get off at every village and ask for a small amount of money, they will give it to you without your passport. I did it—twelve banks in all. I managed to raise my money in 15 hours and pay my way out of that horrible country.

I came home, where I am a famous writer and wrote an article. The Greeks were supposed to be our friends. After the piece came out the Greeks explained that the problem was the size of the sum. Different rules applied to small money. As far as big money was concerned, they'd break the rules to help Serbian people, same goes for Cyprus. But who do you think the big money belongs to? Certainly not me. In '99, exactly a year ago on the 24th of March when the bombings started, I met my Italian friends from the Italian cultural center, one block away from my home. They were all leaving.

You know what I learned? We couldn't get visas anymore, not even women and children, but that day the son of our President got his family a one-year visa. They called that high diplomacy.

Yours,

Jasmina

Saturday, March 11, 2000 01:52:44

Dear J,

Yesterday on BBC TV they showed the farmers of Zimbabwe fighting for what is, according to them, their land, while the poor blacks have nothing. They showed these giant white well fed chaps in shorts with their big four wheelers strutting about, and the poor blacks grasping sticks, trying to stake a bit of land for themselves.

I love that the blacks of Zimbabwe are asking the Brits for compensation and I don't see why not. How come the Jews are the only people to have been compensated? These poor blacks were treated like slaves in their own country. "Might is right"—is that always the law of the jungle? All this talk of democracy is for the birds.

Love,

N

Saturday, March 11, 2000 16:01:36 +0000

My dear Nuha,

My friend from Uruguay says, great the "Globalization of Evil," but I'm amazed at the globalization of understanding, how you two get along. That is actually the most amazing part—our two countries and our poor people with their cultures, habits, their rights destroyed and humiliated by sterile political correctness and money. I cannot say I hate Americans, I can only say I despise them. For example, even before this war I could never imagine falling in love with an American, they are too "thin" a personality for me. I had a similar feeling about Italians, after being brought up in Italy. They were too infantile.

My mother on her deathbed was rambling semiconsciously saying, "Please do not let Americans occupy us, they are so primitive." What an obsession. On the contrary, everything here is Americanized. We follow their technology, updating ourselves from cellars to attics without ever living in a proper flat.

Papers and radio stations are being closed here these days and the police have questioned many journalists. I'm very puzzled by what is going on. It's not sheer repression. I have a feeling that the police want a way out of Milosevic's regime. I have a feeling they are splitting and that his autism and criminal deeds have exceeded their patriotism. I hope it is not wishful thinking.

Love,

J

Saturday, March 11, 2000 06:32:07

Dear J,

I have a lot of American friends, and America is a beautiful country but if you paid me I wouldn't go and live there. (I hope I am not going to have to eat my words.) Their politics and politicians stink. I think it's Zionists that keep American politicians going.

It's funny, in my mother's lifetime half her friends were Jewish and after they were forced to leave Iraq, throughout her life, she used to visit them in London. Iraq had a huge Jewish community. If there was one good thing about Iraq, it was that it was not sectarian. It was with the creation of Israel that animosity grew.

Love,

N

Sunday, March 12, 2000 12:14:23

Dear Nuha,

I hope you know that the Serbian people are not behind Milosevic. Here we hear that people from Iraq are behind Saddam. There used to be graffiti around town that read Slobo/Saddam. It used to make my mother crazy. She was pro Milosevic till the very end and she used to say, he may not be perfect, but he is not a dictator like Saddam. I don't know what Saddam is like. On the BBC I heard an old exiled Iraqi writer, fighting bitterly against the sanctions in his country, with the same arguments I would have used saying: Saddam is actually a person whose many good intentions went wrong. He was educated, democratic—in the beginning.

Well, that is definitely something I cannot say for my president. I met him before he became important and he was anonymous, typical of certain communists, primitive Serbs. With him it was difficult to see where his career would lead. Yours,

J

Date: Sun, 12 Mar 2000 05:08:22 PST

Dear J,

I think there is a difference between Milosevic and "Suds," as I call him, first, Saddam is not very educated. He fears nothing and is an evil killer. I once asked Patrick Seale, an expert on Syria, if Hafiz Assad and Saddam were two of a kind. He said no, Assad was a killer but Saddam was a serial killer. There's a difference. Suds knows there is a coup rising against him before the thought has even occurred to those plotting one. Sometimes I think he should be applauded for standing up to the West, but he doesn't do it intelligently. He doesn't know how to fight using their language.

Iraq is a very difficult country to rule. You always need a strong man. Our history is a bloody one. It's because we have such a difficult climate, so extreme, sometimes 30/35 degrees difference in temperature between day and night. It makes concrete break up so what must it do to humans? People have never known if Saddam is an agent of the West, because he plays into their hands. Perhaps he cut a bargain with them, "Let me stay on, Mr. president, and I'll give you cheap oil, let you have an army, navy, and airforce base in the middle of the oil fields, let you control the Middle East." But Iraq is now a ruined country, what more could they want? The west will never allow an Arab country, rich and educated to survive.

I don't know how one can control evil.

Love,

N

Date: Sun, 12 Mar 2000 20:03:39

Dear Nuha,

I have many friends in the US and I even love a lot of things about it that nobody does—fast food, the style of clothing, alienated big towns—but when I'm there I thin out and begin to lose my fantasies, maybe because I am a decadent European who smokes and drinks, a wild Southern who stays up all night and still goes to work. The US has this kind of "nice girl" atmosphere.

I think that evil is always far easier to spread than good. Maybe because evil is such a large and infinite category. It's so easy to be evil. It costs nothing to close your eyes to injustice.

I think it is the talent for violence that is appreciated in our dictators, that there's a difference between the fear of death and the fear of dying, as Freud would say. The first one is vital, it brings adrenaline to your blood. The second is decadent. You die day by day, suffering the loss of your hair, good looks and health. There have always been wars. There have always been dictators. All wars could have been avoided. You see it afterwards and yet when they start they seem inevitable. If I believed in God I would say, "the Devil's work," and it would be easy.

Since I can't, I write.

J

You *Tell Us What to Do*

Faiz Ahmed Faiz

translated by Agha Shahid Ali

When we launched life
on the river of grief,
how vital were our arms, how ruby our blood.
With a few strokes, it seemed,
we would cross all pain,
we would soon disembark.
That didn't happen.
In the stillness of each wave we found invisible currents.
The boatmen, too, were unskilled,
their oars untested.
Investigate the matter as you will,
blame whomever, as much as you want,
but the river hasn't changed,
the raft is still the same.
Now *you* suggest what's to be done,
you tell us how to come ashore.

When we saw the wounds of our country
appear on our skins,
we believed each word of the healers.
Besides, we remembered so many cures,
it seemed at any moment
all troubles would end, each wound heal completely.
That didn't happen: our ailments
were so many, so deep within us
that all diagnoses proved false, each remedy useless.
Now do whatever, follow each clue,
accuse whomever, as much as you will,
our bodies are still the same,
our wounds still open.
Now tell us what we should do,
you tell us how to heal these wounds.

Sally Grizzell Larson, *Untitled (Number 51)*

Contributors

Agha Shahid Ali was born in New Delhi and raised in Kashmir. He has published six collections of poems, including *The Half-Inch Himalayas, A Walk through the Yellow Paces,* and *A Nostalgist's Map of America.* His poems, essays, translations, and reviews have appeared in *Poetry, Paris Review, Grand Street,* and *Tri-Quarterly.*

William T. Ayton is a British artist living in upstate New York. In the 1990s, he had a widely exhibited series of paintings on human rights. His work has appeared in publications such as the *New York Times,* the *Wilson Quarterly,* the *Citizen,* and *Tamaqua.*

James Barilla is currently completing his doctoral degree in English at the University of California, Davis. His research focuses on the intersections between ecological restoration and literature. He has published essays in *You Are Here: The Journal of Creative Geography* and *Men and Nature.* His study of Aldo Leopold is forthcoming in the American Writers Series.

Mario Benedetti is a Uruguayan writer. Born in 1920, he belonged to the critical literary movement called the 45 Generation. He went into exile for more than a decade but has returned to live in Montevideo. Benedetti is considered a political writer though he has perhaps written the largest number of love poems in Latin America.

Marilyn Booth's most recent books include *May Her Likes Be Multiplied: Biography and Gender Politics in Egypt.* She has translated fiction and autobiography from

Egypt and Lebanon. She has taught at Brown University and the American University in Cairo and is currently a visiting professor at the University of Illinois.

Frederick Buell is the author of two books of poems and three books of cultural criticism, including *National Culture and the New Global System* and *Apocalypse to Way of Life: Environmental Crisis in the American.* His poems have appeared in *Poetry,* the *New England Review,* and *Southwestern Review.*

Jan Clausen's poems have appeared in *Bloom, CrossConnect, Hanging Loose,* the *Kenyon Review, Luna,* and *Ploughshares.* The recipient of National Endowment for the Arts and New York Foundation for the Arts fellowships, she has published nine books, among them the memoir *Apples and Oranges.* She teaches at the New School and at Goddard College.

Adam Clayman is a documentary photographer living in Brooklyn, New York.

Kerry Stuart Coppin is an assistant professor of art at the University of Miami, Florida. Coppin is a documentary-style photographer producing provocative photographic interpretations that elaborate and celebrate positive aspects of the black community experience.

Ellen Dissanayake is the author of *What Is Art For?, Homo Aestheticus,* and *Art and Intimacy: How the Arts Began.* She has lived and worked in Sri Lanka, Nigeria, and Papua New Guinea, and is currently visiting scholar at the Center for the Humanities, University of Washington.

Fazi Admed Faiz (1911–1984) was a two-time Nobel nominee and winner of the 1962 Lenin Peace Prize. His evening radio readings in Hindi/Urdu-speaking regions drew thousands of listeners. Associated with the Communist party in his youth, Faiz later became an outspoken poet in opposition to the Pakistani government.

Kathleen L. Housley has written poetry and essays for many journals, including *New England Quarterly, Image,* and *Christian Century.* She is the author of two biographies: *The Letter Kills But the Spirit Gives Life* and *Emily Hall Tremaine: Collector on the Cusp.* Housley is an affiliated scholar at Trinity College, Hartford, Connecticut.

Ibra Ibrahimovic has been documenting the devastated environment of north Bohemia since 1991. He focuses on industrial landscapes and collects the stories of people living in those areas. A picture from his series "Farmer Jan Rajter" was awarded Photo of the Year by the Czech Press in 2003.

Ryszard Kapuściński is a Polish journalist. While working for the Polish Press Agency, he gained critical and popular praise for his coverage of civil wars, revolutions, and social conditions in the Third World. He is the author of celebrated books of literary reportage such as *Shah of Shahs, The Soccer War,* and *The Emperor,* all of which have been translated into many languages.

Lorrinda Khan lives in Brighton Beach, U.K., with her husband and two-year-old daughter, who was born in the Dominican Republic. She completed her B.A. at Ohio State University and her M.F.A. in creative writing at Goddard College. Her writing is influenced by her global travels.

Naomi Klein, born in Montreal, is an award-winning journalist and the best-selling author of *No Logo.* Her articles have appeared in numerous publications, including the *Nation,* the *New Statesman, Newsweek International, New York Times, Village Voice, Ms., Baffler,* and *Saturday Night.* She writes a weekly column in the *Globe and Mail,* Canada's national newspaper.

Sally Grizzell Larson is a visual artist based in Philadelphia. Her work has been exhibited at Artpool Research Center in Budapest; the Centro de Cultura and the Picasso Foundation in Malaga, Spain; the Brooklyn Museum of Art and Exit Art in New York; and many other venues.

Roberta Levitow has directed over fifty theatrical productions in New York, Los Angeles, and nationally. Her work has been featured in the *New York Times, American Theatre* magazine, and the *South Atlantic Quarterly.* Levitow teaches at Bennington College.

Alphonso Lingis is professor of philosophy at Penn State University. His books include *Excesses: Eros and Culture, Deathbound Subjectivity, The Community of Those Who Have Nothing in Common, Abuses, Dangerous Emotions,* and *Trust.*

D'Arcy Martin is a union educator and writer. The translation of Mario Benedetti in this book was done for a coauthored book, *Educating for a Change,* that applies popular education values and methods to the situation of workers and community activists in Canada.

Inna Mattei grew up in Odessa in the former Soviet Union. She is a graduate of the Kennedy School of Government at Harvard University and the New Jersey Institute of Technology. She was an editor of *Koja Magazine* in New York. Her poetry has appeared in *Black Box, Trumpeter,* and *Magazinnik.* She is completing her first collection of poems, *First Identities.*

Jenny Matthews has been working as a documentary photographer since 1982, documenting social issues in Britain and abroad. She has worked extensively in Latin America, the Middle East, Africa, and Asia for major development organizations. Her photographs have appeared in newspapers and magazines worldwide.

C. M. Mayo is the author of *Miraculous Air, The Other Mexico,* and *Sky over El Nido,* which won the Flannery O'Connor Award for Short Fiction. Recent work has appeared in *Chelsea, Fourth Genre, North American Review,* and *Tin House.* Mayo is also founding editor of *Tameme,* the annual bilingual journal of new writing from Canada, the United States, and Mexico.

Audrey McCollum is a writer and retired psychotherapist who lives in New Hampshire. Her most recent book is *Two Women, Two Worlds: Friendship Swept by Winds of Change.* Her four previous books have focused on child development, teenage violence, life transitions, and the peace movement.

Robert McCollum, a physician specializing in infectious disease epidemiology, is dean emeritus of the Dartmouth Medical School. His interest in Papua New Guinea was first inspired by reports concerning *kuru,* an illness transmitted by cannibalism.

Bill McKibben is a former staff writer for the *New Yorker.* His books include *Hundred Dollar Holiday, Maybe One, The End of Nature, The Age of Missing Information, Hope, Human and Wild,* and *Enough.* McKibben is a frequent contributor to a wide variety of publications, including the *New York Review of Books, Outside,* and the *New York Times.* He lives with his wife and daughter in Vermont.

Edie Meidav is the author of *Crawl Space* and *The Far Field.* She directs the Writing and Consciousness program at New College of California in San Francisco.

Tim Parks grew up in London and studied at Cambridge and Harvard. In 1981 he moved to Italy, where he has lived ever since. He has written ten novels, including *Europa, Destiny,* and, most recently, *Judge Savage;* three nonfiction accounts of life in northern Italy, most recently *A Season with Verona;* and a collection of essays, *Adultery and Other Diversions.* His many translations from the Italian include works by Moravia, Tabucchi, Calvino, and Calasso.

Nuha al-Radi was born in Baghdad. An artist working in various forms, including ceramics and painting, she has taught at the American University of Beirut. Her book, *Baghdad Diaries,* was published in 1998. She has lived in exile in Beirut, Lebanon, since 1995.

Richard Robinson is an award-winning photographer based in Virginia. His work has appeared in *Smithsonian, National Geographic Traveler,* and the *Washington Post Magazine.* He won the Lowell Thomas Gold Award for Travel Photography for his piece "Old Man and the Keys" in *Spirit Magazine* (Southwest Airlines).

Arundhati Roy was trained as an architect. She is the author of the novel *The God of Small Things,* for which she received the Booker Prize. Her recent nonfiction works include *The Cost of Living, Power Politics,* and *War Talk.* Roy lives in New Delhi.

Mark Rudman's poetic trilogy consists of *The Millennium Hotel, Provoked in Venice,* and *Rider,* for which he received the National Book Critics Circle Award. He is also the author of *Robert Lowell: An Introduction* and *Realm of Unknowing.*

Arpita Singh lives and paints in Delhi, India. She has exhibited in India and abroad. Her works are represented in various collections in and outside India.

Paul Spencer Sochaczewski lived for many years in Southeast Asia, first with the U.S. Peace Corps in Sarawak, Malaysia, then as creative director of J. Walter Thompson advertising. He writes regularly for leading international publications on nature, conservation, and things that go bump in the night.

Jasmina Tesanovic, born in Belgrade, is the author of *The Diary of a Political Idiot.* She cofounded the first women's publishing house in Serbia, 94. She has published eight books of fiction and nonfiction, which have been translated into twelve languages.

Carol Van Houten is a librarian who lives in Jersey City. She is the editor of the on-line journal *The Constant Reader.*

Najem Wali was born in Al-Amarah, Iraq. Shortly after the outbreak of the Iraq-Iran war, he emigrated to Germany. He now lives in Hamburg, working as a cultural correspondent for the largest Arab newspaper, *Al-Hayat.* Wali is the author of the novels *War in the Destruction of Pleasure, The Least Night to Mary, Place Names Kumait,* and *Tel Al Leham (The Mountain of Meet)* and the short story collections *There in the Strange City* and *Waltzing Matilda,* all in Arabic.

Ingrid Wendt is the winner of the Yellowglen Award for *The Angle of Sharpest Ascending.* Her other books include *Moving the House, Singing the Mozart Requiem,* which received the Oregon Book Award for poetry, and *Blow the Candle Out.* She lives in Eugene, Oregon, with her husband, poet and writer Ralph Salisbury.

Daniel E. Weinbaum is completing his M.F.A. at Hunter College and is currently at work on a novel. He divides his time between Brooklyn, New York, and western Massachusetts, and works as a cabinet maker and teacher in addition to writing.

Hannes Westberg is twenty-three years old and an aspiring writer in Gothenburg, Sweden. His other passion is music, which he produces and plays as a DJ. He has fully recovered both physically and mentally from the shooting that he writes about in this book. For now, his newborn daughter occupies most of his time.

Wandee J. Pryor is managing editor of Terra Nova projects and the author of several plays.

David Rothenberg is the author of *Sudden Music, Blue Cliff Record: Zen Echoes, Always the Mountains,* and the recently published *Why Birds Sing.* He is professor of philosophy at the New Jersey Institute of Technology and the founding editor of the Terra Nova book series.

Sources

Mario Benedetti, "Why We Sing (Por que cantamos)," translated by D'Arcy Martin, from *Educating for a Change,* Toronto: Between the Lines, 1991. Reprinted by permission of the translator.

Faiz Ahmed Faiz, "You *Tell Us What to Do,*" translated by Agha Shahid Ali, from *The Rebel's Silhouette,* Amherst, Mass.: University of Massachusetts Press, 1991. Reprinted by permission of the publisher.

Ryszard Kapuściński, "The Snow in Ghana," from *Granta* (September 1989). Reprinted by permission of the author.

Naomi Klein, from *Fences and Windows.* Copyright © 2002 by Naomi Klein. Reprinted by permission of Picador USA.

C. M. Mayo, "El Halloween and the Día de Muertos," originally published in the *North American Review,* was excerpted from *Miraculous Air: Journey of a Thousand Miles through Baja California, the Other Mexico,* Salt Lake City: University of Utah Press, 2002. © C. M. Mayo. Reprinted by permission of the author.

Audrey McCollum, portions of "Two Women, Two Worlds" were adapted from *Two Women, Two Worlds: Friendship Swept by Winds of Change,* Netna, NH: Hillwinds Press, 1999. Reprinted by permission of the author.

Bill McKibben, "An Alternative to Progress," from *Mother Jones,* May–June 2001. Reprinted by permission of the author.

Arundhati Roy, "The Ladies Have Feelings, So . . . Shall We Leave It to the Experts?" from *Power Politics,* 2nd ed. Cambridge: South End Press, 2001, pp. 1–33. Copyright 2001 by Arundhati Roy.

Arpita Singh, *For Anjum,* 2002. From Nature Morte and Bose Pacia Modern in association with Tulika Books, India.

Najem Wali, "Waltzing Matilda," translated by Marilyn Booth. © 2003 Marilyn Booth. First published in *Words Without Borders* [www.wordswithoutborders.org], October 2003. By permission of *Words Without Borders.*